A Mouthful Of Petals

Three Years In An Indian Village

Wendy Scarfe And Allan Scarfe

16pt

Copyright Page from the Original Book

Wakefield Press
16 Rose Street
Mile End
South Australia 5031
www.wakefieldpress.com.au

First published by William Heinemann Ltd 1967
Revised edition published by Seaview Press 2011
This new edition published 2020

Copyright © Wendy Scarfe and Allan Scarfe, 1967, 2011, 2020

All rights reserved. This book is copyright. Apart from any fair dealing for the purposes of private study, research, criticism or review, as permitted under the Copyright Act, no part may be reproduced without written permission. Enquiries should be addressed to the publisher.

This book was first published by William Heinemann Ltd in 1967, printed in Great Britain by Cox & Wyman Ltd, London, Fakenham and Reading.

Other Children, a 20-minute colour CD with subtitles showing life in Sokhodeora village and some of Wendy and Allan Scarfe's work there is available from the National Film and Sound Archives, Canberra.

Edited by Julia Beaven, Wakefield Press
Cover designed by Liz Nicholson, Wakefield Press
Typeset by Jesse Pollard, Wakefield Press

 A catalogue record for this book is available from the National Library of Australia

 Wakefield Press thanks Coriole Vineyards for continued support

TABLE OF CONTENTS

PUBLISHER'S NOTE	xi
FOREWORD	xiii
1: SOKHODEORA	1
2: THE START OF THE PIONEERING	18
3: SCHOOLS AND HIBISCUS FLOWERS	41
4: BLIGHTY MILK	70
5: LITERACY AND A BUFFALO	98
6: KESURWA	133
7: NEW-FANGLED PUBLIC INSTRUCTION	160
8: FAMILY PLANNING	174
9: HEADS THAT PLANNED AND HEADS THAT ITCHED	195
10: THE STATE VERSUS MISS VIDYA	220
11: MEALS FOR MILLIONS	244
12: SHOVA	279
13: PEACE THROUGH THE AGES: A VILLAGE ENTERTAINMENT	296
14: THE GIFT	311
15: THE HOUSE WITH THE POMEGRANATE TREE	351
16: WORK AND WORRIES	379
17: MAHADEV'S WEDDING	399
18: DEPARTURE	411
EPILOGUE	423
POSTSCRIPT	484
ACKNOWLEDGEMENTS	486
BACK COVER MATERIAL	489

FROM THE REVIEWS OF *A MOUTHFUL OF PETALS*

This lively and appealing book describes in warm human terms and with a refreshing absence of sentimentality the experiences of two young Australian educationists during their three years residence in a poor backward and remote Bihar village. Confronted as they were by apathy, resistance to change, and chronic malnutrition hovering on the brink of actual starvation, they never lost courage in spite of the grimness of the whole picture. The lesson which they carried away from their experiences was not one of despair but of opportunity.
The Times Literary Supplement, 1967

This appealing and very humane book is very well worth reading. The project described is largely in the tradition of Gandhi's *sarvodaya* – the welfare of all program. Gandhi held that a small number of selfless workers – and the Scarfes come into that category – could produce a successful social welfare enterprise.

The Times Educational Supplement, 1967

The writing is of the most unpretentious, as artless as a diary, a startlingly vivid picture of this one small remote spot on our earth. Most of it is an account of hunger, misery, ignorance crushing human beings almost below the level of humanity. There are gleams of light in the darkness – even in such a place of wretchedness, the reader is left to hope inextinguishable human faculties are only waiting to be released from their prison.

New Statesman, 1967

What can individuals do to ease conditions in an under-developed country, to combat misery, poverty and ignorance in such lands? Probably a great deal more than most of us imagine, as Wendy and Allan Scarfe are able to show from their own experience. One can learn a great deal about the actualities of life in rural India in this perceptive and frank book.

Press And Journal, 1967

Allan Scarfe and his wife are Australian teachers who in 1960 began a three year stay in a Bihar village where they tried to advance education, health and a community spirit. The many pictures of Sokhodeora are nightmarish in their cruel vividness: the alleys strewn with dung, slimy gutters forming greenish puddles, emaciated mangy dogs lying exhausted with hunger, the brilliant gold patches of sunlight on the cow-dung fuel cakes still bearing the imprint of the fingers of the woman who kneaded them, the children peeping through dusty lice-ridden hair or running to hide in their dark windowless homes. The title comes from the misdemeanour of some of these children who stole hibiscus flowers – to eat. The photographs of famished babies would wring tears from a block of granite.

Irish Times, 1967

For three years they found that the natural beauty and serenity of the village lived side-by-side with anxiety, poverty and misery. Their work was not only school teaching but their activities

extended to sanitation, milk and food distribution, instruction on first aid, health, nutrition and family planning. Their experiences in the village are related with warmth, humour and understanding and their account of their work will be of value to other voluntary overseas workers.
Guardian-Journal, 1967

They worked in blistering heat during the day, held literacy classes in a mud-and-straw buffalo hut at night, travelled on elephants to reach remote places and during their holidays taught Tibetan refugees at the foothills of the Himalayas. The book written with uncommon frankness and perception born of the moral impulse that directed the authors' adventure, brings out the live characters of the villagers, their longings and their limitations, their dreams and their despair, their fears and their friendliness.
Shiv Sharma, Sheffield Morning Telegraph, 1967

The magnificent *A Mouthful of Petals* (is) amongst the most important

documents of our time on the nature and problems of our great neighbour ... a distillation of the experience and wisdom of ... Australian(s) who ha(ve) a real understanding and knowledge of mud-brick, cow-pat, village India. It is to Australia's international credit that the Scarfes are now widely known abroad, especially in Asia, for their sensitive and important works on Indian themes ... their achievement has been remarkable.
Dr Stephen Murray Smith, Editor, Overland, 1977

...an interesting social document. It describes with warmth, sympathy and occasional near-despair, the life of an Indian village from the inside.
Nancy Cato, Age, 1967

...a book that is not only beautiful but also important ... a work of deep understanding and major importance ... the beautiful style of writing ... Perhaps it is its profound humanity that is the most lasting impression of this book.
J. Jordens, Overland, 1968

The book is free from sentiment, unpretentious, factual and lively ... a fresh, realistic and accurate account of life in one Indian village.
Mary Martin, Australian Book Review, 1967

A Mouthful of Petals

Wendy and Allan Scarfe graduated from Melbourne University, gained qualifications as teachers and taught in Australia, England and India before settling with a young family in Warrnambool. Together they wrote nonfiction books revealing their interest in history, political conflict and social injustice. Separately they wrote poetry, novels and short stories.

Allan died in 2016 but Wendy still lives in Warrnambool and continues to write. Her novel *Hunger Town* was long-listed for the prestigious Nita B. Kibble award for women writers. She has a son and three daughters, and four grandchildren.

BY WENDY SCARFE

Poetry

Shadow and Flowers
Dragonflies and Edges (with Jeff Keith)

Novels

The Lotus Throne
Neither Here Nor There
Laura: My Alter Ego
Miranda
Fishing For Strawberries
Jerusha Braddon, Painter
An Original Talent
Hunger Town
The Day They Shot Edward

BY WENDY AND ALLAN SCARFE

A Mouthful of Petals: The Story of an Indian Village
Tiger on a Rein: Report on the Bihar Famine
People of India
The Black Australians

Victims or Bludgers? Case Studies in Poverty in Australia
Victims or Bludgers? A Poverty Inquiry for Schools
J.P. His Biography
J.P. His Biography (Revised Edition)
Remembering Jayaprakash
Labor's Titan: The Story of Percy Brookfield, 1878–1921 (eds)
All That Grief: Migrant recollections of Greek resistance to fascism, 1941–1949
No Taste for Carnage. Alex Sheppard: a portrait, 1913–1997

BY ALLAN SCARFE

Novels

A Corpse in Calcutta
The Dissident Guru

Short Stories

The Scourge of Termite-ists

*To the memory of Kesurwa,
who had her longed-for baby a year
after our departure,
but died while we were writing her
story.*

PUBLISHER'S NOTE

This is a revised edition of *A Mouthful of Petals,* originally published in London and New York in 1967. The book now has an epilogue, detailing Wendy Scarfe's return trip to India in 1967.

The original book occasioned an Oxfam project in the Indian village that it depicted; inspired some individuals to do aid work; and for years served aid agencies as a primer for intending field workers.

It remains a unique secular Western insight into the 1960s Indian village, and illuminates that renaissance in Indian history when, newly independent of British rule, people had awakened into a new dawn of freedom and were experiencing the heady sense that Indian society could be transformed. It provides domestic glimpses of the famous Indian national leader, Jayaprakash Narayan, whose statue stands outside the national parliament. It is a contribution to the history of international humanitarian aid. Above all it is a moving personal story of what individuals can do to combat the poverty and misery that affects so much of our world.

This edition invites comparisons with today's rural India. To what extent have the dreams of independence days come to pass? Have the village poor been uplifted, as Gandhi enjoined, or left behind?

Three generations have been born since *A Mouthful of Petals* was first published but we hope this unique narrative will fascinate today's readers as much as it did readers more than half a century ago.

Wendy and Allan Scarfe are the joint authors of *A Mouthful of Petals,* but to simplify matters for the reader the story is narrated in the first person, by Allan Scarfe.

FOREWORD

'Gandhi has played a revolutionary role in India of the greatest importance', Jawaharlal Nehru remarked a generation ago, and 'the main contribution of Gandhi to India and the Indian masses has been through the powerful movements which he launched.'

Prominent among these movements, of course, were Gandhi's 'non-cooperation' campaigns against British rule, so that today's assessments of his 'revolutionary role' invariably focus on his leadership of India's struggle for independence. Yet, Gandhi himself would not have wished his role interpreted in this narrow light. For, throughout his thirty years of national leadership, he constantly emphasised the necessity of a social and economic revolution in India, if the fruits of her political independence were ever to be fully enjoyed. Of all Gandhi's movements, therefore, his pet concern was always with the 'constructive programme', a social welfare enterprise grounded in such concrete aims as rural health, education and sanitation, and revival of village handicrafts. The ultimate goal of the constructive programme Gandhi called *sarvodaya,* 'the welfare of all'. For the realisation of this ideal, he believed, 'no speech making is necessary, nor is there any need of legislative councils or legislation. One thing only is essential, and, that is, a small number of selfless workers – men and women. They can by their example and spirit of service get the requisite improvements made'. Another example, to be sure, of Gandhi's irrepressible optimism; but an example and spirit, nevertheless, of which *A Mouthful of Petals* gives a living and vibrant confirmation.

If no social ideal was cherished by Gandhi more than *sarvodaya* then no Indian today has better understood and interpreted the meaning of Gandhi's commitment than his distinguished follower, Jayaprakash Narayan, the leader of the Sarvodaya Movement.] ayaprakash is the central figure in Allan and Wendy Scarfe's narrative, and a word about his background is indicated here, to complement the Scarfes' story of their personal friendship and association with him in India.

Jayaprakash, like Gandhi, was a leader of the independence movement; and, like Gandhi, he commanded respect not only as a political thinker and strategist, but above all through his example of high moral courage. Unlike Gandhi, Jayaprakash received his higher education in the United States, in sociology. Returning to India in 1929 after eight years in America, he joined the freedom struggle as a confirmed Marxist, and urged a path of armed revolution directly antithetical to Gandhi's insistence on nonviolence. Disillusionment with the Soviet experience, however, accompanied an increasingly close association with Gandhi, and after the latter's assassination in 1948, Jayaprakash felt drawn to Gandhi's teachings. By 1953, he had found socialism and communism unsatisfactory, and concluded that 'Gandhism, to my mind, offers the third alternative – that of revolution by non-violent mass action'. Following the lead of Gandhi's teaching, and, more especially, the recent example of another Gandhian, Vinoba Bhave, Jayaprakash renounced his leadership of the Praja Socialist Party, and dedicated his life to Vinoba's *bhoodan* (land-gift) movement for social reform.

Since this critical decision to disassociate himself from 'political parties and power politics' Jayaprakash's reputation has steadily grown. In Europe and America he is widely regarded as the most original and challenging of Asia's contemporary political and social thinkers. Among educated Indians, he is often called a 'sage' rather than an 'intellectual' or 'philosopher'; that is, his ideas are sometimes dismissed as visionary, but few challenge their moral rightness. Among the common people of India, Jayaprakash, like Gandhi and Vinoba, is not only respected, he is revered.

In this last decade, then, Jayaprakash has turned entirely to the task of 'constructive work' that Gandhi had urged. The great aim of the movement which he leads is to continue and accelerate the social revolution begun by Gandhi, until the ideal of *sarvodaya* is realised. In keeping with

Gandhi's predilections, the movement has concentrated on India's villages, where the need for social and economic uplift is staggering. The Government of India is, of course, involved in the effort for rural development, and Jayaprakash's cooperation has often been sought and received. But his prime concern, like Gandhi, is with the encouragement and direction of voluntary civic enterprises. He now serves, for example, as President of the Association of Voluntary Agencies for Rural Development (AVARD), an organisation which brings together more than fifty groups devoted to social service and rural uplift. The 'Gandhian Movement for Village Development', through which the Scarfes served in the north Indian village of Sokhodeora, represents, as their account indicates, an aspect of the Sarvodaya Movement, and as such is personally directed by Jayaprakash Narayan. In response to his warm encouragement, Allan and Wendy left their teaching jobs in Australia for their three years' experience in Sokhodeora. And so it is to Jayaprakash, as well as to the

Scarfes, that we are indebted for this remarkable series of insights into the life of an Indian village.

A Mouthful of Petals gives us far more than a mere description of an Australian couple's volunteer work in India. The multi-faceted nature of their work is understandable, given the scope of village need: schoolteaching formed the basis, but efforts in village sanitation, milk and food distribution, and instruction on first aid, health, nutrition and family planning are all there too. Beyond this however, there appears an admirable balance of view, a sensitive appreciation of the good as well as the bad aspects of village life. In their own words they found Sokhodeora 'a dot on the plain, beautiful, serene'; yet co-existent with this beauty and peace was an inescapable 'anxiety, poverty and misery'. Indeed, the anecdote from which the title of the book was chosen illustrates well this omnipresent duality, which assumes such stark contrasts in India. The Scarfes convey this situation with an uncommon frankness and perception born of the moral impulse

that directed their adventure; and they exhibit everywhere an understanding that could only emerge from the type of intimate relationship they established with the people of Sokhodeora.
Dennis Dalton, PhD,
Department of Economic and Political Studies,
School of Oriental and African Studies, University of London, 1967

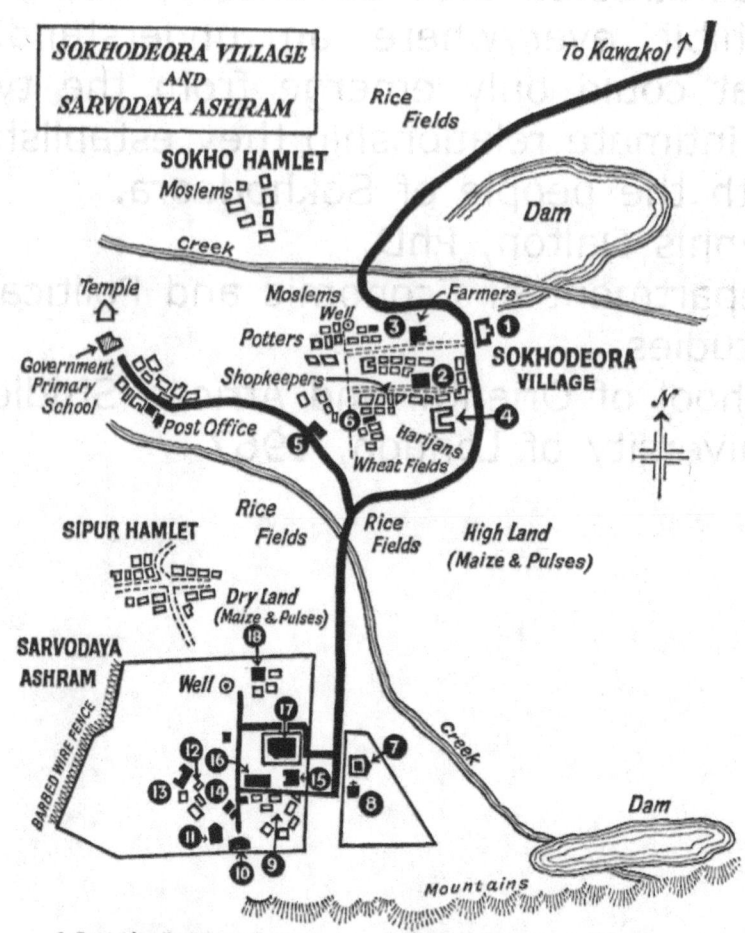

1

SOKHODEORA

Shortly after the scattered township of Pukri Brawan a dirt track branches off the bitumen road and points towards a range of jungle-clad mountains. Deeply rutted by bullock carts and cut by creek beds, this track threads the villages together for the next fourteen miles. Occasionally a truck uses this route to collect bamboo from the mountain sides or a Government jeep comes from the capital, Patna, a hundred miles away.

For the fair-weather bus the terminus is Kawakol, the police station town for the 63,000 villagers of a subdivision in the Gaya District of Bihar. Kawakol straggles along the track for half a mile from a mosque framed in feathery bamboos past the market where the bus stops to the Government hospital outlined against black outcrops of granite.

The shopkeepers here squat on their front steps at five in the morning cleaning their teeth with frayed sticks from the neem tree and spitting into the gutter. Dairymen lead their cows and milk them in front of the householders to prove they have not watered the milk. Gardeners' wives bring cucumbers in bamboo baskets on their heads and squat on the roadside selling.

Three miles farther on, under the cliffs of the Monghyr-Hazaribagh hills, clusters the compact jumble of low chocolate and bronze walls which house the 2000 people of Sokhodeora – farmers, carpenters, potters, shopkeepers, Muslims, toddy tappers, washermen, barbers, bamboo workers, leaf-plate makers, shoemakers, woodcutters, and oil-pressers. The mud walls are only as smooth as hands can shape them, but coloured with earth ochres. The roofs are made of straw or red-earth tiles. These houses merge with the yellow-brown fields and the red sandiness of the road, looking more of the earth than of man; or as if, here, no separation exists between man and nature, no loss of identity with the universe.

Sokhodeora is a dot that is part of the plain; beautiful, serene, full of a sense of continuity with the very beginnings of human civilization.

But to enter the narrow, zigzag alleys between the congested houses *is* to lose much of the impression of beauty and to realise the antiquity of man's anxiety, poverty and misery. Just wide enough to walk through, the alleys are strewn with animal dung and twist closely past accumulations of rubbish. Slimy gutters issue from home kitchens and form greenish puddles. Goats wander with protruding ribs and backbones; emaciated mangy dogs lie exhausted from hunger; pigs fossick for edibles, including human excreta.

The sun breaks the deep shadow of houses, throwing here and there brilliant gold patches on the rows of cow-dung fuel cakes. Slapped on the walls to dry, these still bear the imprint of the fingers of the woman who made them. Where the cakes have dried and fallen there are round stains on the walls.

Some children are naked, others wear only a shirt. The older ones are covered in tattered, discoloured rags of cotton. They peep through matted, dusty and lice-ridden hair or run to hide inside their dark, windowless homes.

To the north, in the foothills of the Himalayas, Pahari people keep flowerpots outside their houses; but here in Sokhodeora no flowers or fruit trees lighten the oppression. As the distant view suggests the beauty and potential of man's life, so the inner reaches of the village contradict this with the closed-in ignorance, the empty-stomached apathy, the hopeless, disease-prone poverty which are Sokhodeora's tragedy in a world that is rich.

There are about 600,000 such villages in India, in which live some 80 per cent of her people – about 350 million. Generally these villages are similarly congested and have neither formed streets, drainage, sanitation nor electricity. Water is drawn from wells and carried for cooking purposes to the houses. A daily bath, if taken, is taken at the well. The fuel is cow dung. Two meals a day are eaten, the chief item being rice. The remnant of the night meal may be eaten at dawn, before work, and a coarse pancake is eaten in the field about midday. The poorest families use the cooking water of rice with spices to replace pulse soup or vegetables.

Members of the castes and sub-castes often live in separate sectors of the village and there is almost no regular association or friendship between castes or between men and women. Most villagers are illiterate. Farming is archaic and unproductive. A mirror, a bicycle, or furniture other than beds, are rare; a village clock or radio even rarer. There is a high incidence of disease and a tragic lack of medical, dental, hospital and educational facilities.

Sokhodeora represents another world, the world of two thirds of mankind, so different that it is almost beyond the imagination of Westerners. And yet someone from London or from Sydney could get there in three or four days.

*

Our first visit to Sokhodeora had been arranged by a friend in London. For about six months we did unpaid educational work for the Gandhian Movement for Village Development, at the invitation of one of India's leading national figures, Shri Jayaprakash Narayan, who at that time was widely considered likely to succeed Mr Nehru. We developed an enduring affection for India before returning to Australia. Two years later Jayaprakash invited us to return and we agreed.

His letters are an interesting record of our arrangements:

London, 27 November 1959: 'I would strongly advise that you lose no time now and return to India as soon as you can. At Sokhodeora there will be a house ready for you and many warm hearts to welcome you.'

Patna, June 1960: 'I want with all my heart that you both return to India: first of all for personal reasons – I want you to be with us. Secondly, and no less importantly, for the reason that it is in the heart of both of you to serve India, and thirdly, for the reason that your service – even though its shape and form may not be very clear yet – would be of great value to us and would add to that international good-will and understanding that are so badly needed.

'I therefore suggest that you prepare to return to India at the beginning of winter this year, i.e. some time in November. You come prepared to stay for at least three years ... we have a new house fitted up for you. We shall arrange for an allowance of Rs.400* a month for you, i.e. Rs.200 a month for each of you.

* Whenever specific sums of money are mentioned in the text we shall refer to these in rupees. At the time of writing, one Australian dollar was worth 8.3 rupees.

	Rs.	$A	£ST.
$A 1 = Rs. 8.33			
£ST. 1 = Rs. 20.98	Rs. 5.28	$A1	8/-
$U.S.A. 1 = Rs. 7.50	Rs.13.30	$A2.51	£1

$A 1 = $U.S.A. 1.1100
Rs. 1 = $A0.12 = £ST. 0/0/11½d = $U.S.A. 0.133
100 naya paisas = 1 Rupee
Old Indian currency: 16 annas = 1 Rupee

'I shall be anxiously waiting to hear from you. I'm going to Europe on 14 June, and will be back by 7 July...'

Patna, 11 July: 'I returned to Patna from Europe (via Delhi and Bombay) yesterday. At Delhi 1 was told to expect a call from Australia at noon, but the telephone exchange informed us that the call did not materialise on account of the Calcutta line being out of order. I was disappointed...

'I had gone so far as the above when the message came that the Australian call had come through. I left off and hurried to the telephone – it is in another house some distance away ... I must express my sorrow that our talk was so unsatisfactory. For me the line was not clear and then I had difficulty in following your accent...

'I feel equally excited now that you are coming. Nothing in our country runs or will run as smoothly as in Australia and you will face problems. But isn't that life? And there will be others facing them with you...'

Sokhodeora, 14 October: 'The question of pioneering arises because it is after all not common for Europeans or Australians or any other foreigners (I hate to use this term) to live in the interior villages of India and do educational work ... In another sense too you will have to pioneer. This is the backward East; so please don't expect all practical details to have been settled for you. You will have a lot of heartaches, but if you do not lose faith in us and in the simple people of this country, I am sure you will never have a heartbreak.'

Tilakpur, 20 October: 'Now I am anxiously waiting to hear from you the exact date of your departure and the approximate time of your arrival at Bombay ... so that I might make all necessary arrangements for your being received and your travel to Sokhodeora.'

New Delhi, 10 December 1960: 'A most warm welcome. Kusum, who is like a daughter to me, will take you to her flat and you may stay in Bombay as long as you wish to recover from the sea journey and get acclimatised to India again...'

*

From Bombay we took the train to Patna, a city accused by a Delhi politician of being the dirtiest in India, where we were met by old friends, including Jayaprakash's wife, Shrimati Prabhavati Devi. There was a party to welcome us and the next morning, accompanied by Shri Brahmanand,

Jayaprakash's private secretary, we set out on the 100-mile trip to Sokhodeora in a station wagon that the Gandhian Movement provided for us.

As we passed through Sokhodeora that evening people and children stared curiously at us, and then a quarter of a mile farther on we reached Jayaprakash's ashram (resting place), quite literally the end of the road.

Men and boys were bringing their cows home to the village from the jungle beyond the ashram and dust rose high from the hooves in the orange evening light. One lad sat cheerfully astride his black buffalo.

The ashram consisted of sixty acres of land, reclaimed from the jungle, and fenced with barbed wire. On the east side of the track were the dairy and maternity hospital separated by an orchard, but we turned through the ornamental wooden gateway into the western half of the institution.

'Goodness, haven't the *gol-mohar* trees grown since we were here before,' Wendy exclaimed to me, as we drove slowly between the communal hall and agricultural students' hostel on one side of the track and two circular colonies of houses on the other.

Since we had left four houses had been built in a square at the village end of the ashram. We unloaded outside the farthest of these, the Western Guest House, distinguished from the Indian Guest House because it had a Western-style lavatory.

Its brick walls had been lately coloured with orange-earth ochre, the iron bars and wooden shutters of the windows freshly painted green, the roof of potter's tiles renovated, the concrete floor in the three rooms newly swept. There was a verandah the full length of the house at the front and a shorter one at the back with a small kitchen at one end and a bathroom and the lavatory at the other.

Wealthier section of Sokhodeora looking south towards the ashram and the Mongyr-Hazaribagh hill track (view from the top of the abandoned landlord's mansion).

Sokhodeora Village. One of the widest streets and the better constructed homes.

The authors with Vidya.

Our kindergarten teacher, Shrimati Kesurwa.

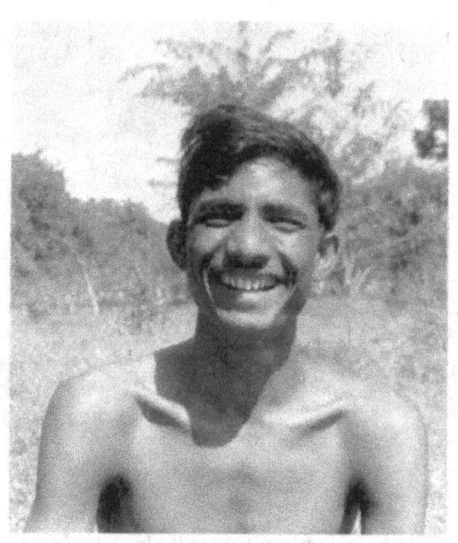

Our helper, Mahadev.

We unpacked bedding, mosquito nets and our Primus camping stove and, after eating, talked and drank tea with Brahmanand by lantern light.

In the morning our servant arrived and asked what work he should do. Mahadev Mochi was a skinny, nervous lad of sixteen with a long thin face, broad flat nose, square jaw and protruding ears. For the occasion he had dressed in his best shirt and dhoti.

'I don't want a servant,' Wendy insisted vehemently to Brahmanand.

Mahadev timidly balanced on one bare foot and then on the other.

'But Jayaprakashji has told me you are to have a servant,' Brahmanand said.

'I'll tell Jayaprakashji that I don't want a servant,' she replied.

Mahadev simply stood, his hands clenched together, frowning miserably, in considerable fear of us. Since we were speaking English he did not understand what was taking place. But our failure to relieve his obvious anxiety was unintentionally cruel of us. We were simply tired and overwhelmed with the many other adjustments we had to make in our new life.

He accompanied me to the office of the Secretary of the Village Construction Board, the non-profitmaking body which ran the ashram with money from private donations and Government subsidies. The Secretary sat cross-legged on the blue cloth which covered the earth floor of the small mud-walled room. He looked up from the papers on a low desk and exchanged greetings.

'Could you find some other job for him instead?' I asked.

He explained gently that it was Jayaprakashji's wish that we have a servant because life here was difficult for foreigners; that the two Japanese agricultural experts had a servant, Mahadev's elder brother; and that the ashram would pay Mahadev's wages. However, he would not insist on our having Mahadev.

I returned to our house alone to find Brahmanand using all his persuasive talents to win Wendy's consent before he had to return to Patna. In the end she agreed reluctantly and presently Mahadev reappeared.

But he passed a miserable and lonely day, for apart from pumping up the water and buying kerosene we did not know what to give him to do.

A stone's throw from our back steps was a well with a pump and hydraulic ram for filling the square tank on a high brick stand from which the water ran into the house. The two guest-houses were the only houses with taps in them. The other ashramites had to carry their water from their well. Pumping was a task Mahadev came to hate, his evasions of which caused the only angry moments between us, while mending the pump became my chief irritation.

We set up house with a pressure cooker, handle-less steel saucepans, a dinner set, cutlery and curtains for the windows and doors, all of which Prabhavati had bought for us. Early on Christmas morning our kerosene-powered refrigerator arrived by bullock cart and unpacking and starting it, arranging books and belongings and washing clothes in buckets of cold water fortunately left us little time to feel how lonely we were or how much we missed our families.

Shortly after our arrival we received a letter from Jayaprakash in Calcutta saying: 'I feel very ashamed that I could neither welcome you at Bombay nor at Patna or the ashram ... I expect to return to the ashram on 2 January Lots of love till then...'

2
THE START OF THE PIONEERING

The news that Jayaprakash was coming with guests jogged the ashram family from the serenity of its daily routine into hurried, nervous activity. Everyone hustled himself and was quick to prod everybody else to look sharp. Each day's arrangements were made at the end of morning or evening prayers.

For two hours before breakfast the men bustled to chip grass from the paths and hurriedly weeded borders, calling fussily to each other, searching for enough mattocks and trying to be first to finish their section. Communal breakfast in the hall was taken in a commotion of chatter instead of in the usual sober silence. Files, papers, accounts flew about the office rooms; hired labourers from the village hustled about the plots and trees in the nursery. Jayaprakash's house was swept, painted, and decorated with pot plants.

The blacksmithy and the soap and carpentry departments were tidied and swept; stray village cows or goats were hurried out the gate. In the Indian Guest House we could see a fluster of bringing of lanterns, bedding and cooking braziers while hired village women mixed cow dung with water in buckets and swept the mixture across the earthen floors to make a fresh, carpeted surface.

When the station wagon arrived, the ashram workers and their families, in their best clothes with hair newly oiled and combed or oiled and plaited, met it at the front gate and were warmly greeted by Jayaprakash and Prabhavati.

Then the driver brought it down the track to the Indian Guest House next to our house.

Jayaprakash had recently inaugurated in South India the Tenth Triennial Conference of the War Resisters International and had brought with him two of the delegates, a Frenchman and an African. Looking about the rooms they were to occupy he issued instructions on the making of beds and the provision of towels, mosquito nets and soap, all of which were promptly fulfilled. He shook our hands affectionately.

'You look very nice,' he said, meaning that he was pleased to see us there. Then promising to visit us for tea he turned his attention back to lanterns and cooking arrangements, before he went to take his bath and lunch. He was wearing traditional *kurta* (shirt), *dhoti* and sandals and somehow managed, as he invariably did, to look fresh and clean in spite of more than a day's travelling in heat and dust.

He was a tall, slender man of somewhat above six feet, erect despite shoulders which were slightly stooped with his fifty-eight years. The fine hair had receded a little from his high forehead. He had a long upper lip and delicately chiselled bow of mouth over a square chin. His eyes, full of movement behind fine-rimmed spectacles, had worry, gentleness and impatience written in them. In repose his face bore a sad, frowning expression, which possibly had been what had given rise to a *Time* characterisation of him as being 'nearly as prominent, and as much of a brooding Hamlet, as Nehru himself'.

His flesh was drawing in slowly on the high cheekbones and wide jaw-structure which newspaper cartoonists enjoyed exaggerating, but he remained extremely handsome and youthful-seeming, vital, sensitive, idealistic, compassionate, a leader of men.

When our nervous Mahadev saw him coming to our house that afternoon he made himself invisible. Jayaprakash rested his carved, rosewood walking stick against our doorway and was about to slip out of his sandals when Wendy assured him: 'We don't bother to remove our shoes, JP, because the floors are concrete.' Jayaprakash is known affectionately throughout India and beyond by the initials JP.

'You are both looking very well,' he remarked with solicitude. His first query whenever he met us was for our health.

To begin with we were all awkward. Although affection had passed between us in letters there was still shyness and reserve between us on meeting again. He inquired about Kusum and our journey, which was natural enough. But it was also characteristic of him, whenever there was an embarrassing pause in conversation or a discussion he did not want to begin abruptly, to talk about travelling arrangements; probably because he spent so much of his own time travelling.

'Is the house comfortable enough for you to manage?' he asked. 'You must let me see how you have been able to arrange everything. I am only sorry that we are not able to accommodate you as comfortably as you would be in your own country.'

'We are quite comfortable,' Wendy assured him, showing him through the house. It was the most modern house in the ashram and for at least thirty miles around.

'You have mosquito nets and bamboos for them,' he murmured approvingly in our bedroom.

Our twin beds were pulled together in the middle of the room. Each of the nets hung on four pieces of bamboo caught behind the bed legs.

'You must also have a dressing table with a mirror. You will be used to that and you will need it. I will have one made for you.'

'No, please don't,' Wendy protested.

'Most Western women have them, don't they? Are the beds comfortable? They were made here in the ashram.'

'Yes, quite comfortable, thank you. We are spoiled having mattresses.'

The base of the beds was strung with a criss-cross of springy webbing, and the mattresses were about an inch thick, stuffed with cotton. Ashram beds were normally string-strung or made of planks, like low tables, and the sleepers used only a cotton sheet underneath themselves.

We had also been given a teak wardrobe and beside it was our kerosene refrigerator, the only other piece of furniture in the room.

'It's a funny place to have it,' Wendy laughed, 'but just there seems to be the least draughty spot in the house.'

'It is the same model as we have in the ashram maternity hospital. I brought that one from England,' he remarked.

'I hope you didn't have all the trouble we had getting it through Customs in Bombay,' Wendy said.

'Someone else handled all the baggage for me,' he replied vaguely. 'What was your difficulty?'

We told him the story as we went through into what we called our workroom, which we had furnished with a table and chair and a glass-fronted cupboard to store our crockery, cutlery and food free from flies. He looked with interest at the two trunks of children's projects, display charts and pictures, reference books and kindergarten equipment we had been given.

'How are you managing about your food and cooking?' he then asked.

'Very well,' Wendy replied. 'Come and see our stove.'

The kitchen was a tiny room with two small glass windows. Glass windows were most unusual, the nearest being thirty miles away in the shops of Nawada. There was a tap in one corner over a concrete sink set at floor level. Concrete shelves ran along two walls. As we had installed a small table, a wire cupboard and the Primus on the box it had travelled in (arrangements which allowed Wendy to stand instead of squatting like Indian women), there was only space for her and Jayaprakash to go in.

'See, these two burners on the top are for saucepans and here's a third burner underneath for the oven.'

'What is the purpose of the oven?'

'I make our own bread and I can make cakes.'

'What a marvellous thing,' he commented, with the sense of wonder he usually showed about the ingenuity of mechanical gadgets.

'It's just a camping stove,' she replied. It was simple enough beside the electric stoves of Western homes but it was not available in India. Middle-class city people had eyed it enviously. Village women made their own mud stoves, or *chulas.*

Wendy made the tea as they talked.

'Is Mahadev cooking for you?'

'No, he does the chores that are time-consuming for us – pumping up the water, sweeping the floors, going messages.'

'You will have to train him. He will not be accustomed to your kind of food.'

'I'd rather do my own cooking, really, JP.'

'Won't it be very difficult for you? You shouldn't have to worry about these things.'

'I'm used to working and keeping house in Australia.'

'But it's more troublesome here. There are not the conveniences.'

'Don't you worry. We'll see how it goes.'

'Do not hesitate to take work from him. He can wash your clothes and boil your drinking water. He comes from a very honest family.'

We went back into our middle room, which just fitted a table and chairs. Wendy served the afternoon tea, apologising for her chocolate cake because it was too moist. There were also dry biscuits with tinned butter and tinned Kraft cheese. The butter was Indian and cost 50 naya paisas an ounce. The cheese was imported Australian at twelve ounces for Rs 7.50. Items such as these we had to bring from Patna. Finally we had a tin of shortbread, given to us as a farewell present.

As Wendy offered them he demanded sharply and suspiciously, 'Where did these come from? From the bazaar or from your country?'

He was as exacting about the cleanliness of food and drinking water as he was punctilious about his clothing.

'They're from Australia.'

'They would be all right then,' he said, taking one.

Mahadev made an appearance in the workroom, where he hovered apprehensively. 'What's the matter, Mahadev?' Wendy asked, but he was too worried to reply. 'He feels he should be doing this, not you,' Jayaprakash said quietly. He added in Hindi, 'It's all right, Mahadev.'

'Now we must talk about your work,' he said. 'I wholeheartedly agree with all that Allan wrote about environmental education in his letters. Though I still would not agree that my idea of a peripatetic school would serve no purpose. The equipment could be moved by bullock cart every three months.'

'I don't say no purpose,' I protested, 'but just that education has to be continuous and repetitive and I think it would be better to establish a permanent school in one place. I really can't envisage a moving school except in terms of a mobile film unit.'

'Even now,' Jayaprakash continued, 'I must say frankly that I don't know what specific, clear-cut work to give you. You received the books I sent you on Gandhian Basic Education? Our Sarvodaya (Uplift of All) Movement adheres to ideas of Basic Education but these ideas are not peculiarly Indian or Gandhian.'

'Yes, we received them, thank you. It's all most appropriate to village conditions. Possibly it was from Gandhi that UNESCO developed its programme of Fundamental Education. We've brought some beautifully illustrated books, too, that you might like to see.'

He flipped through the illustrations to Langford's *Guidance of the Young Child* and Lowenfeld's *Creative and Mental Growth* and, looking up in surprise, remarked: 'I didn't know so much had been written about education.'

'There are libraries of them I'm afraid,' I replied.

'The main difficulty with education in this country,' he said, putting down the books and resuming the conversation, 'is that education is desired mainly to obtain Government employment. The result is that education from the top to the bottom is under Government control in one way or another. Every school wants official 'recognition'; recognition brings with it all manner of controls and regulations and interference.

'I have long been thinking of establishing a school which will flaunt a signboard with the words: "Not recognised: Education Here no Passport to Government Employment." Perhaps you could help with something along these lines. You may not know that we have a primary school here in the ashram.'

'Yes, we have visited it.'

'The ashram artist, Shantiranjan, began a little art class on his back verandah, and then Boddh Narayan, from Sokhodeora, voluntarily taught them some Hindi and so forth for six months. He is paid now. You could give some advice there on the proper way to run it. It is hard to say what you will do. First of all, in any case, you must learn as much Hindi as you can.'

Having given us our assignment he called Mahadev in and asked him kindly and gently in Hindi whether he liked the job and what tasks he did for us. Continuing in the same tone of voice he instructed him in all the work he was supposed to do, such as washing our clothes, which we never did ask of him. There was scarcely a change in Mahadev's blank, awe-struck expression as he made short, almost whispered replies.

'Good,' Jayaprakash said, which was his usual way of ending a conversation, and with a goodbye to us left with the abruptness characteristic of his departures.

Was he disappointed with our talk? We had been anxious and over-eager and not adaptable enough to see the practicality of his scheme for adult extension classes, the 'peripatetic school'. And in such terms he never mentioned it again.

Certainly we were disappointed. We were keen to achieve all that we could in our three-year term, so had hoped for concrete instructions and a delegation of the authority necessary to put them into effect.

It is perhaps worth reflecting that defining goals seems to bring about a similar kind of problem when Westerners and Easterners work together. There is some difficulty in translating high ideals into practical applications without the Westerners seeming to the Easterners to replace vision with materialistic technique, or the Easterners seeming to the Westerners to be impractical organisers.

*

At the mountain end of the ashram, the end opposite us, the houses had been built in two circular 'colonies'. Number 4 in the Western colony had housed us on our first visit here about three years earlier, without the present amenities of taps, shower, cement floors or septic-tank lavatory. Now two Japanese agriculturalists lived there.

The house next to theirs had been made over into the school. It was a room thirty feet by twelve, somewhat longer than the average English or Australian sitting room, with mud walls and earth floor. The roofing poles were supported by whitewashed brick piers spaced along the verandahs and inside the room. At one end of the back verandah there was a kitchen and at the other a bathroom, for both of which the school had no use.

It was late winter weather. Brilliant sunshine dispersed the morning dew and mountain mists by lunchtime. Consequently the children were sitting cross-legged on very dusty coir mats in the sunny part of the yard behind the building. The yard had been given a coating of cow-manure paste across its level surface to reduce the dust and it was enclosed by a fence of bamboo matting, painted with bitumen to discourage white ants. Two shady neem trees with dark, feathery foliage grew there. From one of these hung a faded blackboard made of strips of plank.

There were two men teachers and one woman, Mataji (Respected Mother), who was daydreaming on a low wooden bed. She was short and plump and moved extremely slowly. Her grey hair was combed and braided meticulously into a long plait framing a pretty face that disappeared into double chins. She wore the white handspun, hand-woven sari and blouse worn by all women of the Gandhian Movement. On the other wooden bed the two men sat chatting. Like Mataji, the thin elderly man, after a polite greeting, ignored us; shortly afterwards, before we knew his name, he left the ashram for another position.

Boddh Narayan greeted us effusively: 'I am *very* happy to meet you Respected Brother and Respected Sister. We are all so glad that you have come to our country. Please tell me everything about the proper running of this school. You are my elder brother and sister and I must do everything you tell me. I will be greatly privileged to be allowed to become your disciple and learn from you.'

He was about twenty-one, gracefully thin, with a long fine nose and an eager, boyish expression on his long, narrow face.

Thanking him, we merely asked if we could observe his school for some days. Jayaprakash had gone from the ashram but he obviously had left few or no instructions with the teachers on what our role was to be. So we observed.

There were some thirty children from about three to thirteen years old, although they did not know their own ages and their grades were little indication. One boy in the first grade would have been about twelve. But the older ones in Grades 3 and 4 all told us proudly that they were married – what we should call betrothed. Two girls from ashram families were cleanly clothed in dresses over shorts, with their hair oiled and plaited. Boddh Narayan's two nieces, Vidya and Chandra, who came from the village, were similarly dressed and groomed. But the remaining village children were grubby, with torn, inadequate scraps of cotton cloth round them, and dusty matted hair.

The classes were all mixed in together and made a hubbub of noise, for when a group was told to read they all did so, from different places in their readers, at the top of their lungs, making it impossible for anyone else to hear another teacher. In the main, however, they sat without any task allotted to them so that there were frequent rushes of children on to the slide, from which no one seemed in a hurry to remove them. In addition, there was a constant movement of boys to the urinal, where they lingered and played. The unwatched, unmotivated pupils on the mats fought each other, so that someone small was crying at most times.

Three boys in particular seemed to be the special victims of aggressive urges, but most often it was Durgi who was attacked. He looked a physically robust lad, was clad in torn rags, and spoke with a perpetual whine. He did no reading or writing, insisting that he could not, but spent much of his day lying on the mat being pummelled. We guessed these attentions partly sprung from the caste attitudes of his teachers who laughed about his plight saying: 'Oh, he's just the village washer-woman's son'.

Coming from a society where the standard of education was so established it was disturbing to us to see that there was no encouragement of curiosity, creativity or initiative; no training in application, concentration or persistence; no purposeful repetition of work; no testing or checking to assess individual progress. It seemed, too, that the teachers only concerned themselves *in* the classes with teaching the two or three children to whom they were related or of whom they were fond, or favoured the children of the higher caste.

Some children had slates and slate pencils; some had dog-eared, dusty textbooks, exercise books made of sheets of plain paper sewed together, a steel-nib pen and an ink bottle; but a large number had nothing and the school had nothing to lend them.

Children of kindergarten age, who had been brought along and were protected by an elder brother or sister, were not taught but sat sulkily passive for hours. The one exception was Chandra, who wrote the numbers to a hundred in cramped columns on her slate over and over and over.

What were we to suggest first in this school where no syllabuses were prepared or followed? Where there was no daily timetable? Where learning did not progress from day to day? If the teachers felt satisfied with this kind of teaching how could we encourage them to new ways? Could they see that only the children who were particularly intelligent or persistent learnt, while most were losing the talents they had?

Assuming we were to take charge, we set about separating the classes so that the smaller ones were not continually frustrated by having their abilities and achievements compared with those of an older group. To our teachers we repeated the slogan: 'One Teacher, One Class, One Place', in the manner of television commercials. Not knowing ages we divided the children on knowledge, size or teeth – anyone with baby teeth was counted as being under six.

To begin with, little brother and sister were most aggrieved at being removed from elder brother or sister and vigorously insisted that he or she could do the work of the senior class. To help us staff this arrangement one of the Japanese agriculturalists, Ikeda San, a plump, cheerful, slow, moon-faced man, gave up his spare time. We only needed to watch him for a few minutes to conclude that education in Japan resembled that in Australia. For he responded happily to the children, made use of their activities and interests, kept them all busy, checked each one's work with an encouraging word, explained difficulties and made progress through the textbook. But he only stayed a few weeks.

However, whether it was because we explained the advantages of separating classes carefully enough to be convincing, or whether the arrangement resulted in easier work, this innovation was continued.

Nevertheless it had been the pre-school children's passivity that had most upset us. Any excitement, keenness or joy was being destroyed before they had begun their education. So we took charge of them ourselves.

They objected. They were afraid of being apart from the others and afraid of us. And we did not know enough Hindi or village dialect to reassure them in the face of our newness and strange clothes. One little boy, who had sat almost motionless for days, his eyes clogged with yellow mucus so that he could scarcely see, bawled for so long with such terror that he had to be left in Second Class.

In addition we offended Mataji. She resented losing the group for a reason we learned a year later. For the Social Welfare Board in Delhi had sent her to this ashram to conduct a kindergarten. Before long word found its way back to us that she thought we disliked her. Going to her house before school we assured her that she was mistaken, but our relationship continued to be strained.

We could see no happy solution to this problem because she was elderly and could hardly be expected to be harassed with new tricks: on the contrary, by ordinary standards, Wendy should have been learning traditions and ways from her, paying her the deference which the other younger ashram women did.

Still, the pre-school group was soon fascinated by the building blocks, animal insets and highly coloured plastic constructional toys we brought. Everybody was. Seeing them allowed free play the children from the other classes deserted their teachers and conquered the kindergarteners with pushes and slaps, snatching the trains and balls for themselves.

Two months later things were improving due to our exasperated slapping of offenders' legs – we were not fluent enough to stem the invasions with words. But we realised they suffered unjustly, for they should not have been allowed to run out of class and they, too, should have been allowed such constructional joys. Village people should have been able to afford toys for their children.

3
SCHOOLS AND HIBISCUS FLOWERS

I held the village-industry soap high above my head as I cut each cake into smaller pieces with a pocket knife. The soap had been boiled up in the ashram from the oil of seeds crushed out by bullock presses in an adjoining room. In front of me twenty boys shouted, jostled each other and reached up their hands for a piece. Then they jerked away at the pump on the well behind our house and smothered themselves with lather. That was the beginning of the daily bath at our school immediately before lunch.

The oldest, most serious boy, Jodhan, who was about thirteen, we quickly elected as Health Minister. He took charge of the soap, replenished it as it was used, and distributed it to the children in orderly rows. His most difficult duty was collecting it after the bath, as some of the boys attempted to steal pieces to take home for their families. There was much pocket frisking and shaming of offenders, our students being stern disapprovers of stealing when someone else was caught at it. Not that our disapproval was less stern, but it was consciously dishonest because we knew that to many village families soap was a luxury. Wherever you go in India you can see women washing their waist-length hair with ashes or mud.

Many of the children took the chance at bathtime to wash their clothes and either walked around naked stretching their bodies like cats until clothes dried on the grass or else put the wet things on again and shivered. As they only possessed one set of clothes we decided on a school uniform which could be hung on a named nail before the children left school and worn during the day while their clothes dried. The manager of the ashram *khadi* shop, selling hand-spun, hand-woven cloth, measured our children and arranged tailors to make shorts and shirts for the boys and shorts and dresses for the girls.

Boddh Narayan wrote the names on the clothes when they arrived and each child walked about proudly, fussing with the way the shorts sat on his hips or getting Mataji to adjust his collar. To have new clothes was an experience they only had, if they had it at all, at the colour-throwing festival of Holi in March. Fat three-year-old Prakash was the only one whose clothes did not fit. Two of his friends plumped on their knees to grapple with his pants, but pull and tug as they might the waist would just not fit over his ungovernable paunch. The sight of him frowning and wincing as they yanked would have been highly comic but that his distended stomach was due to roundworm.

'I didn't get new clothes,' protested a new boy who had come from another school.

'I didn't get new clothes,' complained a poor attender who had missed measuring day.

The nights and mornings were cool for the children in cotton clothes, so in addition we bought cheap black blankets which we cut into four, each piece to serve as a shawl. That was some compensation for the aggrieved as we had no more funds for more uniforms.

The experiment was a failure. We did not know enough disciplinary Hindi to make the children leave the uniform at school so that it would serve the purpose of cleanliness as we had intended, and, for whatever reason, our teachers would not make the effort to keep control. When we found more than thirty garments strewn about the earth floor one afternoon with the children walking over them we called all uniforms in and had the children wash them. Then we sold them from our house. For two hectic days, from 6am until nightfall, parents and children arrived. What had cost the equivalent of five rupees went, depending on the poverty of the family, from one rupee to 50 naya paisas. The proceeds we spent on books for the school library for which the Ashram Management Committee donated a cupboard.

Thus from our point of view some village families were helped without humiliation, and they shouldered the problem of caring for the clothes.

But not everyone saw it in that light. A couple of parents used the episode as an excuse for not sending their children to school, saying: 'I'm not sending them to that school because you don't give them clothes.'

Perhaps it was their exasperated response to our regular request throughout the village: 'Why don't you send your children to school?'

We did this because only a quarter of the children in the area attended school. Forty per cent of boys attended but not quite eight per cent of girls. Education to Grade 3 was compulsory but not enforced. There was not the machinery to enforce the law nor would there have been room to accommodate all children. For the higher grades, fees had to be paid which many could not afford.

Daily attendance at our school was so irregular that we used to have an accounting each month praising the most regular attenders and Jhodan won the prize each year. When there was harvesting we might have as few as twenty students, while at other times 120 might arrive.

Most of them looked sturdy and energetic yet the majority had a cold all through the year. There is little information about child morbidity in India, but UNICEF reports indicate that more than 40 per cent of Indian children have acquired tuberculosis infections by the age of fourteen.

Suresh was covered with scabies, three had trachoma, one was going blind, and one boy had large white blotches on his foot that to our ignorant eyes might have been leprosy.

There seemed no use in the children learning to read and write if they were going to die or go blind, but the parents were clearly not seeking medical treatment for their sick children. Were an illness to become serious they might resort to forest herbs, or quacks, or even superstitions, such as the use of spells for tetanus; but only the educated would go to a qualified doctor. Happily, we were able to arrange regular medical inspections at the ashram hospital. We kept health records, dispensed doses and talked with parents. Normally a quarter of the children were suffering from either anaemia, parasitic worms, typhoid fever, trachoma, malaria or malnutrition sores.

'Our school is not enough to generalise from,' we hesitantly remarked much later to two doctors, 'but if it is in any way typical, then up to a quarter of India's village children could be in need of and not receiving medical attention.'

'More like a half,' they both replied.

The seriousness of such health problems was emphasised when a girl of eight in Mahadev's quarter of Sokhodeora died from tetanus. They all got thorns in their bare feet. Hers was fatal.

Boddh Narayan arranged for a visit by the Government vaccinator and his arrival was spectacular. In an instant our attentive classes were darting across the ashram fields while we stood puzzled. The new Health Minister, Shiva, hid in the jungle until the afternoon, for which poor example he was demoted. But pursuit, shouts, threats, cajolings brought most of them back to the elderly, unshaven man with the small black box.

Seated on a wooden table he swabbed forearms with a quick dash of methylated spirits, squeezed a globule from a small tube and twisted firmly into the flesh with a four-pointed prong. The old-fashioned method. He was supposed, too, to clean the prong with spirit after each patient.

The girls went first. They took the vaccination in silence. The boys hung back. They cried, bellowed, jumped and tried to snatch the prong away, all the time making agonised faces. Then they all stood or sat about, holding their arms extended, looking at the abrasion with wonder, now laughing and brave once again.

We felt responsible for warning the mothers of the ensuing reaction. A week or so later a number came to us anxiously wanting both reassurance and instructions in what to do for the fever.

On his next visit, Jayaprakash, seeing what we were doing in the school, suggested that we visit the schools of the Kawakol Police Station area, meet the teachers, and think of ways to help them. He must have spoken of this also to the Block

Development Officer, Shri Sharma, for we were taken to meet him a day or two later.

The Indian Government had brought the whole of rural India under the Block Development Scheme, setting up a Block for each group of villages with a population of up to 100,000 to serve a variety of administrative and developmental purposes. Like most, Kawakol Block had the characteristic flat-topped, concrete office buildings and residences within a fenced area in which gardens, trees and a children's park were being developed. It had clerical, agricultural, engineering, medical and welfare staff. Its look of newness, spaciousness and cleanliness contrasted sharply with Kawakol town.

The Block Development Officer must have sent the Schools Inspector. He arrived at our house on his bicycle full of enthusiasm, drew sketch maps and jotted down teachers' names and even planned meetings of teachers who we would address. From another quarter we were asked to prepare a report of school conditions for the Central

Government's Khadi and Village Industries Commission.

When Jayaprakash had written to us about returning to India he had asked seriously: 'Can you ride bicycles?' Then he had added in some amusement: 'Our Prime Minister Mr Nehru has said that India is just entering the bicycle age.'

We had assured him amusedly that we could. Our experience, of course, had been mainly with bitumen or formed roads. The tracks spider-webbing out from Kawakol were another proposition, as we were to discover two mornings a week. We borrowed the two ashram cycles from their caretaker, Yogendra, an earnest young man who amused us with his almost rapturous pride in them. And after we had dusted and repaired them they did us very well. Of course village children and youths besieged us to let them learn to ride, some even offering 50 naya paisas for an hour. Mahadev shared the longing and practised frenziedly, getting the bike going before him at a run and then trying to leap on from behind.

Our winter visits to schools were delightful. There was a freedom and gaiety about spinning our bicycles together along the narrow, rutted tracks through villages where women stared disapprovingly at Wendy. Doubtless a woman cycling, bare-legged in a Western skirt, accompanying her husband, seemed immodest to them. Reaching sluggish green streams, where people washed after toileting, we recklessly put on speed down the banks and lifted feet high off the pedals when our wheels hit the water hoping our momentum would carry us across and not dump us in the middle. Village men, carefully wading across, with black furled umbrellas invariably tucked under one arm while the other hand held their *dhoti* up to their knees, looked at us as if we were most eccentric. Perhaps we were a little intoxicated with youth, a sense of adventure and of freedom from inhibitions.

Sokhodeora was soon left behind. It had three private schools: an elderly, courteous Muslim teaching Arabic script to a handful of Muslim children in a dark room of his house; a young Hindu with shaven head who seemed a little unbalanced and was utterly irregular about time, or attending at all, wielding a stick in an open spot on the eastern fringe of the village; and a surly middle-aged man with a huge stick in hand sitting in a chair with his feet up blocking the door to the village library, which was in the lane alongside most of the shops. Trapped inside were thirty or forty children in a space nine feet by twelve. He, too, was often late and irregular. To teach he shouted 'Read!' and everyone did full blast. The din could be heard from the village outskirts. Each month this teacher banged a drum through the village to collect the fee of one rupee a month per pupil.

Sokhodeora Government school had two mud-walled rooms. The two men teachers lived in them and the children normally sat on the earth verandah or on the few feet of ground the school had in front. Like the average school it had no lavatory: health was a subject in the curriculum but it did not usually take much practical form. The teachers were expected to follow the syllabuses and daily routine published by the Bihar State Government, the overriding principle of which was to try to make schoolchildren happy, to provide some active joy for village children and people and an appreciation of things that were apart from the daily struggle to exist.

It was sad to see the way they carried this out. When the children began to fight or run about too much the teachers wielded a stick and shouted, 'Sit down! Read!' They took their baths and washed their clothes during lessons. At times they were simply 'Gone away' and the children sat for hours awaiting their return; at times they had gone to their family or had 'temperature' for a couple of weeks; occasionally the children had all gone home for lunch or a drink of water at the strangest times. Once they tried to illegally extort enrolment fees from the Harijan (the lowest caste) parents. However, we did not find them sleeping in front of the pupils like the teacher of a nearby village, and perhaps some excuse may be found for their unprofessional conduct in the fact they were paid only Rs.60 a month.

Occasionally Wendy took a spill in ruts or a sandy creek bed but the road to Kawakol was comparatively smooth. It swung out of Sokhodeora in a semicircle on the top of a low dam wall then turned where an old *mahua* tree threw shade for passers-by to rest on their journey. It then crossed by a brick bridge over a sluggish, slimy rivulet where frogs croaked and slender ibis hunted them and finally turned sharply round a house into the crowded, filthy main street of Kawakol.

On either side of the street were brick shops where blouses or shirts were made on old sewing machines, where rice, flour, spices and pulse were kept in earthenware pots, where sweets attracted flies and bees and cigarette and betel shops were made from the rusty sides of kerosene tins. Hens, goats, dogs and children scattered before bullock carts carrying timber, bamboo, handmade baskets or bags of rice. Pools of water from the shops gathered dust in hollows in the earth road. During the dry season the unpunctual bus squealed, rattled and coughed down the street, covering people and foodstuffs in a cloud of dust.

Squeezed in the middle of the shops was a brightly coloured Hindu temple in the entrance of which was a private Lower Primary School that enrolled children for the first, second and third grades.[2] Eighty youngsters sat cramped together on the concrete floor and were kept in some order by the teacher's liberal use of a stick. They chanted their lessons aloud or wriggled

We observed at least seven schools in Kawakol and its hamlet, Rani Bazaar, the most successful one being a girls' school of thirty-two pupils in a new, two-roomed brick building with a cleanly dressed, cheerful lady teacher who had delivered a baby two days previously.

Opposite the Block gate there was a Lower Primary School on a house verandah where it seemed to us the teacher was paid for keeping away.

---

[2] Unlike our ashram school, which eventually spanned from kindergarten to Grade 7, Government schools were divided into Lower Primary (Grades 1–3), Upper Primary (Grades 4–5), Middle School (Grades 4–7), and High School (Grades 8–matriculation).

Nearby, Shri Rameshwar Prasad's private school was on a verandah five feet by twelve, which jutted into the dusty road and a wood yard. But it seated twenty-five boys whose legs he periodically belted with his stick without moving from his chair. There was the usual sight of a boy of fifteen in third grade.

The biggest was the Government Middle School taking Grades 4 to 7. It had a well, a lavatory and a children's vegetable garden, but for the first month or six weeks of a new year the teachers sat at a table in the sun taking enrolments. Any children who attended played volleyball.

We most frequently visited the Upper Primary School, a dilapidated brick building with three rooms, a sagging roof and a well with broken brickwork. The three men teachers generally sunned themselves or read an out-of-date newspaper, not venturing much into the ill-lit rooms where their pupils droned or quarrelled. But one of them, a slight Muslim with a grizzled beard, was charming to us, frequently requesting our help to build a brick wall to keep out goats and enable the children to have a garden. He proposed very simply that we give him the money.

He was greatly disappointed with our more cautious proposal to deliver him two hundredweights of wire. Nevertheless he assured us that he and the children would cut poles from the jungle. As the posts never arrived, neither did the wire, and we went down in his estimation.

It was always pleasant to rest in a tree's shade on the outskirts of Kawakol and admire the graceful mosque, white with golden and heliotrope designs, looking pure and removed from the clouds of dust and heat. Winter was moving into summer; the thermometer reaching the nineties.

The road split before it reached another dry river. One branch led through barren land towards the other mountains on the north side of the plain. About a mile farther on in that direction the ashram leprosy centre and model village had been built. Near the corner was a private high school with straw roof and brick walls only to head height, some of the bricks not even cemented together. Most of the matriculation students had no other ambition than to farm their father's land and no idea how their studies of Sanscrit and English would help them become better farmers.

Taking the left branch we then rode towards Pukri Brawan and the outside world. We took frequent spills from the holes and the deep ruts of bullock carts. We walked where a layer of clods had been thrown on to the track to build it up above the rice plots, which would be flooded in the monsoon.

At Saraunia the teacher greeted us warmly and showed us his school with pride. The village people had built it themselves four years earlier. It was a mud-walled room nine feet by eighteen in which sixty-one children were squeezed, sitting on the earth floor as usual, and behind them was a tiny room for stores – five maps, palm-leaf hand brooms and some rope made by the children. There were three tiny, wooden-barred windows giving some light, and doorways but no doors.

We were moved by his effort. There was no blackboard, lavatory or playground, but he seemed to stick carefully to the Government timetable, kept Grades 1, 2 and 3 separate from each other, encouraged silent reading and the children showed competence in their work. An atmosphere of orderliness and affection existed between him and his pupils and there was no stick in evidence. As a gesture of encouragement we left them some lead pencils and illustrated magazines in Hindi, suspecting that he would not prevent his pupils from looking at something off the syllabus.

With us, too, we carried a box of pictures illustrating the Japanese method of rice cultivation, which we had been given by Shri S.K. Dey, Minister for Community Development, on his visit to the ashram. But they were a little advanced for Grade 3 despite the children's pleasure at being shown large pictures.

And so until late in March – Bandichuk, Bararaji, Bhorambag, Lower Primary, Upper Primary, middle schools, Government and private – the temperature passing 100°F and forcing us to return home by midday.

The only Government high school for the area was at Phuldih. It had spartan residential quarters for children who lived too far away to walk there daily and the boarders kept their own vegetable garden. The staff were proud of their small library and simple science equipment, and we watched the only science lesson we saw, the teacher demonstrating a chemical experiment to his students who sat on long wooden benches. The grade of pay was higher than in primary schools, the headmaster earning about Rs.100 a month.

Chairs were brought and morning tea courteously served us in the office. When it had been poured there was an anxious, whispered consultation as to what our custom might be in the order of serving. Evidently deciding that it would be the same as theirs they served me first. Quite automatically I passed the cup to Wendy, then saw their expressions of confusion and embarrassment.

Mudrapoor Upper Primary School was the last we visited for our survey, but our experiences formed the basis of the speeches I was invited to give to meetings of teachers and Block Development Committee meetings, where I pleaded primarily for lavatories, medical inspections of children, wells, and for abolishing the stick.

Mudrapoor was some miles into the eastern sector of the area, which was harsher and here the villagers were poorer. Passing between the black, pyramid-shaped rocks behind the Block we rode perspiringly through a wide expanse of sand and stones that flung up the glare of the sun into heat haze and mirage.

The teacher was a fat, middle-aged man who emanated both confidence and severity. The usual springy palm stick lay in threatening readiness across his table, but he and the children had built a lavatory and he later sent some boys to us at the ashram to learn soap-making.

Very reluctantly we got our cycles out of the shade and pushed off on the track which, bypassing Kawakol, skirted 'Bear Mountain'. We stopped frequently under trees and looked regretfully at our empty thermos. Wendy's front tyre took a puncture and the patch would not stick, so we walked most of the way back.

Near the ashram we took a shortcut across country and along the top of a big earth dam that had been built in the times of village landlords to catch the monsoon run-off from the mountains. In Wendy's estimation it was, like most of my shortcuts, more difficult than the long way and we had to drag our bicycles over beds of rocks and up and down steep, water-cut gullies while the sun hammered the cracked earth and the west wind hurled leaves and dust. We reached the ashram fence in such a state of weariness that we just leaned on it while Yogendra, who was working in his vegetable garden, brought us a long drink of water, and we did not care whether it had been boiled or not.

We settled back to the problems of our own school until we went to the hills near the end of April to escape the relentlessly increasing heat that dried out our energy as it climbed towards 127°F in the shade in June.

Our teachers needed training as much as we needed to know more Hindi and more about village customs and thought patterns. The textbooks were inadequate, and learning in basic subjects was weak. There were conflicts with parents for time wasted on bathing and medical treatment, and conflicts because we had introduced practical craft activities, creative work in art, and 'toys'. There were currents of Government versus private schools and students removed to get a 'recognised' education. There were irritating visitors who wanted us to talk instead of teaching, or to use a stick, who felt that there was nothing to understand about children except that they were 'naughty' and we were odd to fancy otherwise. There were those who thought that teaching was the last resort of the desperate unemployed.

We took nature walks instead of studying nature from a book and we introduced a new kind of art lesson. Boddh Narayan's occasional art lesson consisted of him drawing a stylised mango or peacock on the blackboard and telling the children to copy it. This was the way his teachers had taught him and neither our long and careful persuasion nor the abrupt scorn of a visiting Japanese artist ever changed his mind. But we had no differences about clay modelling.

For our part we stimulated children's thoughts on a topic or took them to watch an activity like irrigation or wheat cutting and then they created. When we ran out of paper we allowed each a section of the whitewashed walls. They drew just what Lowenfeld had observed Western children draw except that they were years behind in development. The most bold and original child was chubby, huge-eyed, dreamy Latoo Mistri, whose father was the Sokhodeora blacksmith. Although he was in Grade 3, a man to him was nothing but a huge lurid head about two feet across. Unfortunately his father disapproved of our new ways and sent Latoo to the Kawakol Middle School and Latoo ever afterwards looked at us with a furtive, guilty expression.

The most interesting painting was done by a boy of thirteen or fourteen in which anything of significance was exaggerated, as in the paintings of Western seven-year-olds. The scene showed the school roof being repaired. The man laying the tiles had enormous hands, the one on the ladder gigantic legs, the one carrying the basket of tiles on his head had an enlarged head. It clearly illustrated the retarding influence on mental development of the formal copying by rote kind of education that was in evidence around us.

Seeing the children's work Jayaprakash made us a present of a Hindi book on child art and we were able to lend it to Boddh Narayan, but it did not change him.

We had a taste of what staffing problems could be when Jayaprakash found us a plump, middle-aged teacher who was an ardent Gandhian by his own report. He was bullying and had to be prevented from using bad language and sadistic punishments but he had the children sing Gandhi's favourite hymns. He tried to borrow Rs.200 from me and others and became obnoxious when refused. He temporarily turned Boddh Narayan against us by arousing his envy of our wealth. For

Boddh Narayan's wage was Rs.45 a month, which we later managed to have raised, but only to Rs.60; Mataji too he quickly allied to himself.

The end of our tolerance at school was reached when he had the children fetch his wood and cook his meals and had toddy tappers bring him palm juice, which he drank in front of the children. We presumed it was at its intoxicating stage without accepting his offer to share it and found it necessary to insist that he have his lunch during the school lunchbreak.

All this however was the fringe of the storm. By the time of Jayaprakash's return in March he had antagonised most people in the ashram, but most of all the bearded artist Shri Shantiranjan Gangopadyaya.

By contrast with Sokhodeora the ashram was a spacious and beautiful place, a model of planning to inspire village people to want a more gracious life. There were trees of many varieties, flower borders and gardens in front of each house. Shantiranjan had created some lovely bas-reliefs on the hall and on the Village Industries building. He had also cast two large concrete sculptures – stylised forms which harmonised perfectly with the expanse of mountains and sky. One of them represented Mother India and the other Aspiration. All his sentiment, philosophy and patriotism had gone into their making.

But to our new teacher the forms were obscene. In the night he dressed them with bags. In the day Shantiranjan fumingly undressed them.

That quarrel between creation and destruction seems to be as old as man. Jayaprakash took the side of beauty and promised us to go on looking for more promising teachers.

This beauty extended to our more newly developed end of the ashram. Trees and shrubs were much younger but the eye of a gardener had been there nevertheless. Jayaprakash used to say that he wished he had spent his life as a gardener and he always toured the ashram grounds with the head gardener in the evenings when he came there.

In front of our house there was a flowerbed along the verandah edge and farther out a row of shrubs and trees, including a eucalyptus, which linked together the four houses in our colony. In the centre of the cut grass was a mango tree surrounded by whitewashed rocks.

At the back of our house hibiscus plants were growing into a hedge down either side of the path and outwards round two rectangles. The flowers were crimson – a glad relief from dust, illness, poverty and struggle.

The schoolchildren used to detour past our house to call 'Are you coming to school, Wendy sister, Allan brother?' or to say something on their way home. They would even call out hello from a quarter of a mile away. They were often around at weekends, too, as we sometimes gave them ice and answered all sorts of questions about it, like whether our egg beater was our ice machine, and a group led by Durgi and Sambo played with the constructional toys on our front verandah. The only modern object they thought of making was a jeep, for a jeep and a plane passing overhead were the only mechanical conveyances they had seen. Still they adored coming to make jeeps.

Often the presence of children was pleasant but sometimes they were a nuisance. One of their misdeeds was to steal the hibiscus flowers.

They stole them to eat.

We would catch them with guilty, apprehensive expressions and a mouthful of petals, the ends protruding and then disappearing between their lips like the wings of beetles and insects in the mouths of the almost transparent lizards on our house walls.

But it was a tragic kind of misdemeanour, which symbolised for us the way in which hunger and poverty consumed the efforts people made to create beauty in their lives.

4

BLIGHTY MILK

Jayaprakash had arranged with the Minister of Education for us to spend the summer months of May, June and July teaching in the Birla Vidya Mandir at Nainital in Jim Corbett country. On a peak over 7000 feet high in the foothills of the Himalayas it boasted of being the second highest public school in the world and from the deodar forest grey apes swung on to its corrugated-iron roof. When the monsoon began and our room was lost in clouds that surged upwards and downwards like gigantic seagulls we returned to the plains.

In Lucknow we broke our return journey to visit the family of the Director of the United States Information Service, and, as a result of their pains to introduce us to people who might be able to help us, much of the future course of our work was decided. Mr Eckersley, an Englishman employed by the World Health Organization, invited us to his office to inspect latrine moulds. We sat around a deal table looking at blueprints of wells and concrete roofs that we hoped would be helpful in building our school. A huge, gently spoken Yugoslav with blond hair and blue eyes joined us, slipping through the dark green door curtain, which stirred under the whirr of a fan.

'Can you stand going outside into the heat to see the latrine moulds?' Mr Eckersley asked. 'They're sold in threes so that casting the parts is a whole day's work for a mason. We don't make them ourselves. That has been passed over to a local industry to provide employment.

'Our target is to install five million village latrines in the United Provinces. We've already installed 10,000,' he said with a sudden smile at his own earnestness. 'We don't bother to persuade people about hygiene or the control of cholera. It's much simpler and they respond more if we show them how convenient it is to have such a clean unit in their homes.'

He added: 'But we're not exclusive. If you would like to introduce them in

Bihar State you may. I'll forward on your order for the moulds and they'll come by train.'

From Lucknow we returned to Patna by train and from there travelled by jeep. The usual fourteen-mile track between the bitumen and the ashram was impassable and the ashram jeep brought us over high ground at the foot of the mountains round the entire perimeter of the funnel. Jackals slipped away into the brilliantly green jungle. Pink-edged cumulus cloud drifted overhead. High land was springing with maize crops. The patchwork of rice fields held brown water that mirrored trees and sky. There was a pervasive swamp smell.

Farmers were levelling their plots with teams of bullocks dragging a wooden bar across the water-covered earth. Two or three at a time stood on the bar holding an animal's tail for balance and shouting to keep them moving. They wore only loincloths and were mud spattered from hair to feet.

Men, ankle-deep in water in the beds of rice seedlings, were pulling the plants until they held a double handful.

Then they twisted some of the stalks to bind the bundles and sent them with a child to the women. Knee-deep in water the women planted the seedlings in erratic rows.

In the ashram, Shimada San, now the only remaining Japanese, was training students of the Agricultural School in the Japanese method. Two held a rope so the seedlings were planted in straight rows and could later be kept free of weeds. A few of the Sokhodeora farmers followed the method and had the small rotating hoes that cleaned between the rows of plants. Shimada persuaded me to help with the planting. He, himself, worked at it barefooted and contracted hookworm.

The days lacked the biting heat of summer but the humidity made us lethargic. The perspiration never dried on us and we took up to five cold baths and changes of clothes in a day. Both Shimada and I suffered from a skin rash.

In the three months of the monsoon most of Sokhodeora's forty-five inches of rain fell. It came in sudden squalls, roaring nearer through the jungle on the mountains and then bursting out in a white sheet that found holes in roofs and dangerously softened the base of mud-house walls.

The trouble with having Mahadev with us again was that we came to think of him as the accusing eye of the village farmers, which saw all our lazy Western ways. They and he rose at 4am, worked seven days a week until dark, had almost no leisure and no belief that people are entitled to leisure. His presence soon shamed us into working every day too.

In any case leisure activities were very limited. We could stroll through the ashram, or through the fields or along the wall of the dam beside the jungle. But the going was slippery and the water threw heat up into our faces as if we had been sealed into a steam-filled bathroom. The schoolchildren sternly warned us against walking in the jungle: 'There are huge snakes there. They hang down from trees and swallow you. They are as big as – as – as Allan *bhai* (brother).'

Mahadev told us an even more cautionary tale. 'There is a very bad snake during the monsoon. It drinks milk. If a mother of a young baby goes into the jungle the snake will chase her until it catches her. It twines itself all around her body so she can't move and then drinks her milk.'

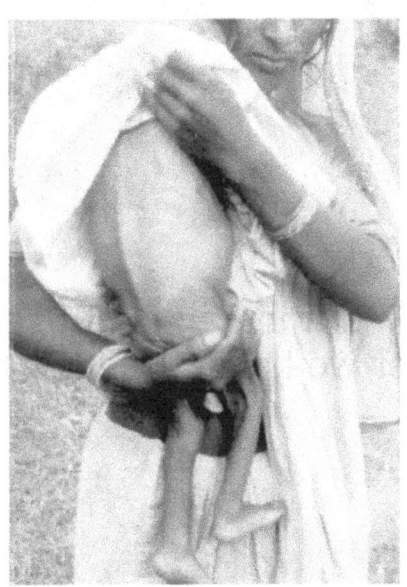

Shova about three weeks after we began her treatment.

Shova, with her mother, about seven months after we began treating her.

Some of the sick babies. Adjhodia on the right.

Schoolchildren carrying Multi-Purpose Food from our house.

But one Sunday afternoon, while taking a stroll, we discovered that the ashram had about 1400 pounds of American powdered milk waiting to be distributed. It had been in storage for some time because of the difficulty of finding someone to work consistently at giving it out, and the task was willingly handed over to us. So began eighteen months of milk distribution, daily in the school and thrice weekly in the village.

We discussed what to do with it between ourselves and decided that we might be able to use it to bribe the village people to clean their own caste sectors regularly. While the village had no system of sanitation such cleaning could be only partial improvement, but we hoped to introduce Mr Eckersley's latrines.

So we went to see the village headman, who was sitting with Ganesh Mahto in the latter's home in a narrow room built between the inner courtyard and the street. Ganesh Mahto was our teacher Boddh Narayan's elder brother and head of one of the wealthiest and most influential families. To Mahadev he seemed enormously rich because the family owned six acres of land. But it supported at least six adults and six children. Two string-strung beds were placed on either side of the opposite doorways opening into the street and courtyard and on these several men sat cross-legged. Maluk Das, with his young bright face alive and welcoming, jumped up as we entered.

'Greetings,' he shouted at us. Maluk Das always shouted – it was somehow part of his zest for life. He was a Harijan but also a member of the village council and he was very proud of his position and conscientious about it.

Vishnu Dev, an older, soberer friend from Phuldi village, twinkled at us through his glasses. Everyone moved up and we sat on one of the string beds.

Ganesh Mahto sent his four-year-old daughter, Chandra, running for tea and a fan. We drank the strong, tobacco-coloured liquid, and Chandra with her close-cut, shining, boyish hair and small serious face knelt on the bed beside us waving the fan up and down. We protested laughingly.

'It will make her small arm ache, Ganesh Mahto, we can fan ourselves,' but he shook his head.

'This weather must be terrible for you. It is even difficult for us.' Boddh Narayan entered and seated himself self-effacingly on the far end of the bed. He smiled at us half apologetically, as if he should not intrude on his elder brother's councils. Seeing how used he was to deferring to the opinions of older members of the family, it was easy for us to understand why he found it difficult to take decisions by himself in the school.

They asked us about our summer vacation and we told them something of Nainital built around its deep and beautiful lake. Then I mentioned our experience in Lucknow.

'These latrines are extraordinarily simple and cheap.' Picking up a sharp stick I roughly outlined the pit structure and the piping on the earth floor. 'A total cost of twelve rupees.'

'Twelve rupees,' Ganesh Mahto repeated in amazement. 'There are no proper latrines in this village,' he added. 'Have you seen the road from Kawakol where it enters the village near the Zamindar's (landlord's) house? Ugh.' He wrinkled his nose in disgust. And well we knew he might. Even in the jeep the smell had been sufficiently unpleasant and we remembered the times when we had walked to Kawakol picking our way carefully through the human faeces left there.

'Our family has a latrine,' he added, 'but it is not good.'

He led us across the road behind some houses where a kind of marrow trailed over the walls into a thatch lean-to. Here some boards across a pit partly concealed a cesspool.

'It is difficult,' he said, 'because when the water underground rises in the monsoon this overflows.' Such a latrine was no solution to the village sewerage problem and we all knew it. 'Will the water level rise in these pits you have described?' he asked.

'Yes,' I replied, 'but they should be deep enough to cope with it and they are also enclosed so that seepage cannot occur over the surface ground and contaminate your wells.'

Everyone was interested and we returned to Ganesh Mahto's house. 'The ashram has 1400 pounds of powdered milk,' Wendy continued. 'We want to distribute it in the village. We were hoping to use it as a bribe to persuade the village people to clean their streets.'

The headman looked doubtful. He was never very keen on plans which involved him in action. However this time the enthusiasm of Vishnu Dev, Maluk Das and the others forced his hand. He reluctantly drew out his little notebook.

'We'll begin in the Harijan sector,' Maluk Das yelled at us. We felt that he also raised his voice because he thought that we would understand his Hindi better.

We were happy with this arrangement because we knew the Harijans as a group better than we knew anyone else in Sokhodeora and as they were the poorest and greatest in need it seemed appropriate to begin there.

So we planned with the headman for twice a week in the Harijan sector, the cleaning to be done on the Sunday before, and then twice a week in each of the other sectors. The Harijan children were, however, to come to all the distributions because they were the worst fed children in Sokhodeora village.

The following Sunday I borrowed mattocks from the ashram and we set out to clean the streets. Our work force met in the small Harijan square where meetings were held, where wheat was laid on mats to dry, and where cows were tramped over sheaves of wheat or rice to crush out the grain. The area was littered with the decaying stalks of maize and animal manure. We collected the headman, whose enthusiasm had grown, and some shallow baskets. The few lads who were squatting around the square were recruited at once to bring small reed brooms and I went searching for more helpers from the homes along the alleyways.

The refuse from the square was scraped into the baskets and emptied into a pit on a vacant piece of land adjoining the square. This land belonged to the headman and was deep in rank grass.

Black goats and white, with ridge-like backbones and indented flanks, wandered around the square, nuzzling in the refuse for something to eat; a couple of village dogs, their rib bones heaving as they breathed, lay listlessly flicking their ears at the flies. Occasionally, with a soft patter and loud squeals, a small herd of bristly black pigs pursued by a little boy with a pointed stick rushed across the square and disappeared into one of the alleyways. The Harijans were the only group in the village who kept pigs.

As we worked, the tall madwoman, who lived alone in a tiny kennel in Seepur hamlet, appeared in the square. She cried out wildly, shaking her long black matted hair and stared about with her obsessed dark eyes. Then gathering to her flat breast the white kid she often carried she hurried away. It was almost as if a character from biblical times had appeared.

It was several hours before the alleyways of the Harijan sector were clear of refuse and my wet shirt clung about my shoulders as I accompanied Wendy back to the ashram. The headman was excited and went with us as far as the road to the ashram.

'See how nice it looks,' he beamed and made a special and unnecessary note in his little book that the next day would be a milk distribution day.

When we arrived in the square early next morning a crowd had already gathered. Anyone asking what we were making was told by his neighbour, 'Blighty Milk'. Milk that came out of a tin was so strange that it seemed it must come from England. Several of the village musicians were seated on woven palm mats, pumping a small harmonium and beating with twinkling fingers on the *tabala,* the small drums. Groups of women and children squatted on the ground and some of the children beat time to the music on the bronze bowls they carried. There was an air of festivity. So little variation occurred in their daily lives that they always made the most of an unusual or unexpected event.

Mahadev fanned a smoking cow-dung and wood fire laid in a small pit at one end of the square and over it steamed a big bronze cauldron now blackened with smoke. On the ground, occasionally sniffed at by a passing goat that was kicked out of the way, stood several tins of powdered milk. Mahadev had not been in favour of boiling the water since his caste folk drank it unboiled every day. We decided, however, for milk without germs.

While the water came to the boil I talked to Mahadev and the group of young men with him, and Wendy sat on the string bed brought for our comfort. It was hot and the perspiration ran down the brows of the musicians.

The headman joined Wendy and the collection of women who had drawn close to watch her curiously.

'Tell them something useful for them, Wendy sister,' the headman said a little pompously.

Wendy looked at him in some embarrassment.

'What should I tell them?' she replied and looked at the faces of the women about her. A couple smiled cheerfully and bounced the babies planted on their hips up and down. But a number looked at her with suspicion. She was an alien there and they did not accept readily either new people or new ideas.

'Tell them something to help them,' the headman insisted.

Driven by a desire to make contact with those closed faces but unprepared and inexperienced as yet in this type of work, Wendy began haltingly.

'There is a lot of water in the streets in the monsoon. If you planted banana palms near the drains they would drink the water, your streets would be dry and you would have bananas to eat.'

The idea was sound enough but the ground for receiving it infertile. It was as if she had suddenly walked into a room where everyone was talking, the last guest, and in that momentary silence had remarked, 'Wholemeal bread is better for the health than white.'

Doubtless the village women thought her a little mad and she certainly felt foolish.

The water boiled and saved her further embarrassment. I opened the tins and she ladled in the milk, stirring away the lumps and beating the liquid until it frothed. Several of the older boys organised the children into two long rows and we ladled the creamy hot milk into each bowl. There were naked little boys, girls with ornaments in their pierced ears and nostrils, and one girl with a streak of vermilion colour across her forehead and down her nose. They all fanned their milk to cool it and keep off the flies. It was very satisfying. The milk was so creamy, so full of all the wholesome goodness the earth could offer human beings, and to us it somehow represented the universal necessity of caring for the child.

At school the children reacted very conservatively.

'What's this stuff?' they asked. 'We've never had this before.'

'It's milk. You've seen milk before,' we replied.

'Yes, we've seen it,' Johdan gently explained for us, 'but we don't drink it. I don't know what it tastes like, truly, Allan brother and Wendy sister. I've never drunk it.'

It was not a child's exaggeration. When their mothers weaned them at about two years old they immediately ate the food the rest of the family had – rice, dal and spices. Through the years when their bodies most needed protein they had no meat, milk or eggs.

This came about because of the poor breed of cows, the inadequate grazing and the village ignorance about growing fodder crops. Local cows averaged three foot six in height and gave a quarter of a pint of milk night and morning.

To improve breeds the ashram had a stud Brahma bull and an Australian Jersey cow, and there were artificial insemination facilities at the Pukri Brawan Block.

On the following Sunday morning we took mattocks to the village for a clean-up of the shopkeepers' sector, but our intentions were soon set at nought, for none of this caste would take part. It annoyed us for the rubbish was their own and the headman had been able to demean himself to street sweeping the Sunday previously. In the afternoon Wendy walked down to enlist the headman's help in the next day's milk distribution. He promised to come. Mahadev was to have the water boiling by 7.30am.

The Monday was a holiday, Republic Day – 15 August. It proved eventful. At about 5.30 Wendy put water on the stove in the kitchen and came inside to set the table for breakfast. She noticed the liquid in the tray underneath the Primus and assumed it was water. However, it was kerosene from a break in the pipe.

There was an explosion. We rushed to find a sheet of flame. The burning fuel in the tray had melted the solder which held the two halves of the tank together and its contents were spurting in a jet of fire. Hurriedly we threw buckets of earth over it all: that was the next best to burial our stove got.

The kitchen roof was very low and its tiles were laid over a layer of straw, and now the stove was out we could see that the straw too had caught alight.

'Heavens, what will JP say if he comes back to find the house burnt down?' Wendy exclaimed.

First we threw water upwards, which had little effect. Then I ran for a ladder and removing the tiles we carried buckets from the well and poured water from above.

But the longest part of the misadventure was cleaning the burnt straw and mud out of the kitchen.

As a result Wendy went to Sokhodeora at 7.30 not in the best mood for village work since we were now in such difficulty without our stove.

Even at that time the day was humid and unpleasant. She slipped through the ashram fence at the side of our house and took a meandering path across the unfenced fields beside

Seepur hamlet. From a high bank that kept floodwater out of Seepur she descended on to the grassy bunds between the water-filled rice fields, where the crop was tall, luxuriant, green. Bare feet had worn the top of the bunds into slippery black mud. She balanced along, frequently stepping over human excreta.

The water smelled rank. Across the breaks in the bunds, which let the water flow between the fields, farmers had set fine bamboo lattices to trap small fish. This was the season for small boys to make fishing lines and take home proudly a few silver scraps to be spiced and savoured at the evening meal. Wendy jumped some of these channels, landing precariously in the mud, until she reached a channel several feet across.

She turned back searching in the criss-cross of bunds for another way and a black snake slid silently into the water. Having reached the road between the ashram and Sokhodeora she looked along the opposite side for a way. Jumping the creek at a narrow point she followed a thorn hedge which enclosed a maize crop, clambered round the roots of a huge *mahua* tree and found another bund through rice plots which led to high land beside the village.

The only person awaiting her was Mahadev who was trying to light a fire in a mud *chula* he had brought with a couple of cow-dung cakes. It smoked and smelt but gave no heat.

'Where's the headman, Mahadev?' she asked.

'I don't know,' he replied, blowing furiously on the smouldering dung.

'Hasn't anyone brought you any wood?' The answer was obvious enough. Summoning her patience she asked, 'Did you ask anyone for wood?'

He looked uncomfortable and she realised he would not be able to go into the houses of another caste. Feeling irritable she squelched along the muddy street until she reached the entrance to a house courtyard, where she knocked on the wooden door lintels. There was no door and when no one answered she hesitantly entered the courtyard. Against one earth wall was a pile of wood. In one corner lay a pile of bronze cooking pots that had been carefully scoured with mud or ashes until they shone. Under the small verandah encircling the yard a few tattered lengths of discoloured white sari hung to dry.

She called tentatively again and an elderly man appeared.

'We have come to distribute milk to your children and need some wood to boil the cauldron. Could you give me a piece?' she asked.

The man looked helpless and replied: 'We haven't any wood, Memsahib.' She looked from him to the pile of wood against the wall. He followed her gaze but said nothing.

'Isn't that wood?' she insisted.

'Yes, Memsahib.'

'May I take a piece?'

He inclined his head. Taking it she hurried out.

After she had been to several more houses, Mahadev had enough fuel for his fire. An hour later the headman, Shri Goverdan Sau, appeared. Newly bathed, freshly shaven, with hair oiled and combed and freshly ironed white clothes he almost sparkled. Wendy was hot and annoyed with the muddled arrangements and unfriendly reception.

'You said you would be here at seven-thirty and have the milk ready,' she reproached him.

'I have to go to a meeting, Wendy sister,' he replied. He looked at her helplessly and then called a friend. With a 'He will help you, Wendy sister' he was gone.

'Attending meetings is always more important round here than doing something practical,' she grumbled to herself. 'Just the opposite from Australian attitudes. If I were in Australia I'd say to myself I've got to waste my time at a meeting.'

The water was beginning to freckle on the bottom of the cauldron but was far from boiling. However, a noisy restless crowd of children had gathered and they were pushing, thrusting out their bowls and getting in the way in their efforts to see her and the tins of milk. She sat on a rickety chair the headman's friend had brought, fanning her perspiring face with her hand.

'Could someone clean the street?' she asked him. 'So that the children can sit in rows while we give the milk out.'

He called to a boy, who promptly turned his back and pretended not to hear. The crowd in the narrow alley was seething backwards and forwards to a loud babble of laughter and comment.

She mixed the milk and as the man seemed inclined to give up she persisted: 'We won't give out the milk while the street is so dirty. What is the sense of making the milk hygienic and then distributing it amongst goat manure?'

He grabbed a small boy by the arm and sent him to find a hand-broom. After what seemed like fifteen minutes the boy returned. He sketchily swept a space where the children could sit.

In some dismay Wendy surveyed the mass of about two hundred undisciplined children, and turned to Mahadev for help.

With a flow of village dialect Mahadev grabbed children and pushed them down by force into a sort of row until slowly two undulating lines stretched along the alley. Wendy filled a container and began to pour the milk. Immediately those who had been served hurried away and others farther up the rows ran and jostled to fill their places. She had to stop.

'Explain to them,' she said to the headman's friend, 'that they'll be served but they've got to wait.'

The lines had become a milling throng. He shouted and shoved until there was order again. Beginning to pour again she noticed that the lad before her looked familiar and his wet bowl had obviously just been washed. There was no doubt that he had emptied his first bowlful into another container at home and returned for more.

She served him, but as he and his two companions jumped up to leave she shouted exasperatedly at them. By dint of a continuous stream of similarly angry orders the cauldron was emptied.

The crowd dispersed with noisy rapidity. Mahadev took the cauldron to the well to clean it with mud and grass. It was eleven o'clock and thanking the headman's friend Wendy returned to the ashram exhausted. And since the following distributions in other quarters went no better, eventually she only did them in the Harijan sector where things always went smoothly and where the need was greatest.

5

LITERACY AND A BUFFALO

'On his fifth journey the sailors broke a Roc's egg and ate the young one,' related Mahadev, 'and then the parent birds threw rocks from a mountain on their ship and broke it. But Sinbad got to some place and he met an old man' – broom under one arm he followed Wendy from our workroom into the kitchen – 'and he carried him on his shoulders across a river, only for kindness, and then he couldn't get him off.

'You listen to this bit—' He broke off. With almost trembling eagerness he opened *The Arabian Nights* in which his finger had kept the place and read slowly and blunderingly to her.

'Isn't that wonderful?' she responded.

'This is the first story I have ever read like this,' he commented excitedly and went on reading. In the end she had to break his rapt enthusiasm.

'How about finishing the sweeping, Mahadev, and telling me afterwards?'

He emerged with a start from another world that we had gleaned from Patna, Lucknow, Nainital, Bombay and Delhi for our school library. It is doubtful whether the intoxication of his break-through to the printed word could ever be conveyed to Westerners who have all been to school.

Not long before he had tentatively asked me, 'Would you write my name in Hindi for me on a piece of paper?' 'Goodness,' I replied, 'how could I write it in Hindi for you? You should be able to do that better than I can.' Nevertheless I wrote *Mahadev Ravidas* for him.

Mahadev picked up the paper lovingly.

'I will take this home and practice writing it over and over until I can do it. Then I can sign for my wages, instead of having to put a thumbprint, and they won't be able to laugh at me. They think you're stupid if you have to give your thumbprint.'

I ignored his impersonal 'they', knowing who had laughed at him. I was to witness some time later a person who should have been kinder ask very condescendingly, 'Can you sign?' to which Mahadev replied, for all his poorer clothes and station, with a proud toss of his head and an 'Of course I can. What do you think I am?'

'Didn't you go to school, Mahadev?' I asked.

'Yes, I went up to the fourth grade at Sokhodeora school.'

'Why couldn't you write your name?'

'Forgotten.'

So we encouraged him to learn. Between chores he would sit on the front verandah if the day were sunny or in a corner of our workroom if it were cold. At first he read aloud to himself in an expressionless monotone, fumbling with the letters and sounding them all through before he could say the word they formed, repeating the word, then going back over the last two or three words, only managing to read sentences when they were short. It was our school pupils over again.

But gradually he learned to read silently and without a finger under the lines. He took books and magazines home to read at night by lantern light.

He was developing a mind which before then had been acquainted only with local farming methods, local beliefs, Hindu religion and the story of the Ramayana. His understanding of cause and effect, particularly in matters of pain and illness, was tragically limited, his inability to draw sound conclusions from his observations resembling the thought processes of Europeans before the coming of the scientific method.

One day, for instance, he asked our help for an inexplicably aching thumb. There was no sign of cut, bruise or swelling and we were baffled. It was only some time later that an explanation occurred to us.

'Mahadev, when you were making the fowl house for me, did you hit your thumb with the hammer?' I asked.

'Yes.'

'Didn't you think of that? That's why it's sore.'

He felt anxiety at the recurrence of the thirteen-year period when Nag, the

Great Serpent, Causer of Earthquakes, walked the earth, and did not know what to think about the news that Holy Men were gathering in Delhi predicting the imminent end of the world. But there was a part of his mind that could accept our information about planes, satellites and rockets because of the kind of life that we were able to live, which seemed somehow the result of this kind of knowledge.

He had no way of knowing that an unscrupulous quack was less reliable than a university-trained doctor, or of realising that the quack's diagnosis and medicines were useless when he did not bother to see the patient. He was certain that women were men's inferiors and that educating girls was pointless. Custom allowed him no association with girls of his age: his father would arrange a marriage for him.

Eventually he said that there were some other youths of his part of the village who also wanted to learn to read and write.

'That's good,' I said and waited for him to elucidate.

'They wanted me to ask you if you could teach them at night.'

We discussed this over a period, for some compromises had to be made – they were unwilling to come to our house at night and we did not want to have a class every night of the week.

In the village there was an unused building, belonging to the ashram, which had fallen into disrepair. Monsoon squalls had damaged the mud walls but the roof was sound. We began our night class there in a long room once used as a pit-loom weaving centre. Now, as no one interfered, people were using it as a cowshed, tethering their animals between the deep square pits in the earth floor. However, it was cover for our students who could not sit out of doors in their thin cotton clothes.

Many of the wooden window shutters were broken or missing, so that in winter the wind whistled through in chilly gusts. There was a low wooden bed to sit on once the hens and their droppings had been removed, but we quickly found it better to squat on the floor since the bed was infested with bugs.

On the first night Mahadev and I went from house to house to collect anyone who wanted to come to make use of the time before he had his evening meal. The intense light of our Petromax incandescent mantle lantern attracted people out from the darkness of their homes. Some had only the light of the cooking fire, some a wick burning in a small clay saucer of oil, and Mahadev's home had a kerosene lantern. Nightlife consisted, in warm weather, of men sitting in groups outside their homes chatting about the events of the day.

Since Wendy was there we were also able to find for the class five young women and two girls – Mahadev's young sister, the sparrow-like Chamilwa, and a girl who had attended our school for a time. Lakshmi and Suji were giggly adolescents in coloured saris. Bhagia was a serious, frowning girl who brought her baby sister on her hip. Kesurwa was a young married woman with marriage tattooing right up her arms to her plump shoulders. She had a broad, short nose, very full mouth and a pretty triangular face with widely spaced eyes. None of us guessed how much more closely we were later to be associated with her.

We went three times a week. By the time we reached home most of the ashram was in darkness, asleep. One old man came and watched for several nights but would not join in for fear of ridicule.

'Come,' I encouraged him.

'I couldn't learn. I'm too old.'

'Can you hold a pen?' I asked gently.

'Yes.'

'If you can hold a pen, you can learn to write and if you can see the letters you can learn to read.'

The old man smiled nervously, but after a week or two he sat with the class and when he read his first group of words his trembling excitement left us feeling moved and triumphant.

Our students had to find their own palm-leaf mats or bags to sit on, for the mud floor was cold. Our first night consisted of testing everyone with a few simple books. We noted quickly that a few could read with reasonable comprehension but the large majority could not read at all. A middle group had learned the alphabet and read by the halting method of sounding their words letter by letter even to stating dental 't' and palate 't'. Of course, after they had struggled through a group of words in this manner they had no understanding of what they had read.

We decided that if we wanted to keep the group happy and confident that adults could learn to read and write, then our methods must bring speedy results. So we printed sets of words and sentences, which would be generally known to village people, and abandoning the alphabet for the time being, launched into a word-recognition campaign.

Wendy worked with the small group of girls and young women and I managed the large group of youths and boys. There were about sixty. We had one Petromax lantern and two hurricane lanterns. Lighting was inadequate, congestion and confusion great. With just the two of us it was almost impossible to keep each person interested and progressing, especially the children, who required constant attention. We were at last to decide sadly to expel the children. It was a hard decision to make because a number of the little boys could not go to day school. They were employed looking after animals, work for which they earned a few paisas a month, or in other field or household tasks. But we had begun the class for adults and we felt that they had first claim on our attention.

However, when Jayaprakash came to visit the class we were still sorting all this out.

As there was nowhere to sit in the room except on the bed with the bugs we instructed Mahadev to take a stool from our house for Jayaprakash to sit on. It was not unusual to see people carrying furniture around the village for the comfort of a visitor. There was little of it and it was generally in a worn-out state.

I went earlier that night so that I could collect the attenders in good time. I usually called them, few people knew when it was seven-thirty.

I took the Petromax lantern and by its brilliant beam Wendy watched my progress across the fields. When the light finally disappeared in the Harijan sector Wendy waited a few moments and then heard the *thud thud* of the drum used to call people's attention. Then she saw the lantern light reappear and bob about as I crossed a small section of open fields to the disused weaving room.

When Jayaprakash arrived at our house to meet Wendy he took the kerosene lantern from her and she collected the remainder of the matching cards. Their conversation was desultory.

'I'm afraid that you may not be very comfortable,' she said apologetically. 'I sent Mahadev with a stool but perhaps I should

have sent a chair.' Our chairs were of pleasantly polished teak but were very heavy.

'I shall be quite all right,' he replied, helping her over the stile at the ashram fence. 'But how often do you and Allan do this? It must be very cold and difficult at night.'

'Three times a week, and we enjoy it. It's muddled at the moment but wonderfully exciting. You will see how enthusiastic the young people are, and we even have some women and girls. Bhagia – you know Akloo her father? He works in the ashram agriculture department and is crippled – well, Bhagia is extraordinarily bright. Her memory is particularly retentive, which is amazing, for she is thirteen or so and has never had any schooling. She will read in a few more lessons.'

'Do you only teach literacy?' They picked their way across the stream which cut the road where the track from the ashram swung right skirting the village.

'At the moment, but we would like to extend the education later. Perhaps Shimada San might give some lectures on the Japanese method of paddy cultivation. I would like to see the women having lectures and demonstrations on diet, care of children and hygiene. But it's a matter of progressing where they feel the need. I've had to adjust the kindergarten programme because parents say, "My son has been coming for a month and he can't read or write yet." I try to show them by throwing a ball to the children that they haven't the manual dexterity to catch it and therefore can't be expected to hold a pencil and write. But even then they are doubtful and we've had to introduce some look-and-read cards.'

Her foot slipped off the narrow bank and she caught her dress in the prickly hedge fencing the adjoining field. Jayaprakash held the lantern while she extricated herself. On either side the wheat was high and Wendy at last stopped in embarrassment at an intersection of bunds.

'I'm afraid I'm lost,' she said ruefully. 'I always come with Allan.' Jayaprakash smiled and turning right led the way to the door of the class.

Everyone rose at their entrance. Jayaprakash was respected and deeply loved in Sokhodeora but village people are uncertain of themselves and there was a shy silence in the room. Several of the little girls drew their tattered saris across their faces and giggled nervously. Jayaprakash wished them all 'Good evening', expressed his pleasure at being with them and sat down.

A noisy babble of talk and reading broke out and everyone hid his embarrassment behind a word card or a book. We went to work squatting in front of our pupils, dodging the lantern light shining from the centre of the floor. At one stage Bhagia and Lakshmi suddenly covered their faces with their saris and turned away. Wendy looked up and Jayaprakash, who had been bending down to watch them, smiled. Then he moved away quickly to save the girls' confusion.

Lakshmi could read quite well and occasionally her friends rested to listen to her or to follow her reading down the page. She was reading a chapter about the diet necessary for a pregnant woman. The word *footna,* meaning to germinate, puzzled them all. Wendy's Hindi vocabulary was not extensive but she knew the alphabet thoroughly. As this was completely phonetic she was able to read fluently, even if the meaning of some of the words escaped her. Usually once the word was spoken the girls recognised it and so they progressed. But *footna* baffled them. They appealed to Jayaprakash who explained that it was used in relation to *gram,* a high protein vegetable which should be eaten when it is sprouting.

We stopped earlier than usual so that Jayaprakash might speak to the class for a short time. He was always fatherly with the village people and this night he was particularly gentle. He removed his glasses and passed a hand over his eyes and forehead in an habitual gesture of thought before speaking and looked around sadly at the dirty, ragged group of young people, the unbeautiful room.

'Poverty and dirt often go together,' he said. 'So often that we tend to make one the excuse for the other. You are all poor but you can also be clean. Cleanliness is a matter of pride in yourselves. I can see that you all have this pride or you wouldn't want so eagerly to learn to read and write. I would wish for you all that you strive to be clean even though it is wearisome and difficult for you. We must do something about this room, too, so that you may learn in pleasant surroundings.'

Again he thanked them for inviting him and expressed his pleasure at being there. On our return the village was quiet and from a *mahua* tree in a nearby field an owl hooted dismally.

'Mahadev believes that if a person hears the owl hooting his name he is doomed to sicken and die,' I remarked. 'It is not hard to imagine things like that when it has such a mournful sound.'

'It has sad memories for me,' Jayaprakash replied quietly. 'When I was in jail I had a friend who heard the hooting of an owl the night his father died. He discovered later, when he had been released, that the bird's melancholy cry had come at the same hour in which his father died.'

'It is strange how many people have had similar associations,' Wendy said, 'and how birds and their cries have been used as symbols by poets and writers for centuries.'

'"Quoth the raven 'Nevermore'",' Jayaprakash replied and Wendy smiled for the same line had occurred to her. That he associated his sense of foreboding with the same reference made us feel very close.

'The village people need a lot of help,' he said, returning to his earlier thoughts, 'but they are often not prepared to help themselves. They want and expect God to do it all for them. I often say to them that they would do well to think about the English saying "God helps those who help themselves". You must have experienced their apathy.'

'I believe it's nutritional,' Wendy replied. 'People can't have physical and mental vitality on two meals of rice and pulse a day. A huge proportion of village women suffer from anaemia and they must be just dragging themselves around.'

He nodded.

'You live physically because you can't help it,' I said, 'but to think, adapt or change requires an added energy. It seems to us that the tragedy of it is they can't find that energy and yet they have to find it if they are to escape their hunger.'

It was after ten o'clock and everyone in the ashram was in bed. We were reluctant to let the companionable moment go.

'Would you like to come and have some coffee with us,' Wendy suggested. 'Unless it is too late for you?'

She heated milk on the one-burner Primus we had bought in Patna while he and I sat in our middle room at the table.

'You will need extra help with these classes,' Jayaprakash remarked as Wendy poured his drink. 'You might perhaps explain this teaching method to some others so that it might be more generally used.'

'I have introduced it in the kindergarten,' Wendy replied. 'The parents are a bit suspicious of it so I compromise between that and the customary alphabet method. But it does serve the purpose of preventing our adult classes from feeling that reading is an unattainable skill.'

As the ashram seemed so deserted and lonely we lit his way the few hundred yards to his house. The stars were brilliant in the cold, remote sky. The universe seemed particularly aloof from the red-mud village hugging the earth.

Jayaprakash's path of striving had been incomparably longer and harder than ours. He had joined Gandhi's Independence Movement before we had been born and had spent ten years in jails. Knowing this we were suddenly overwhelmed by our respect and affection for him. I wrung his hand and Wendy, breaking the rigid Indian conventions, kissed him on the cheek. Stooping quickly he gave her an enveloping hug and walked quickly into his house.

*

On Christmas night we were very aware of how people like ourselves in the Western world would be celebrating the occasion. Our Christmas Day was milky-white overcast with a white effulgence for a sun that brought the temperature only as high as 44° F. Mahadev arrived in the jumper I had given him and the shoes and shawl we had bought him, but he was still shivering. He was puzzled too.

'Allan brother, what is the white stuff on our roof this morning? It was on all the roofs. I have never seen it before.'

It had been eighteen years since this part of India had experienced frost. 'It's frost, Mahadev. Like in our ice machine. Because it's so cold.'

'I've never seen it before,' he repeated.

When the schoolchildren straggled along in their cotton shirts with teeth chattering, bare feet blue and arms clasped about their chests I suggested they play a game of soccer to warm up. It was the only time Boddh Narayan turned angrily on me.

'It's all right for you,' he reproached. 'You've got woollen jumpers you can put on after you've been playing. They've got nothing extra to put on and they'll catch pneumonia.'

So instead he and I lit a fire in the little disused kitchen at the back of the school and the children squatted around it while the cauldron of milk heated. After they had drunk it we dismissed them so they could sit by their house fires. Then, with Mahadev, Wendy and I carried the cauldron to Seepur hamlet and boiled up more powdered milk for the children there who did not go to school. Finally we dispensed it in Sokhodeora.

'You're not going to your night class tonight are you?' ashram friends asked as they headed towards bed.

That night the wind howled and pounded through the shutterless windows and our students shook. They lit a fire in the middle of the floor but it smoked badly. Coughing and gasping with eyes smarting tears, we heated more milk and served biscuits Wendy had baked for the occasion with our new Primus underneath our burnt-out oven. Biscuits were a treat they seldom had so they were soon eaten.

We returned home sadly, wondering again how people in the West were spending Christmas.

*

We had fifty rupees' worth of army disposal blankets bought for us in Gaya and cut each blanket into three pieces. After we had stitched the cut edges by hand we gave them for shawls to the children in our adult literacy classes. The sixty of them were becoming too noisy to manage and we objected that they should be sent to school by day. So having given them the shawls we expelled them, and a day later, thanks to Mahadev's shaming some parents, thirty of them arrived at school.

For the remaining adults we had books from Literacy House in Lucknow – another result of our visit there – which dealt with everyday village experiences in simple, repetitive Hindi. They described how to make chutney, how to build a pit latrine, what vegetables were good to grow and how they should be nurtured, what diet pregnant women needed. It was with one of these booklets that Mahadev next pursued Wendy about the house, his thirst for practical knowledge being even greater than his liking for fiction.

'Wendy sister, do you know what to do when a snake has bitten you?' he asked, unable to keep his remarkable discovery to himself.

'Yes,' she replied and told him quickly before she realised she was deflating him.

'A number of Sokhodeora people have been bitten by snakes,' he said, 'and nobody knew what to do. They just died. But it's easy what you have to do.'

The next time, when he found what to do when someone's clothing had caught on fire, she let him explain excitedly how to roll the victim in a blanket on the ground. It was not that the average Sokhodeora person had a blanket or quilt, but he was elated to know because, again, he knew of people whom the accident had befallen. Their clothes had caught alight from the pot of coals underneath their string-strung beds.

It was clear to us from his eagerness and amazement about such simple measures of first aid that our literacy classes could be of great help to young people who had never dreamed of what knowledge twentieth-century men have.

Bhagia's progress was another triumph. For some time she had been torn with conflict for she could not concentrate on her alphabet with her baby sister crawling and crowing over her. Wendy had suggested that she leave the toddler at home; perhaps she used the remark as an excuse to her mother. In any case she worked at her study fanatically and in eighteen lessons, over a period of six weeks, she began to read her first book. Even though it consisted only of Intelligent Anand learning to read and then teaching his wife to read, she was elated. Spurred on by seeing her progress the other girls asked each class night if they could borrow 'Anand fellow' to read at home.

Now every morning we awoke to bright, warm sunshine and day-by-day or week-by-week the temperature relentlessly went up a degree or two. Soon we would go to the mountains again for almost three months.

The wheat was cut with sickles, a leg-aching task as we knew from cutting rice at the end of the monsoon. To protect their harvested or ripening crops from animals and thieves the farmers built temporary pole-and-straw perches in their fields. By day the children sat in them and the men by night. Some sang for hours into the darkness while others preferred to beat an empty kerosene tin. As we came home from the literacy classes we met groups of men making harvest offerings and prayers under sacred trees.

Some men employed workers to thresh the wheat by beating the sheaves on a wooden bed. Others spread the sheaves on hard ground and walked cows round and round over them. Then the grain was dropped into the wind so the chaff could be separated. During this time we searched Sokhodeora for people to train as volunteer teachers so the classes would be permanent. They were to go to a training course at Literacy House in Lucknow. But in the whole Kawakol area just under sixteen per cent of males over fifteen were literate. Of these, two-thirds had passed Grade 5 Primary School and one third Grade 7. In the population of 63,000 there were only sixty-nine who had passed Intermediate or Matriculation Certificate, three qualified doctors and thirty-one graduates who were mostly outsiders in Government service.

The task of finding a woman was even more difficult, for slightly fewer than two per cent of women over fifteen were literate. Of these, seventeen were Matriculates; the remainder Grade 5 Primary School Pass. Again the highly educated group was mostly outsiders employed in the area.

For weeks Mahadev seemed the only choice. As March and the Literacy House Training Course in Lucknow approached his fear grew of having to go alone and he too searched. When he had almost settled things with a lad of his caste the boy decided to go to the mines at Jheria to find work.

At the last moment he found Shri Ugra Narayan Mahto who was thoroughly literate and brought him for us to meet and approve. He appeared extremely nervous, only speaking a brief 'Yes' or 'No' when a direct question was put to him, so it was impossible to form an estimate of him, but we endorsed Mahadev's choice.

We were unable to find a woman.

Both youths were afraid of the city and of the long train journey. Mahadev had never ridden in a train. We happened to be in Patna on our way to Delhi on the day they passed through to their two-week training course, and we found them so frightened that we had to go with them to the station and see them on to the train.

The fares and fees were well invested for the new experiences Mahadev had. He had never seen an aerodrome, the wide, traffic-covered streets of a city, the tall buildings. Nor had he met fellow countrymen from other localities and states. But he was deeply upset that his protege, Ugra Narayan Mahto, had received a Pass Certificate while he had not. Because his Hindi was weak he had only gained a Certificate of Attendance.

He brought back with him a cheap novel he had bought at a railway station stall, a little shocked at himself for the extravagance. Its romanticised picture of Westernised city life quite amazed him.

At the end of their training each had been given a free Literacy Kit, which would remain the property of his class if he conducted it regularly for a year. The kits were an invaluable gift to Sokhodeora. They arrived by rail at Nawada in big wooden boxes and consisted of slates, books, cloth blackboard, alphabet chart and a Petromax lantern – educational requisites far beyond the means of their classes to provide for themselves. The Petromax alone, which cost the equivalent of two months' wages, was immensely prized because of the brilliance of its light.

They took charge of the classes, and I went periodically to encourage them, although they treated my visits as inspections. Wendy stopped teaching because we had adopted a baby in Delhi. As Mahadev assumed what seemed to us to be a superior air to the women's class he was lectured on the importance of educating women, but the women stopped attending because learning from a male teacher infringed their social customs.

Later Ugra Narayan Mahto asked to be released to teach the illiterate of his own caste, and so began a men's class in a tiny, straw-strewn room of his house. Both he and Mahadev taught every night for the following year without payment, earning the right to keep the Literacy Kits.

By the beginning of April the sun beat the fallow earth with a glare that screwed up your eyes until it had beaten a headache into the middle of your forehead. The Loo, a savage wind from the west, said to come off the Rajput Desert, rose early in the morning and tore through the house until nightfall. It thrashed to strings the leaves of the banana trees I had planted by our back verandah as a windbreak. Dust and leaves raced along the ground rasping your ankles. Some days it blew the sky and the sun murky white like a fog. On our verandah the temperature was 106ºF, and inside the house 102°. There was no escape from the heat. If we kept the window shutters open our teeth chewed grit and the wind nagged like toothache making us irritable and distressed, but to shut it out made us feel as if we were suffocating.

It was our second experience of early summer. Everyone walked slowly, hugged shade, covered the head and licked dry lips. The great *mahua* trees had lost their leaves as though it were autumn. Heat haze trembled over the sand of the creek bed between the ashram and Sokhodeora. Whirly-whirlys spun giddily into the sky. The mud walls of the village houses flung the heat back at the alleys well into the night. Because of its low roof our kitchen became too hot to cook in.

It was a time of idleness, for the only crops were a few vegetables kept alive by irrigation close to the village. It was a time of endurance, for there would be no cool change to bring relief; a time of chills, colds and flu because everyone slept out of doors under clear sky and immense stars, catching the night breeze and the goose-pimple dews of early morning.

For the aged it was the time of death. Men carried the stick bier with its body in red and white cottons to the deep beating of a drum past our house into the jungle, where the body was burned.

Near the end of April the Indian Government sent us to the Tibetan Refugee School at Mussoorie in the foothills of the Himalayas behind Delhi. We returned after the monsoon had broken to find that Mahadev's class had been meeting outside until the rains began, for the room they had used had been repaired and leased to a Bihar State Handicrafts Training Centre and he had been unable to find any other room in the crowded village.

So he had taken his students into the low mud-and-straw buffalo hut beside his house.

The night I visited it Shri Kurian kept Wendy company in the flickering lantern light. This, by all local standards, made her an immoral woman. Kurian, a diminutive man from Kerala with tremendous energy and a flair for the dramatic, had recently returned from learning ceramic work in Japan.

It was a humid evening. Myriads of insects and small, flat, black and stinking beetles flopped about the light or crawled at the base of the lantern stand. The beetles were disgusting creatures, for when squashed, swept out, or even touched, they exuded a loathsome smell. A small brown frog also sat at the base of the lantern stand and even he did not seem to care for adding the beetles to his menu.

He came each evening hopping across the verandah to pursue the insects about the light in our room, and we used to ask each other jokingly before we went to bed: 'Have you put the frog out?' In the mornings we used to ask: 'I wonder if a snake has got him today.'

Wendy and Kurian talked in a desultory manner while she kept looking through the barred windows for a glimpse on the road of my lantern. She had two fears. One was of being left alone in the house with the dim, fluttering light of the lantern making deep shadows against the walls and across the verandah. For the dimness seemed to emphasise the scuttering of rats in the roof, the sound of bats chewing small frogs and dropping pieces, and the swish and rattle of banana fronds against the kitchen and bathroom walls, noises that conjured up all kinds of frightening fantasies.

The other fear was for me, in case I met a black bear on the road. Kurian had not helped matters by giving her a graphic description of a man's face after it had been torn away by a bear's claws.

The black bears were greatly feared by the village people, particularly in the toddy season, because they climbed the palm trees and stole the fermenting sap that was collecting in small earthenware pots suspended under cross-cuts in the palm trunks. After drinking this intoxicating liquor they would attack without provocation. They came, *too,* into the sugar cane crop just near our house.

'If you see a bear sleeping beneath a palm tree,' Kurian said, 'tip-toe quietly past and do not disturb the fellow.' Both of them laughed at the image this conjured up in their minds.

'I can tell you another good recipe,' Wendy chuckled. 'The schoolchildren showed me some tiny seeds and I'll get you some if you like. All you do is give them to a tiger when he comes to eat you and he will fall down dead.'

At last I appeared, clumping on to the verandah in the boots I wore to cope with slippery bunds, water and muddy alleys. I smiled at Kurian and thanked him for keeping Wendy company.

'Where was the night class?' Wendy asked.

'In Mahadev's buffalo hut,' I replied dispiritedly.

'In a buffalo hut,' Wendy repeated in amusement and consternation. 'My God,' Kurian said. 'Where was the buffalo?' 'Evicted to a small verandah under the front of the thatch. There wasn't room for everyone inside,' I said, and then my sense of humour got the better of my frustration about the plight of the class. Chuckling I ducked my head low and stooped, lifted one leg high and stepped with exaggerated care over an imaginary creature on the floor. The mime amused Kurian and Wendy and they laughed heartily. Perhaps there was also something in our laughter of a need to momentarily escape from the general lack of beauty or graciousness in village life.

'What are we going to do?' Wendy asked anxiously.

'I don't know,' I smiled, 'unless we house train Mahadev's buffalo.'

'My God,' Kurian repeated.

'The Harijans are suggesting we might build a room for them.'

'How much would it cost?' Wendy asked.

'Goodness knows, but if we're not going to build a new building for our school we'll use the money we've got from Australia. Anyway a literacy class can't continue in a buffalo hut. It's undignified and an insult to their efforts and aspirations.'

The buffalo herself brought matters to their climax. She delivered a stillborn calf and continued to be very ill afterwards. The Block veterinary surgeon insisted that she occupy the hut until her health was restored. So now something had to be done.

6

KESURWA

Luttan came on to our verandah slowly because he was timid and apprehensive. Behind him, with head lowered, as befitted a woman, followed his wife Kesurwa. Both of them had been attending our night literacy classes, but that did not diminish their present fears. Still, in Kesurwa's quick step and free swing of the hips, rounded as an ancient sculpture, there was an independent spirit far removed from Luttan's plodding and his almost apologetic efforts to efface himself.

We drew up four chairs and almost commanded them to sit down, whereupon they perched on the edge. It was, of course, against their custom to allow men and women to sit together, and they were in public view, but we ignored this.

'What work do you do, Kesurwa *bahen* (sister)?' we asked.

'Cow-manuring floors in the ashram. Only now and then.'

'How much do you earn a month?'

'Sometimes twenty-eight rupees if I get work most days. Not usually.'

'We want someone to teach in the kindergarten. We will be here only three years and we want to train someone who can carry on after we have gone. The ashram found Annapurna sister for us, but she is having a baby and won't be working after that.'

They both looked unhappy. Luttan was worrying about getting back to his work in the ashram dairy although we had arranged for his absence.

'But Wendy *bahen*, I have never been to school,' Kesurwa murmured in a frightened voice.

'We've searched the village and there's only one other woman possible – the one who is running the Government night class for girls. She's literate but you have doubtless heard that she threw the Harijan girls out a few nights ago, telling them they were dirty, to go back to the pigs. That's not the kind of person we want.'

'But I know nothing, Wendy *bahen*. How could I teach the children reading, writing and sums?'

'They do very little of that in the kindergarten, Kesurwa,' Wendy replied, 'and what you need to know I will teach you. You and I will work in the mornings and in the afternoons you can come here for reading lessons. In a few months you'll be surprised at how much you'll know.'

Kesurwa was unable to respond to her confidence and encouragement and continued to look downcast.

'I don't think I'd be able to do it. I've only done floors.'

'You can start on trial for a fortnight then, from the New Year. If we think you are learning you could continue, couldn't you? To begin with we will pay you 30 rupees a month.'

They were still unable to decide. 'Come and look at the kindergarten and then you can think about it for a day or two.'

They came with us to the renovated storeroom that had become the kindergarten when the problem of overcrowding forced us to separate the pre-school children from the original school. It stood behind Shantiranjan's sculpture of Mother India overlooking the soccer field. To the rear were a banana grove, and bathrooms clustered about a well.

It was an oblong room, which Wendy had determined to make as attractive as possible. She had had the floors levelled and the walls whitewashed and had painted the doors and window shutters blue, green and white. Over the whitewash she had painted rows of animals and illustrations from some of the nursery stories. There were, for instance, the three bears, Michaelovitch, Alexandrovna and Mihaelovitch chasing goldilocks Nastasya, a result of the fact that the only cheap, well produced and beautifully illustrated nursery books in Hindi we had been able to find, had been printed in Moscow. (A friend sixty miles away in Gaya who sought our advice on setting up a kindergarten was alarmed that we might be indoctrinating our pupils, but for us *The Three Bears* did not seem excessively political.)

Kesurwa was delighted with this room. Perhaps this was what decided them to accept.

Her afternoon reading lessons were a painful effort to her, requiring all her powers of concentration, and it took many afternoons of practice on one story before she had any of the fluency necessary for reading before a class. Then, of course, her problems doubled because she had to concentrate not only on the story but on the children as well and story time ended at first in confusion and anger.

However she continued zealously, determined to master *The Three Bears, The Animals Who Lived in The Glove,* and *The Crane who went to Dinner with the Fox.*

Reading was a battle so many village people fought and we felt only the greatest admiration for them. They were prepared without boredom or rejection to read the simplest material over and over again.

It was easier when Wendy prepared a demonstration lesson for her for the following day. If it was in colour identification they placed leaves or flowers in their correct colour groupings and Wendy showed her how to let each child group a small individual collection of things and how to then let them talk about the colours of the objects in the room, or seen from the window.

Sometimes they rehearsed a health lesson. They caught a fly in a glass one day and Wendy explained how she could show him to the children and talk about what a naughty chap he was. She grew wheat on damp cotton wool with the children, although the sparrows stole most of it.

In the beginning Kesurwa had a daily lesson in telling the time from the clock. It was essential, for without this she could not hope to conduct any sort of orderly timetable. First she had to learn the English numerals, for the Hindi numbers were written differently, then she had to master the various meanings of the two hands. In the beginning Wendy helped her by setting the alarm for halfway through the morning when lessons stopped and the children had to be bathed, combed and given milk and medicines. But before many weeks had gone by she could manage without the alarm. She picked up the clock and gazed at it closely and intently, then checked with Wendy and prepared for the next stage of the morning.

Their discussion of the theory of teaching was at the simplest level. Sometimes they talked a little about why children were given free play in the kindergarten but Wendy's explanation amounted simply to the fact that it made them happy, that they learnt to play together and learnt to use their hands. Frequently they discussed how long small children could be expected to sit still as Kesurwa, like so many other people, wanted small children to sit quietly for as long as she could and was surprised and irritated when they became naughty and noisy.

She tried very hard and was always cheerful and willing to help us after hours in our village work. The children's attendance was regular because she collected them in the morning on her way to school and saw their parents if they were absent. She even shamed one mother into dressing a boy who used to come naked. Her social attitudes were sound and she never favoured the children of one caste and as she had the advantage of knowing the local dialect she eased the children's transition to Hindi. It was a joy to watch her affection for the thirty pupils.

Harijans watching the preparation of the Multi-Purpose Food.

Shrimati Kesurwa serving Multi-Purpose Food to the kindergarten children.

Schoolgirls hemming blanket pieces for shawls.

They were, of course, very appealing. There was tubby Prakash with closely cropped hair on his round head and a mischievous, turned-up face who was always disrupting lessons with some humorous remark. There was Lalta, a soft, round three-or four-year-old, with skimpy hair plaited in two thin wisps and tied at the back of her head with a piece of wool. She wore an imitation jewel in the side of her nose, which gave her an oddly grown-up appearance, and at least four petticoats to her ankles. Over them she wore a short cotton blouse. All of her clothes were faded. She not only loved her bath but if not caught in time would wash all the petticoats too, thumping them on the concrete apron around the well in the usual village manner. The two of them liked to chat together, on the top rung of the bamboo climbing frame, and Prakash used to assist her in her imaginative construction of boats or houses.

About midday Kesurwa walked home with them, holding hands with a girl with a damp, newly washed shirt over her head keeping off the sun, or a boy with damp pants over his head and oblivious of his bare bottom.

Periodically she marched them to the ashram maternity hospital, for the kindergarten served a most important function as a health centre. The children waited nervously on the verandah or chased each other about out of bravado, or peered through the barred window to see what the doctor was doing.

For some months Bacchu had the first consultation. Son of a labourer in the ashram nurseries, he was a stolid, unsmiling little boy with spindly legs and a stomach as protuberant as Prakash's or Lalta's. He always wore a green and fawn checked shirt and short khaki pants, and his black hair was well oiled down on his round head. But from the back of his neck to his calves he was entirely covered in malnutrition sores.

Dr Asha sympathetically examined him. She was a frail, immaculately clad young woman who worked in the ashram for about a year, leaving after she had given birth to a baby girl in what was temporarily her own hospital. Bacchu's sores had not responded to daily cleansing and an application of ointment, nor to a first treatment for intestinal worms. The compounder, who was also the Sokhodeora postmaster in the afternoon, made up his new prescription and handed it to Kesurwa.

Sumitri, a slender, elf-faced little girl with long, crinkly hair and a husky voice had pushed into the consulting room and heard Dr Asha's routine questions about worms with great interest.

'Have you noticed any worms after toileting?' Dr Asha asked her, when it came to her turn. Sumitri, imagination aroused, nodded eagerly.

'Were they long?'

By an indication of her hands Sumitri described what was to her a gigantic length. Dr Asha's eyes twinkled.

'What colour were they, Sumitri?'

'Green,' came the thoughtful, husky reply.

'And I suppose they chased you,' Dr Asha laughed and chucked her in the stomach.

Dropping her eyes with an impish smile Sumitri ran off to see if her goat, which always accompanied her to school, was grazing peacefully.

It was a shock to Wendy to find that Lalta's distended stomach was the result of an enlarged spleen from constant attacks of malaria. Lalta looked particularly pretty that day. She had on a dress of shiny blue material and full long pants. For several days now she had said every morning that she was going to 'her country', which meant she was going to the village where her kinsfolk lived.

As Dr Asha questioned her, an old woman joined the onlookers waiting in the room. Her back was curved and she walked with the bow-like hobble of very old village women. Her sari was tattered, her legs sticks of bone on which the large, wrinkled, calloused and cracked feet seemed splayed to an unusual size. At the sight of her, Lalta left the doctor's side and ran to lay her head in her grandmother's lap.

Dr Asha called the next child and laid Lalta's iron tablets on the table for Kesurwa or Wendy to take later. Wendy brought the next child for examination and on reaching for the tablets found that Lalta had discovered them for herself and had consumed at least three.

'Oh, Lalta,' she said reproachfully.

Lalta sucked blissfully at the taste left by the sugar-coated tablets, put her head on one side and gave her most entrancing smile. It was quite impossible to be cross with her.

There was quite a diary of instructions by the time the last pupil had been examined. Wendy moved to the door but Kesurwa seemed reluctant to go. She hovered near the doctor, as if wishing, but somehow afraid, to ask for something.

'What Is It, Kesurwa?' Wendy asked.

She hesitated. 'I have much pain here and here, Wendy sister,' she said, touching her shoulders and upper arms, and then added in a burst of confidence: 'I have so much pain every month.'

'Then you should ask about it,' Wendy moved to Dr Asha's side and explained that Kesurwa wished to consult her.

When Kesurwa returned to the kindergarten to help sweep it and tidy away the things before lunch, she brought some medicine and seemed happier. But this was the beginning of increasing hypochondria, brought on by Kesurwa's failure to have children and the reflections other women made about this.

That afternoon, when Kesurwa's lessons finished, Wendy accompanied her to the village. Kesurwa was to show her where Bacchu lived and help explain to his parents the use of the powders Dr Asha had prescribed.

They found his house at the end of a dark, overhung alleyway. Wendy called at the entrance and his mother appeared with several of the neighbours, including Lalta's mother, a cheerful plump woman who obviously adored her little girl.

'Lalta loves school, Wendy sister,' she said.

'Thank you,' Wendy replied.

Everyone smiled appreciatively.

'I have come to see Bacchu's mother,' Wendy went on. 'He is a very intelligent little boy but not very well. He has worms and Dr Asha at the ashram has given him some powders.' She explained how the powders were to be taken and then asked: 'Do you understand?'

'Yes, yes, she understands,' a couple of the neighbours replied quickly. 'See!' they gesticulated, taking the packets from Wendy's hand. 'This is for night, this is for the morning.' But they all spoke so quickly in the village dialect that Wendy lost the remainder of the conversation.

When the babble of interest had quietened she indicated Bacchu's sores and asked, 'What do you give Bacchu to eat?'

'Rice and potatoes, Wendy sister.'

'And what else? Does he have milk or vegetables or spices?'

'No.'

'Does he have dal?' This was the pulse from which village people obtained their protein. 'No, Wendy sister. No. Rice and potatoes he has,' she reiterated.

'That is one reason why he has sores. He needs other foods as well.'

'What to do, Wendy sister? We are very poor.'

Wendy nodded and, briefly repeating her remarks about the medicine, she wished Bacchu's mother and the neighbours *namaste,* resolving on the way home to add cod-liver oil to the kindergarten daily milk supply.

Actually she used shark-liver oil because it was cheaper. She walked along the line of gaping mouths pouring a spoonful into each one. After the first day's dose, Ajnasia, a pointed faced, impish girl with a front tooth missing, took great pleasure in torturing her slow-thinking friend, Suji. 'That stuff Wendy sister gave you was poisonous and you're going to die.'

It did not occur to dull-witted Suji that Ajnasia too had drunk her spoonful. Throwing herself down upon the dusty road she wept bitterly about her fate. Wendy dispelled the tears and the shark oil healed Bacchu's sores.

Often Kesurwa helped with the milk distribution in the small communal square in the Harijan sector where we continued to distribute it. At one end was a thatch lean-to where the leader of the Harijan caste made doors and windows for sale. Under this, over a pit into which burning logs had been placed, the large bronze cauldron of frothy milk steamed. Mahadev stirred the milk with a long spoon from our kitchen and Kesurwa fanned away the flies or occasionally scooped out the small pieces of straw or ash which the gusts of burning west wind lifted from the ground and deposited on the surface.

There was nothing they could do about this, but Kesurwa had contrived to have the square swept clear of animal dung and the children seated (in a circle) crouched on the flat of their feet, arms resting across their knees.

They placed the container for their milk on the ground in front of them. We poured as equal a portion as possible into each bowl and some stayed where they were to drink the milk while others went home with it. Mahadev took the milky cauldron to the well to clean it and several women came with small woven platters to remove the coals from the pit and take them to their own houses to light their fires for the night meal. Matches were a luxury in the village.

After one such distribution Kesurwa was chatting to Wendy as they walked through the village:

'We have only been in Sokhodeora a couple of years, Wendy sister. We haven't got any land here. We stay with my parents. Before we came here my husband was working in the mines at Jheria. He got high wages, Wendy sister, two rupees a day. He had an accident to his head and was in hospital for some months. Then I said we should come here. Come and look at my house, Wendy sister,' she asked eagerly.

So a small distance along the congested alleyway they turned into the courtyard of her parents' house. It was a space perhaps eight feet square and on the front, alley side, had recently been constructed a tiny room with a thatch roof barely a short man's height. Kesurwa drew her into this tiny, windowless structure.

'See,' she said enthusiastically, gesturing to one end, 'this is where I shall hang my cooking pots.'

Wendy rapidly attempted to compose her shocked, compassionate feelings so that nothing of what she felt might register on her face but she must have failed, because Kesurwa's eagerness died.

'We shall sleep at this end of the room,' she went on more slowly, then added helplessly: 'What else can we do, Wendy sister? We have no land and we are very poor.'

Wendy found herself unable to answer and she had missed the moment when she might have shared Kesurwa's enthusiasm. As she walked back to the ashram this seemed a great failure and she wept.

Increasingly Kesurwa succumbed to bouts of depression and days of moodiness and nagging at the children, which puzzled Wendy for some time.

'Are you unwell, Kesurwa?' she asked one afternoon.

Kesurwa's face took on new lines of anxiety and she crossed her arms so that each hand was resting on the opposite shoulder.

'I have great pains here and in my chest and in my back and every month such terrible pains.'

It was almost exactly what she had said months previously. Wendy remembered the morning in the hospital and her consultation with Dr Asha.

'Didn't the medicine help you?' she asked.

Kesurwa shook her head. 'I went to Kapassia [the ashram leprosy centre where every Sunday a doctor came from Gaya to treat outpatients] and saw the new doctor and he gave me some different medicine, but the pains do not go away. We are so poor, Wendy sister. We eat only rice and vegetables and some dal and spices. I need some powdered milk.'

Wendy was surprised, for this complaining Kesurwa was a new person to her. She knew well enough the extent of the village people's poverty and Kesurwa, without children and with herself and Luttan employed, was far better off than the average. Then she compared Kesurwa's life with her own and felt trapped. She considered herself entitled to milk, bought it and drank it. Kesurwa also had the right to believe that she was entitled to milk but she had little money for it so could only complain. Yet the powdered milk available was for the children. Quelling her sudden irritation, for caught as she was emotionally she had no answer, Wendy explained that the milk was for the children. Kesurwa looked at her helplessly.

'Well, if the doctor gives you a letter saying you need it we will give you some,' Wendy relented and was ashamed for making Kesurwa feel that she had rejected her friendship and withdrawn something of her moral support.

Kesurwa suffered, too, from the envy of her women friends with whom she had once done floors. Finally her rebellious feelings led her to buy a block of land just beside our house but outside the ashram fence.

'I'm going to live outside the village, Wendy sister,' she said. 'I'm not happy there and it is too cramped.' She added excitedly: 'My husband and I went to Nawada and signed the papers for the land. It cost eighty rupees.' Then she fell gloomy again: 'But how are we going to afford to build a house? My husband has become one of the trainees at the Bihar Government Handicrafts Training Centre and he will only get twenty rupees a month for a whole year.'

'You can do a lot of building yourselves,' Wendy replied, 'and we will help you.'

'Wendy sister, could you help us to get a big window like you have in your house?' she pleaded.

'We'll try.'

Their plot was high, dry land which grew at best a few weakly pulse bushes here and there and next to it Mahadev's family had one of their fields. Mahadev's eldest brother, Bindeswar, tried some of my tomato seedlings there. He needed water and Kesurwa would need water, so as Bindeswar and Luttan were companions, both attending the training course for shoemakers, they took up my suggestion that they dig a well.

They dug with mattocks at the intersection of their land with that of a third farmer so that the well belonged to three owners. As they descended Bindeswar dug the earth into a basket, which Luttan raised at arm's length above his head. Their neighbour's two sons, on top, each pulled a rope attached to the basket to bring it up. About thirty feet down they reached water and used it for the tomatoes and building the house. But they had to wait until the water receded in the summer to deepen it adequately. Mahadev went to the Block for application papers for a Government subsidy for bricks to wall the well, but they probably did not eventually succeed in making it *pukhha.*

After work and at weekends Kesurwa and Luttan worked very happily building the mud walls for a small two-roomed house that took up almost half their land. We gave her two windows and they were one of the first things a visiting Japanese nurse from Nepal noticed – and praised – in almost windowless Sokhodeora.

Kesurwa was even more envied and one day a woman gleaning in a field near hers picked a quarrel with her, resorting to the worst abuse village women knew and accusing her of adultery. She came to the kindergarten next morning her face badly bruised and cut, disregarding her physical hurts but enduringly resentful at the unjust slur on her reputation.

The only part of their bodies which village women dared show were the feet, forearms, and midriff between the bottom of their blouses and the waist of their saris. Kesurwa's midriff, like the tummies of the kindergarten girls, was covered with small horizontal scars, and Wendy asked her one day what they were.

'The midwife makes them, Wendy sister, with a knife or anything sharp.'

She laughed self-consciously.

'It is kind of—' she broke off with the difficulty of explaining the custom to her, then added, 'for good luck.'

'I should have thought the baby had enough to cope with in untrained and unhygienic midwives,' Wendy reflected sadly.

'It is our custom, Wendy sister,' she shrugged with a half smile.

After her original excitement the slow progress of her new home began to depress her and her independent spirit seemed to search for new ways of satisfying itself.

'I tell them in the village they are dirty, Wendy sister,' she said, 'and ought to keep themselves clean and send their children to school to learn, but they just ignore me. There was a man in the ashram some days ago talking about nurses' training in Gaya. What do you think, Wendy sister?' she asked.

'I don't know anything about it, Kesurwa, but I do know that trained nurses can earn as much as a hundred rupees a month.'

She gasped, for this was untold-of wealth and that a woman should be able to earn it seemed incredible.

'What other information did he give you and were you thinking of it for yourself?' Wendy asked.

'Yes,' she replied. 'He said it would take two years and that we would live-in while we were trained. But my husband won't think about it.' She added miserably, 'He said if I went away he would get another wife. I don't know anything, Wendy sister, and I would learn to read and write really well.'

Wendy understood then a little more than she had at the beginning of their friendship. Kesurwa was unwell as much because she was unhappy as because she had some complaint. Her remark seemed particularly sad for it underlined all Kesurwa's longings and limitations. She wanted to know so much but was so restricted in experience and by lack of education that the only knowledge she could name or conceive of was that of being able to read and write fluently.

Luttan, Wendy knew, to be narrow and timid. He would be easy game for the sharp, vindictive tongues of others amongst the village women and they would have no hesitation in imputing immoral motives to Kesurwa's desire to go to Gaya. Without the social pressure of the village Kesurwa and Luttan might be able to make some arrangements: with it Kesurwa was ensnared and helpless.

'Perhaps when Luttan completes his Government training you might both go to Gaya,' Wendy said. 'He naturally doesn't want to be without you for two years. It would be lonely for him. Try talking it over again. The extra money would make so many things possible for you.'

But Kesurwa said nothing, aware and despairing in a way Wendy could never fully experience of the rest of her life's pattern – the endless struggle to exist without even a hope that her life might become more secure, more comfortable, more enlightened, more beautiful.

7
NEW-FANGLED PUBLIC INSTRUCTION

It was the time of the Saraswati festival. Saraswati is the Goddess of Wisdom who stands on a lotus flower, the flower which half in and half out of the water symbolises the duality of worldly and spiritual knowledge.

Each year her plaster statue was placed in the Sokhodeora schoolroom, a mud-walled building some thirty by fifteen feet with a small, bare swept space outside and a huge *mahua* tree shading its roof. After the festival she was carried in triumph at the head of a procession, which proceeded with much beating of drums to the jungle, and there she was left.

In the early days of our night class we had bought a kerosene-lantern projector from Bombay. It was the same as any film-strip projector save that there was an attachment at the back where a Petromax lantern could be placed to provide the light for the slides. We were excited because it was an excellent teaching medium and we hoped to be able to use it for general social education in the village. This was in accordance with the Government policy of using adult literacy classes not only for the teaching of reading and writing but for the dissemination of that knowledge which would help raise the standard of living in the village. With the projector were two film strips. We had written for others but had had no success in obtaining them, so we decided to show the two we had – one on the control of cholera, the other on the treatment of TB. Both were necessary but the first seemed of more immediate use, so we ran it through, obtained help in translating the English script on the film into Hindi and set off to our night class.

There were about thirty young adults waiting for us in the dim gloom of the hurricane lantern. We heard the faint murmur of voices as we arrived; a fine dust hung in the air after the sweeping and the still figures, shoulders and heads draped about with thin cotton shawls, presented momentarily a picture of ghostliness.

'*Namaste,* Wendy sister, Allan brother.' It was a loud greeting. The noise suddenly increased and an excited babble followed the opening of the box and the appearance of the projector.

One or two people had seen a film in Nawada, thirty miles away, and had talked of it for months. Now, wonder of wonders, they were all to see a film. Jodhan, the gentle lad who had attended the school and been our first Health Minister, was there. He had left school to work on his father's land. As he was one of those who had visited the Nawada picture house he could not forbear a few comments of innocent superiority.

'It won't be like the film you saw,' I told him smiling. 'This only shows a series of still pictures on the wall.'

We leaned a wooden backrest against the wall and draped a piece of white cloth over it. They all crowded as close as they could to our improvised screen and we had to shift them back.

Slide-by-slide the film showed the symptoms of cholera, the necessity of notifying the village council as soon as a case was suspected, methods of preventing the spread of the infection such as the pouring of bleaching powder into the wells, the boiling of utensils and clothes used by the victim. Everyone laughed at the picture of the sly milk seller who was secretly adding unclean well water to his milk so that it would go further. It was meant to be buffoon-like but was nonetheless true. We ran the film strip through several times that night to the accompaniment of reminiscences about cases of cholera seen by the young people there. Alas, later that year a cholera epidemic in the area was to take a toll of as many as eighty lives from a village some eight miles from Sokhodeora.

News of the projector spread and we were next begged to show a film in the village library. At one end was a rickety table, two chairs and a wooden cupboard with battered green-painted doors and inside a small collection of thin paper-backed books. The floor was covered with straw and so crowded that it was almost impossible for us to find either standing room or a space for the projector. They all squeezed up, sitting on one another's legs.

Boddhu, the village postmaster and compounder in the ashram hospital, took charge of the group. He and Dukharan, the librarian, spoke seriously of the sudden and terrible nature of cholera. The village people were very afraid of it.

When we had shown the first set of slides, Boddhu requested that we also show the strip about TB. We watched sadly the instructions so few of which any of the village people could follow: well-ventilated rooms were unknown; the list of foods – chicken, eggs, milk, vegetables – was impossible for village people to buy; and the problem of isolation in their overcrowded homes insoluble.

However, we thought the fascination of watching the film prevented them from seeing the essential tragedy being revealed to them. They had so little knowledge of the advantages given to others that they felt very little sense of the injustice of living in an age in which many of the diseases they died of were curable had they only the money to buy such cures.

A week later the village was organising a drama for the Saraswati festival and Boddhu asked us if we would show the film in the village Government schoolroom as a preliminary to the drama.

'It will be very difficult if a large crowd comes,' I said. 'We can only throw a small picture on the wall with the Petromax light.'

'No, no,' Boddhu assured me, 'everyone will see. They should see this film on cholera.'

So that evening we again lugged the heavy projector to the village. This time we continued along the dusty, bullock track that separated the two sections of the village – Sokho and Deora. A few people, cleaning their cooking pots with earth outside their doors, looked up as we passed and greeted us. The sharp smell of the cooking fires pervaded the night and a soft smokiness hung in the alleyways.

Already a number of people had gathered at the school. We stooped to enter the low door, buttressed in the mud walls by a heavy beam lintel, and clambered over the seated crowd. A group of chattering women nursing toddlers and babies watched us curiously. They pushed and jostled like a brood of hens and as each new woman arrived, shoved, shifted and abused afresh. Very soon we ourselves were jammed against the projector and it was impossible to throw the picture over the heads of the people packed in front of us. Boddhu came to our rescue. Laying hands on shoulders and arms he shoved the audience to both sides. I stood to explain the meaning of the film to the group. A burst of newcomers pushed by an increasing crowd behind swayed into the room to be met with invective from those already seated. My voice was completely lost. I gave up and threw the first picture on the improvised sheet screen. Immediately half the audience stood in order to see better. They were whacked by those behind to a chorus of: 'Sit, brother, sit, sister.'

My explanation of the first picture was drowned in the surge of hubbub.

We stopped, stood up and attempted to gain silence, but the swaying crowd at the door was too concerned with either getting in or preventing others from doing so and we were helpless.

Boddhu forced his way to the front but he could not make himself heard either. He retreated again to the door and started to evict as many people as possible. We waited until the noise eased a little and proceeded with several more of the pictures. I shouted to be heard above the once more increasing noise. Suddenly all attention was diverted from us to Boddhu who was trying to keep out those he had managed to push out before they had quite realised what he was about.

Angry youths abused Boddhu and were precipitated against him by the shoving crowd behind. He turned to us with a defeated look. We replaced the lantern in the box as he scrambled to our side.

'Take the projector outside, we'll show it there. I'll get rid of this mob.'

In our turn we scrambled over legs and small children and reached the door. Angry shouts still followed Boddhu.

Small evicted groups stood about talking noisily. We decided that this was one of our failures and resolved to creep out of the fast-gathering crowd and proceed home.

We disappeared unobtrusively down the roadway. A few hurrying people on their way to the film show looked at us with some puzzlement but we had passed them before they had a chance to comment.

The next morning Boddhu told us reproachfully that they had searched for us for some time and we might have felt guilty for our exit but for Mahadev casually mentioning that the dispelled crowd took its seats at the drama about Saraswati, which commenced almost immediately after our departure. We had only been the curtain-raiser.

*

'Allan brother and Wendy sister, it would be a marvellous thing for our village library. People would come every evening to listen to a wireless,' said the headman, Goverdan Sau, in his most persuasive tone. He had an appreciative audience in Ganesh Mahto and the village librarian, Dukharan. We were all sitting formally on our front verandah drinking tea.

'Your name would always be remembered in Sokhodeora. People here never have the chance to travel like you have had. They cannot even see Delhi or Bombay or the important cities of their own country. They don't even know what is happening in their own country's affairs and how the five-year plans are going and what the Government is doing for us.'

'We know how much you want to help us,' Dukharan put in. 'When you were here last time three years ago you painted our library cupboard and gave us books and whitewashed the walls. Your services weren't forgotten.'

'We hope we will be able to arrange the money to get a daily newspaper,' Goverdan Sau added, either to demonstrate their sincerity about the lack of information or to give us another chance of offering help.

We knew that there were seventy countries in the world each lacking this ordinary information medium, and whose village people would have also fitted this description, but it seemed best for the present to conceal our sympathy.

'What will happen when the battery goes flat? How will you afford another one?' we asked.

'We can collect money for that,' Goverdan Sau assured us confidently, 'and the council has funds for social education. We'll only switch it on for an hour or so every evening so the battery will last.'

'Would you take proper care of a radio?'

'Dukharan will be the only person permitted to switch it on or manipulate the knobs.'

'Well, we'll see what we can do to help you,' we said finally.

We then asked a number of friends whether they thought we should give Sokhodeora a radio, and to our surprise all were strongly against it – even Patna people who had the advantages of newspapers, radio and cinema themselves. It seemed wisest to accept the advice. However, reassured by the fact that the Australian Friends' Service Council were in favour of us using their gift of AU$80 (Rs.666) for this purpose, we took advice about radio shops in Patna and purchased a set.

First we set up an aerial on bamboo poles in our garden and tested the wireless in our house. Then, having carefully instructed a very nervous Dukharan about the knobs, we took the set to the Sokhodeora library for Christmas. The bottom part of the cupboard had been cleared out to fit the radio so that it could be locked away when not in use. Leading the aerial wire out between the top of the mud wall and the roof we dug in the first pole against the back of the building.

But we were then faced with our most real appreciation of the congestion of Sokhodeora. The wire, which seemed short in our garden, now stretched well into the yard of an adjoining house. Goverdan Sau found the house owner and explained the problem. He willingly co-operated, digging a hole with a 'shovel' – a bamboo-handled crowbar – beside his house door, planting the second pole and attaching it with rope to his roof beams.

The menfolk's satisfaction with their installation was sharply punctured. The householder's old mother came out of the house and launched into a tirade!

'I'm not having that newfangled thing in my house yard. You don't know what might happen to us.'

'Be quiet, Mother,' her son shouted. Turning to Goverdan Sau and me he said, 'Come on, let's go. Don't take any notice of her. She'll have to put up with it.'

A day or two later Mahadev showed a naive but healthy reaction to the new source of knowledge: 'Wendy sister, Allan brother, what can you do about it if the man on the radio tells lies?'

'What do you mean?' we asked in some astonishment.

'He said it was going to rain today but it hasn't rained at all.'

So there was no doubt of the radio being educational. But the question still remained whether it would be cared for.

'You can come any time to see that we are looking after the radio,' Dukharan insisted and we always found him in charge of a group of men quietly listening in darkness with eyes fixed on the green dial light to the news in the erudite Hindi of All India Radio. It must have been difficult for some of them to follow.

'Allan brother,' began the anxious news of the first trouble, 'rats have chewed through the aerial wires on top of the wall!'

'You'll have to twist the ends together again. The difficulty is they will keep doing it.' They solved that for themselves by leading the wires through bamboo. They then nursed ten months' life out of the battery which we had expected to last between three and six months. Long after that an extremely nervous deputation of three brought the radio to us because it had stopped.

'I'm sorry, I don't know how to mend it,' I said. 'You'll need to have it repaired at a radio shop in Patna.'

But Goverdan Sau took the responsibility for this. How the cost of the new valve was collected we did not know but he returned from Patna in a few days with the radio repaired, and we were glad that we had followed our own counsels.

8

FAMILY PLANNING

Near the end of our first monsoon, Shri L.N. Jha, Deputy Minister of Information for the Bihar State Government, invited us to attend, as State guests, a Family Planning Seminar which he himself had organised. We had first to travel the hundred miles to Patna to join his party. From Patna half the group set out in his car; the half, which included us, fitting into the car of Shri Tubid, the Deputy Minister for Forests and Tribal Welfare. Both cars were neat, Indian-manufactured Ambassadors.

After an evening's driving we spent the night at a Dak Bungalow perched in the Hazaribhag forest. Dak (Mail) Bungalows are hostels for the use of Government officials when they are travelling. Curiously enough, Jayaprakash's ashram lay on the opposite side of the hill tract.

'I wish we had time so I could show you all the animals,' Shri Tubid said in the morning as we set off to complete the journey to Ranchi, Bihar State's main hill station, where we had lived for a time three years previously.

That evening we were taken to an outdoor public meeting where we sat with the speakers on a platform facing a crowd of young men, clerks mostly, to judge by the neatness of their white cotton clothes. Our host, Shri Jha, spoke dramatically of the growth of India's population and the urgency of controlling the birthrate. Then we struggled through the crowd into a long room to quietly inspect the exhibition before everyone was admitted. But the doorkeepers struggled unavailingly against the pushing throng and no sooner were we inside than the room had filled.

The exhibition consisted mainly of large photograph panels showing crowds with growth-of-population statistics superimposed over them. At one end of the room three women social workers presided over a small table display of contraceptives. A newspaperman photographed us as we inspected these and the Patna Press next day carried the news of two 'Austrian guests'.

Shri Jha was most pressing that we address the opening session of the conference the following morning, so with his help and that of his secretary I prepared a short speech in Hindi. But the inaugural address was delivered in English by the Governor of Bihar, Dr Zakir Hussein, who subsequently became the vice-president of India, his most important argument being that through family planning Indian families could achieve dignity.

This was followed by addresses by Shri Tubid and Shri Jha and both spoke in English. In consequence I felt not a little disconcerted when I was handed the microphone.

As a preface to my remarks I made reference to Shri Jha's slogan 'Hindi for Commonwealth Language'. Earlier, in private, Shri Jha had cracked a number of bitter jokes about the White Australia policy, charging that Australians would prefer to have a European convict than an Indian professor. Then he had laughed at the implied racial superiority by proposing humorously that on the basis of population Hindi should be the Commonwealth language. Australia, for instance, having only a quarter of the population of Bihar State alone.

Having said this slogan I delivered my speech in Hindi, to the great satisfaction of the newspaper reporters who made an extravagant fuss of the incident.

After this formal inauguration, the seminar proceeded in both languages in a very reticent atmosphere. Leading officials from the Health Department spoke of the State's failure to use its budget for contraceptives; the Chief Civil Surgeon caused a stir of interest among the men with his authoritative assertion that 'Men never lose their fertility'; the women social workers outlined the problems of encouraging city women to come to their clinics and related women's complaints that foam tablets caused local irritation. We were able to contribute information about problems of organisation at the village level and pleaded for the rapid extension of family-planning education and facilities to rural areas, suggesting that training could be given to literate women of the villages. But Wendy's proposal of biology and sex instruction in secondary schools met with a shocked reaction and was rejected.

The most dramatic moment of the conference was provided by Shri Jha's Parliamentary Under-Secretary who began her speech with a heated denunciation of family planning. Heads turned and delegates raised eyebrows at one another in the shocked silence. But breaths came easier when she reached the point of advocating – most passionately – compulsory sterilisation of men.

Shri Jha's sense of humour got the better of him and he whispered to us: 'She's so excited because she has already produced eight offspring. It's a counsel of desperation.'

However, there was more enthusiasm for sterilisation after the fourth child's birth than for the use of contraceptives, and statistics revealed an increasing number of such operations. Nevertheless we felt obliged in private conversation to correct one delegate's misunderstanding that Westerners have small families because they are all sterilised after their second child.

One of the most unusual features of our work was a constant transition from mixing with some of the poorest people in the world in Sokhodeora to meeting some of the most prominent people in India. In addition to the conference, Shri Jha held an official dinner which caused him no small anxiety as the guests had very mixed customs. Some would eat Indian, some Western, some vegetarian, some non-vegetarian food – there was even one woman who would not take salt. Out of the exceptional courtesy always shown to her Wendy found herself seated next to the State Governor, Dr Hussein.

We were also invited to English-style tea at the Governor's residence. There the guests waited in a huge hall until his arrival and then followed him through great double doors into the dining-room where Dr Hussein, in the course of the buffet meal, spoke to every one of his guests. I very tentatively asked him about sex education in secondary schools and, with recollections of the reaction of the conference still strong, was taken aback by the blunt reply: 'Of course there should be.'

Before we parted in Patna Shri Jha undertook to have the ashram declared an official family-planning centre by the Health Department and to supply us with Rs.1500 worth of contraceptives for distribution, proposals which were never actually effected. But the idea was a source of some amusement to him since, as he understood Gandhi's and Vinoba Bhave's attitudes, he thought this was subverting the Gandhian Movement. However, Jayaprakash had written to us expressing his approval that we should do this work and should attend the seminar.

On our return to Sokhodeora I obtained twenty-five dozen foam tablets from the Government doctor at Kawakol, who was not managing to dispense all the supplies he received. Only a few people came irregularly to the hospital requesting contraceptives and he was obliged to let them have a maximum of three tablets. These were usually wrapped by his compounder in a screw of newspaper for the patient to carry home perhaps a couple of miles. To us the arrangement was neither practical nor dignified.

We began by memorising the instructions in Hindi and then debated whether we should approach individuals or give public demonstrations. Although there was much to be said for the latter course we found ourselves for a long time too reticent to undertake it.

Actually Mahadev began our campaign by telling members of his caste about the 'medicine' and reporting to us that so-and-so, whose wife had just had their fourth child, did not want any more children for a time. So the first person to sign for a bottle of tablets was a Harijan shopkeeper whose mud-walled store with lockable wooden doors was six feet square and stocked little more than a couple of packets of Scissors cigarettes, some raw tobacco, some spices in rusty tins, and an earthenware pot of rice. But he never asked for them again nor even admitted using them, replying with silence to any questions.

The next were two husbands in the ashram who asked us anxiously to be sure not to give the medicine to unmarried people.

One afternoon Paro Mochi, Mahadev's father, stopped me in the narrow alley outside his house and asked shyly: 'Do you eat these tablets you've got?' His air of a mature man who understands about these matters and has been enlightening his neighbours quickly faded as I explained, and he was overtaken with embarrassment. But being a respected elder of his caste he gradually won back his expression of confidence. He was not one of the younger marrieds to giggle self-consciously and make a quick exit.

By this time the lane was crowded with listeners. Apparently I was the only one disturbed by the presence of children whom nobody made serious efforts to shoo away. A woman pushed past the listeners carrying a bucket of water from the well to her house and one of the young men shouted facetiously: 'She'll take them! She makes kids too easily!' The men laughed.

'Humph!' she replied, tossing her head indignantly, then pulling her sari over it and hurrying away.

Another young man, despite having just listened, repeated the same question: 'Do I eat them? Does my wife eat them?' To him serious medicine was swallowed; local applications were made from jungle herbs.

I explained patiently how the tablets were used. My questioner appearing puzzled, I explained twice more. I was then asked: 'My wife should eat them?'

'Nobody eats them. They are for local application.'

'Would one tablet a year be enough to see that you wouldn't have more family?' he asked anxiously.

'No,' I replied patiently. 'I've just been explaining all that to you. When did I tell you they were to be used?'

He ignored this question and asked again perplexedly, 'Would one or two tablets a month be all right?' The audience laughed.

'No, it's as I've told you,' I said. 'After all, it's not as though you have to worry about the expense of the pills. The Government supplies them free.'

He thought for a moment. I began to assume, since I had now explained three times in full detail, that the man understood and consequently was quite taken aback by his next question.

'What do the tablets taste like?' he asked with curiosity. 'How many times is it going to be necessary to tell you,' I said, 'that you don't eat them? *Don't.*'

The crowd was thoroughly amused. One of them said sympathetically: 'He's dumb, Allan brother. Don't bother telling him any more. We'll explain to him.'

And so ended the first public indoctrination.

A more sad aspect showed itself a day or two later, with the arrival of the first of the miserably anxious men whose shabby, worn clothes were usually stained beyond the power of soap or rain to bleach and who wanted to ask on behalf of a friend.

'Have you any more of your medicine to kill babies?'

'To stop babies, yes. But not to kill them. And it's not our medicine. It is from the Government hospital. The Government provided it for you.'

'It doesn't make you sick?'

'Is your wife pregnant?'

'It isn't for me. It's for my friend.'

'We haven't got anything like that. And don't you try to kill the baby. You'll end up killing your wife. The quacks will give you mercury or something dangerous.'

They went away without 'medicine', slowly and reluctantly now a hope had been lost, back into their desperation. And we could only hope against hope that they would not go to the unlicensed medicine shops in Kawakol.

Wherever I went in the village I raised the topic of family planning in conversation, so that very quickly I came to know people's fears and their need of independent choice. In their ignorance of biology they feared that the medicine might make their wives ill or unable to have children.

'But what if my children died and I couldn't have any more?'

'You can have more. You just stop using the medicine. That's what is meant by planning.'

'You know how it is, Allan brother. So many people in our families are dead already. All our children might die and then there would be no one to survive us.'

'But that's a different matter, surely. If you want to stop them from dying then take them to the Government doctor when they get sick. You only have to walk three miles and it only costs an anna. But you won't. You hope they will get better until it is too late.'

Choice was very important to the postmaster. He agreed emphatically with family planning at its first mention and pronounced: 'They should all do it,' giving a condescending glance towards the village houses.

'Do you want some for yourself?' I asked.

'No! You're not going to catch me using those,' he retorted, proud of his sophistication. Both he and Shri Ganesh Mahto requested alternative 'medicines', which we were able to supply when there was a change of Government doctors at the Kawakol hospital. Dr Saha left Kawakol for a training course in Canada and was replaced by a younger man, Dr Surendra Sinha, who willingly passed on to us some of the new supplies he had brought with him.

Finally I gave some talks and demonstrations to the Harijan night class on the fine monsoon evenings when the men sat on mats on a hard patch of ground outdoors. I had prepared for these some biological charts which were really quite hideous and doubtless obscene, but the class did not seem to notice this aspect.

By this time it seemed that the greatest problem Sokhodeora people had in accepting the idea of family planning was in accepting the fact that one could plan such a matter. This was the only resistance to family planning that we met from a religious quarter, and it arose from the ingrained feeling that it was not man who planned but God. It is, of course, much less common nowadays in Western society to speak of the First Cause in daily happenings: 'God has blessed your love' has become an explanation in terms of biology.

So I began by saying: 'You have to think about this in much the same way as you plan to build a house or you plan to buy a cow. You have to learn to look forward beyond the next meal, to plan ahead. When you marry you must try to decide how many children you would like.'

'We understand, Allan brother,' Bindeshwar, Mahadev's eldest brother, said sympathetically, 'and we will try to think for the years ahead. It is very sensible. If we have too many children how can we feed them?'

But as the discussion developed, one or two giggles in the circle having been silenced, the question was nevertheless raised again, with a tolerant grin: 'But you don't have anything to do with this. It is God's will whether you have children or don't have children or when children happen to you. We have nothing to do with it.'

Having no inclination to undermine their religious beliefs I approached the problem by asking, 'But God has given man intelligence?'

'Yes.'

'And God wants man to use his intelligence?'

'Yes.'

'So God has given scientists the intelligence to discover how to make medicine so that people can control the number of children they have. Surely God does not want you to have so many children that you cannot feed them and they suffer? Are men mixing God's plan all up if they have too many children?'

The class thought this over in silence but did not reply.

At the end of my demonstrations there were requests for the medicine, which I had now learned to refuse, saying: 'You should not take it until you have talked about these matters with your wives. You must both be agreed about it. And you should have some plan about your family, not some interest which is only going to last for the next week or two.'

Bindeshwar agreed solemnly. 'Yes, you should ask your wife about it. I would like to discuss it first.'

Nevertheless when we were leaving India we had no difficulty in distributing the remaining supplies. In fact, we were asked plaintively, 'What will we do when you are gone?'

'Go to the Kawakol Hospital and get them,' we replied, assuming a cheerfulness we did not feel. For all they could expect after a three-mile walk were three tablets in a scrap of dusty paper handed over indifferently without the effort to educate or sympathise.

It is a pity that all Westerners do not hear the amusing and debunking lectures of India's internationally known population expert Dr Chandrashekhar, such as we heard in Madras when we attended a Quaker International Seminar there. For many have false impressions about India's population problems.

Indian people, for instance, do not, one and all, have huge numbers of children. The national birthrate is less than that of the USA, which no one associates with an acute population problem. In the Kawakol area, 70 per cent of the population lived in joint families averaging 8.57 persons per family. As each joint family normally could include the elderly parents, at least one married son and daughter-in-law, and possibly an uncle or aunt, the number of children was not great. The remaining 30 per cent of the people there lived in single families – that is the married couple on their own

– and their average was 4.28 persons per family. Here again the number of children per married couple could have only been two or three.

It is truer to say that India does not have a population problem so much as a development problem. Her number of people is a problem only because agriculture and industry are too underdeveloped to provide adequately for them and fully employ them. This is not to deny that India should introduce family planning or that the West should give massive aid to her family-planning programmes. But it is much better for outsiders to think in this way about India. Impatience about slow development is preferable to impatience about people's intimate family life.

Unfortunately the publication of population statistics tends to strengthen wrong impressions about Indian fertility and to alarm and annoy rather than arouse a sense of sympathy; to deaden the sense that suffering people are unique individuals with the impression that they are abstract numbers; to undermine the urge to help individuals just because there are many needing help. Unfortunately some Westerners are more prone to thinking, What's the use? It's only a drop in the bucket, than they are to thinking, It will help feed Bacchu; it will send Chandra to school; it will buy Ramesh some chickens.

All along there must have been doubts, which were never expressed to us, arising from the fact that we had no children, feelings that family planning must mean the absence of children; for we discovered after we had adopted our baby daughter, Vidya, that unwittingly we had added a dimension to people's thinking. Some even connected our care of sick children with our family-planning campaign: 'They are cutting down our population with birth control, but they are keeping it up by saving sick children. The idea is OK.'

Of course we could lay no claim to cutting down the population at all. The most we had achieved in a few months was some education, the results of which were incalculable. And before we left, our seedlings of thought in

Sokhodeora had had to withstand the hot wind of a national crisis.

The Chinese–Indian military clash on the border had not subsided when I visited Ugra Narayan Mahto's night class one evening. After it concluded the members stood about in the alley looking at the stars and listening to Shri Maluk Das, the Harijan member of the village council, shouting good-natured abuse at a skinny young man dressed in rags who took his teasing with a cheerful grin.

'Look at him, Allan brother!' Maluk Das bellowed. 'Here is our Communist. He is a Chinese supporter. Do you think he will submerge all of us? We will eat him.'

The situation had humour enough: what sort of Communism the class-mate had, when he was learning to read and write and had little or no other way of contacting propaganda, was difficult to imagine.

'Your family planning is no use to us, Allan brother,' Maluk Das boasted. 'We need lots of strong male babies now to beat the Chinese. We've got to increase our population. We need more and more children, and we know how to get them.'

He triumphantly slapped me on the shoulder.

9

HEADS THAT PLANNED AND HEADS THAT ITCHED

We still had much to decide on the kind of education that was most suitable and necessary for our school pupils. The goal we had found them so ineffectually heading for had been tragically inappropriate, if our English tutorials with Boddh Narayan were any indication. He wanted to pass public examinations of about matriculation standard and came to us early each morning. But the fabled gold at the rainbow's end would have been as easy for him to reach as it was for him to conceive of Wordsworth's daffodils.

The first reality to face was that the average income of the 63,000 people in the Kawakol area was Rs.165 (AU$19.80) a year per person – or 38 cents a week. It was not evenly distributed and the poorest group was made up of 1422 families whose members had an income of less than AU$6 per year. Land was similarly unequally divided – 307 families had over 15 acres each and 767 families were landless, but the average was half an acre per person. Labouring was the main occupation of almost a quarter of the population and farming the main occupation of 55 per cent.

Housing was unsatisfactory, underemployment prevailed, public health was bad, and psychologically the people were backward as almost 90 per cent of them belonged to the lowest, most backward castes. Sokhodeora was a problem village because of the disharmony between castes and between family factions.

The meaning of all these figures was that people sacrificed everything to be able to eat. Most of the children had to take active part in their family's endless struggle to survive from day to day, from harvest to harvest. Education was looked upon as a luxury, not as a necessity in their struggle, which was immediate. All they might hope for was that if God somehow provided, then the children might get an education. But, of course, the education of the child cannot wait. Neither God nor man had provided in Sokhodeora and generation after generation had had no education.

Sometimes it was not necessity so much as lack of vision that kept children from school, and so we constantly canvassed the village arguing for education. On occasion we found a supporter who became embarrassingly outspoken on our behalf. When one Harijan father replied defensively: 'We have to send our boy to look after the pigs,' our ally, Ganesh Mahto, retorted: 'You want to make your son into a pig.'

Ganesh Mahto had the income to allow him to send his daughters Vidya, Chandra and Aasha to our school and his son to Phuldih High School and he had ideas about what education could be.

'It's the same as a jail,' he commented on the private school in the Sokhodeora library, 'with the teacher sitting across the door with a big stick to prevent his prisoners from escaping.'

We had an occasional child who was beyond our ability to help. Insane or intellectually impaired children were usually given the task of herding animals, but it did also seem, as Ganesh Mahto had implied, that herding animals tended towards intellectual impairment. Gwanda was such a boy. Whatever he was asked to draw or write – an elephant, a house, alphabet letters, his mother or father – he always did interrupted scribbles in the form of the number 3.

Wendy talked to him about very, very fat elephants and they described them together with large arm movements. Finally he drew a line following the edge of his paper and so constructed a large rectangle. For a moment he had caught the impression of size, but then he proceeded to fill this space with his old scribbles. We made no progress with him and he returned to herding cows.

But it was, more importantly, a matter of deciding what the normal children should learn to enable them to improve their environment, no matter how unpromising they might appear at first.

One morning thirty ragged Harijan girls appeared at school. They were the ones who had been expelled from our night class and their ages ranged from about six to twelve. By daylight they revealed themselves as the wildest and dirtiest pupils we had ever encountered. They picked their noses or blew them between their fingers, they had never learned to sit still or be quiet or watch or listen. Some brought a goat and tethered it nearby, and they kept forgetting to go to the lavatory as we had shown them.

They could neither be all put in First Class because of their ignorance nor allotted to grades according to their ages, and it seemed not unlikely that our teachers, feeling their own superiority, would ignore them or discourage them from coming. I had the Seventh Grade, and I took them together as a group, receiving unexpected aid from my seventh graders in keeping order. (By this time our school had Grades 1-3, like a Government Lower Primary, and Grades 4-7 like a Government Middle School.

Our aim was a complete ten-year course.)

As it appeared possible that we would not be able to do much with the inside of their heads in the immediate future we decided that at least we could do something with the outsides. A matted shock of hair crowned each head and they scratched at it with grimaces. Out of school they would sit down one behind the other, sometimes in a line of four or five, each girl helping her friend in front by picking out the lice and cracking them between her fingernails. We bought a large packet of Gammexane, a DDT preparation, and prepared to clean their hair.

Lice were an affliction to the village people. Once a family member caught them it was next to impossible to keep the house free of them. Their bedding and clothing was inadequate and could not be washed frequently and no shops there sold DDT. Bugs were easier to get rid of with boiling water.

Kesurwa looked at the grubbiness of our new pupils and said shortly, repeating a remark she often made: 'Village women do not keep their children clean, Wendy sister. I tell them their babies are dirty every morning when I go to collect them to bring them to kindergarten.'

This was a sweeping remark. Some Harijan women bathed and oiled their children regularly and it was not pleasant for them, for they had to go to the well, draw up a bucket of cold water, and hold their screaming, struggling children. Any mother anywhere might have grown weary of the effort to keep them clean.

Such comments, too, fanned the already warm resentments against her for having better wages and more gracious work. However, Wendy only murmured that perhaps she might be a little more tactful with the parents.

The instructions were to mix the powder in water, apply it, wait twenty minutes, and wash it out with warm water, carefully avoiding the eyes. So we built a fire under a large petrol drum full of water just behind the relatively unused pumping shed adjoining the ashram bathrooms.

Some of the children went in search of wood and others hauled buckets of water out of the well. Everyone was very cheerful. Several little boys with short, cleanly oiled hair scratched their heads ostentatiously and looked at us with a grin: 'Wash our hair too, Wendy sister!'

All children like making a fire and soon the dry branches protruded well out from under the tank. The fire was lit and the children organised in various groups, the smallest first.

Wendy had just poured the Gammexane into an old powdered milk can and was mixing in the water when there was a shout and much confusion. She looked up quickly in time to see the flames of our fire licking up under the thatch-and-tile roof of the pumping shed. The thought of our morning's good intentions finishing in a charred and useless pumping shed held her immobile. I ran and snatched away the burning branches so they lay clear of the roof, and Kesurwa, in her enthusiasm, threw a bucket of water over the flames and me. The children jumped up and down in excitement and we all laughed hilariously. Suddenly de-lousing had become great fun.

One by one we poured the mixture into the tangled hair, rubbing it into the scalp whilst the children stood or crouched, hands held tightly over shut eyes because we had warned them, perhaps too vigorously, not to bob about and to close their eyes in case the mixture hurt them. When it was all finished everyone sat around waiting for the water to be hot enough. A few of the older girls had wet, clinging scraps of cloth about their waists but the younger ones were naked and crouched in the early summer sun like a row of little brown birds. A few scratched experimentally and picked out a louse to see whether it was dead or not. Exclamations of surprise and amusement followed their discovery that the louse was indeed dead, and they held it out on the flat of their hands that others might see.

When the water was ready we ladled it over the now stiff hair, feeling the texture become suddenly soft in our hands. Although the sun was hot and cold water not unpleasant the children begged us to tip the warm water over their backs whilst they soaped themselves. For it was a great novelty to them to bathe in warm water.

At last Kesurwa combed the last head and we viewed our handiwork with some pleasure. Suddenly all the children's smiles vanished to be replaced by hunted, frightened expressions. Damp garments were snatched from the ground where they had been laid to dry and in amazement we watched our schoolchildren vanishing in all directions. Some flew down the road to the village, others disappeared towards the jungle. Coming into view for his second annual visit was the Government vaccinator with his little bag and large black umbrella.

On Sundays or after school on Saturdays we took the Gammexane and some soap to a well in Sokhodeora offering them to those whose curiosity drew them or to others just going past. Having such long hair the women were more keen to take part than the men, who tended to ask if they could have a little to take home. As we refused such requests since the stuff was poisonous and might be eaten by children we soon had a group around us washing their hair. Some weeks later we discovered that they had been asking the shopkeepers to stock Gammexane. It was cheap enough for many people to afford and head lice were very uncomfortable.

Shyness and self-consciousness disappeared quickly enough as they knelt and poured water over the long hair covering their faces, and we could normally rely upon a humorist to keep everyone amused with comments cheerfully made about the women walking past.

'Look, she's got them!' would be shouted, starting a laugh at some girl's discomforted face.

'I have not,' she would retort with an indignant toss of her head.

Then, after a minute or two, she would return tentatively.

'I haven't, but my sister has. Could I take some home for her?' Amusement subsiding into encouragement she would join in.

Sokhodeora ashram schoolboys planting cucumber seeds and covering them with chaff to protect them from the sun.

Tibetan Refugee School, Mussoorie, 1962. Boys digging their own playground out of the hillside.

Bathtime after ploughing for wheat-planting.

The influx of unruly children who would remain at school for such a short time and yet needed to learn so much to improve their everyday lives, was one of those many events which brought into sharp focus the wisdom of the plan that Jayaprakash had outlined to us during our second discussion about our work. It had taken place a month or two after our first conversation:

'I would like you,' Jayaprakash had said, 'to set up an Experimental Rural School to teach village people how to improve their farming and houses and health. If they can raise their standard of living in the village there will be less inclination for them to drift into the slums of our already overcrowded cities. I don't think it should be a preparatory school for further education. People get degrees and won't come near the village again.

'I envisage a type of basic training that would fit boys to farm more scientifically and keep their accounts and try new methods, such as the Japanese method of rice cultivation. They should learn new skills to apply to handicrafts and acquire knowledge about sanitation and diet. They should be prepared for participating creatively in the life of the village community, in running its council and setting up co-operatives, in planning village development, aiding its health programmes and its cultural activities. For the girls I think there should be emphasis on the learning of hygiene, dietetics, childcare, spinning, sewing, poultry keeping, vegetable and fruit growing and other home and village crafts.

'I would like it to have a ten-year course, complete in itself. In the senior four years or at the secondary level, the bias should be towards agriculture and science. We need much more scientific knowledge in our villages. The most interesting problem is to create a type of technical training relevant to village conditions, not only for the present stage of development but for later on when electricity reaches this area.

'This problem has been occupying our educational planners for some time, since one of the aims of our third Five-Year Plan is the development of agro-industrial communities in the rural areas.'

He produced a drawing.

'This is a plan the previous ashram secretary drew for the construction of a new school building sometime before you came here. How does it strike you?'

We made a number of criticisms of it – it was too small and had insufficient windows.

'You draw another plan then, please, Allan.'

'Would you like us to prepare syllabuses for the classes so you can see if they fulfil your ideas?' Wendy asked.

'Yes, and would you also draw up a report on staffing requirements for full-time or part-time teachers and what hours should be worked. You might need to have some course for untrained teachers, mightn't you?'

'Yes.'

'Perhaps you could draw up a scheme of teacher training. You should give me an estimate of recurring and nonrecurring expenses for the building and running of this Experimental Rural School. The ashram, of course, cannot afford it. I have spoken to friends of mine about my scheme and I shall try to raise funds for it, but I do not know whether I shall find time to collect donations. We shall apply for a grant to the Government. I would like it to be a model school for this area. If our experiments are successful they might serve as a model for schools throughout India.'

The syllabuses in all subjects for each of the ten years of the course took us more than three months to prepare from Indian, American, English and

Australian courses. They were completed when Shimada San wrote the agriculture syllabus in Japanese, told me in Hindi and I wrote it in English. These were then translated into Hindi by some very friendly and kind staff members of the Patna Teachers' College.

We drew up a succession of plans and estimates but the last plan was prepared by the Block engineer and we had it transposed into a blueprint in Patna. The grant that we applied for could not, however, be obtained. We found in discussions with the Social Welfare Board in Delhi that we could only obtain further subsidies if we continued to use them only for our kindergarten. However, Dr Shrimali, the Minister for Education in the Central Government, promised to consider an application under the terms of a Government scheme for grants to voluntary educational institutions. The paperwork involved stretched finally to an application in seven copies.

Adjoining the ashram was an area of about six acres of land obtained from the village for the new school. The creek from the mountains ran through it and the boys and I, digging a test hole for a well in its dried-up bed, reached water at a depth of only four feet.

Jayaprakash selected the site for the school and gave his permission for us to begin building four rooms with money that we had been sent by wellwishers in Australia. Iron bars were brought thirty miles from Nawada in a bullock cart and used to make eight large windows in the ashram carpentry shop.

Much to our regret the master builder found for us was Mohammed Sherfu Din, head of a large family in the Muslim hamlet of Sokhodeora who had been employed earlier on the ashram buildings. Earning Rs.3.50 a day he was the highest paid workman in Sokhodeora. Our objection was that he lacked a reputation for honesty and had not only withdrawn his children from our school but spread rumours to its discredit. He would not make any estimate of how long the work would take or what it would cost, and being quite ignorant about building I was most uneasy in my role as architect and works supervisor. Sherfu Din did not improve matters by teasing me about my ignorance.

Once I had watched a dam builder who sat in a chair at a table under a tree and spent his day dispatching his servant for betel nut from the village shop. Naturally my labourers found me an unusual foreman, for I swung a mattock with them as they dug the foundations, brought a clock so that they knocked off promptly after eight hours' labour, and paid them weekly when they were accustomed, if not reconciled, to being paid weeks or months in arrears.

But my doubts soon began. Lime would be needed in the foundations and there was an oven for cooking raw limestone in the ashram. Sherfu Din insisted that it was too far away and a new one must be built at the site. When the bricks for it had been bought his son made an unannounced appearance at the same high wage as his father, who insisted that two bricklayers were indispensable. The furnace building continued for days under my increasing suspicion.

It was at this point that we attended the Ranchi Family Planning Seminar. When we got back to Patna the last storm of the year's monsoon broke. Some of the Patna streets were four feet deep in water. The Ganges raged a mile wide. South of Patna a dam broke, spilling water, it was said, eight feet high and a mile wide, devastating thousands of villages.

As we neared Nawada we passed hundreds of people living in temporary straw shanties that they had put up along the margins of the elevated bitumen road. Farther on a river had completely destroyed the road bridge, hurling pieces of brick and concrete as large as a village house a hundred yards downstream.

In Sokhodeora, Mahadev was full of the frightened excitement he had felt during the storm. Twenty or thirty houses had collapsed when the rain had softened their mud walls. We felt deeply the distress of their owners but found no way of helping them. One day Jayaprakash's dream of model villages made of brick houses along wide streets with electricity poles will become reality.

But until that time the monsoon to householders will mean the expense of building again and again, and people being injured and killed by falling roof beams.

Water had smashed the kiln and choked up the foundations of our Experimental Rural School. Jayaprakash came to the ashram for a night, deeply distressed at the suffering he had seen over hundreds of square miles. In the few minutes we had to speak to him he asked us to defer the construction until we received the Government grant.

In the meantime there was one other preparation to make. We had applied to the Bihar Government, under a scheme of assistance to non-Government schools, for three teachers, and had met both the Bihar Education Minister and the Director of Public Instruction. It was understood that we would be able to interview and select these teachers; but events developed differently.

We ended the school year with a Speech Night in the ashram hall. The children practised for weeks and performed songs, plays and physical education displays very well. Prizes were presented. But only three parents attended, the audience consisting of people living in the ashram. In the New Year a school committee was formed and we held an education exhibition, children were promoted, a bookstore begun and more books were bought for the library.

There were now Rs.300 worth of books. We had chosen the new books because they dropped many of the customary myths and idealisations of great men in favour of factual knowledge of a scientific type.

Sokhodeora Government Primary School, which had been closed for some months after the death of the elder teacher, reopened in February, and to our dismay the head man and village leaders assisted the teacher in a campaign to win pupils at the expense of our school. When the derogatory rumours were at their worst we had only twenty pupils.

Wendy had an angry interview with the Sokhodeora teacher for taking the kindergarten children who were below school-attending age. He began to make jeering remarks when he encountered us in Sokhodeora:

'You haven't got your teachers for your famous Experimental Rural School yet? What qualifications are you wanting?'

At this stage we were feeling so frustrated that we were unable to resist being equally petty, and, knowing he was not university trained, replied, 'Oh, people with a degree.'

'I hear they are sending you two Grade 7 passes,' he retaliated.

We had an insidious feeling that this could be true and could only remark to each other in the privacy of our house and with some attempt at humour that we were glad they were Grade 7 passes and not Grade 7 fails.

However, everybody was to be singularly embarrassed. One day the Block Inspector of Schools visited us at our house. 'Have your two teachers arrived for the ashram school? They were instructed to do so a month ago,' he said.

'No. Perhaps they have been delayed in travelling here.'

'No. They have no travelling to do. They are the teacher and his wife from the Sokhodeora school. It has been closed for months so they were told to come to your ashram school.'

'Well, Sokhodeora school is open again. It has about eighty pupils.'

'Then he's done that in the hope of getting the Government to keep the school open to save him from coming here. He knows if he comes here you'll watch him and make him work properly and come on time. Here's the note of his appointment and you kindly fill it in and return it to me the day he arrives.'

The couple arrived next afternoon and unfortunately were not replaced by the Government. Even under surveillance they would leave children idle for periods of up to two hours. But there was no need to give up hope yet because the school had not been built. We had introduced the new syllabuses and it was exciting to see my seventh grade students learning the history of medicine and mathematics that related to their experiences of crops and household expenses.

There was only one existing Hindi copy of the syllabuses, so to protect it we pasted it page-by-page into two large ledgers. In the end our Government teachers lost one of them.

10

THE STATE VERSUS MISS VIDYA

During our second January at Sokhodeora, Jayaprakash and his wife, Prabhavati Devi, made a quick visit to the ashram for planning meetings with Government officials. The Indian Planning Commission had made arrangements with the controlling body of the Gandhian Movement, the Sarva Seva Sangh (Association for the Service of All), to conjointly establish three pilot projects in backward areas to revitalise village handicrafts. The Nawada – Sokhodeora area was one of these.

We were invited to attend the meetings, presided over by Jayaprakash leaning hack on a long, round pillow against the library wall. In front of him the participants sat cross-legged on the carpet looking particularly handsome in pure white, carefully pressed cotton. We enjoyed both the break from our usual work and the high level of discussion, despite occasional difficulties with the vocabulary of engineers or experts from the State Electricity Board.

In between the meetings, since we were in our best clothes and had many friends to talk to and there were new people keen to meet us, we spent much of the time serving tea. On the afternoon of 30 January, the anniversary of Gandhi's assassination, we had a conversation of unforeseen importance when Jayaprakash's personal secretary, Shri Brahmanand, brought Shri Rup Narayan to tea.

Rup Narayan had a business in Delhi and was, for the first time, visiting a village. He was immaculately clad and impeccably courteous.

'Ah, do you take salt in your tea?' he asked, when Wendy served his tea; so politely that there could have been no offence if we did. As he spoke he seemed to peer through his spectacles; the glass in them was so thick that his eyes appeared to be swimming and this gave his face something of an owlish quality.

'No, do you wish to take salt in your tea?' Wendy replied carefully, knowing that there is a wide variety of food habits to be respected in India. 'I'll bring it for you from the cupboard if you want it. It's no trouble.'

'Well, no,' he replied hastily, 'but I thought it might be an ashram custom. I believe eggs and meat are not eaten, but I really do not know what is the custom in ashrams.'

'No, it's not a custom here,' Wendy said.

'I fancied it might be. You know,' he went on to explain, 'I always have my bed tea but when they brought it to me here' – through our barred window was a view of jungle that harboured bears and occasional man-eating tigers and it made the idea of bed tea comically incongruous to us – 'you know I couldn't drink it. So I didn't ask for any this morning. It is not that I object to salt, you understand, but there was so much salt.'

'They must have got the sugar and salt mixed up,' Brahmanand commented.

We had begun to laugh. 'And Indian people,' Wendy said, adding to the merriment, 'take such an awful lot of sugar in their tea.'

The joke dissolved all formality and he soon had us talking freely about the village and children and the work we were doing.

'You two are so fond of children,' he observed after a time, 'but you have none.'

'No, but we are thinking of adopting a baby. There are so many children wanting parents and they can only be helped by individuals. We met two American nurses in Delhi who have eighteen-year guardianship of twelve children. The children were charming and their home was so delightful that it gave us the idea. Do you know of any places where you can adopt babies?'

'Yes, I know two or three in Delhi.' Naming them, he added encouragingly, 'I will do anything I can to help you. I will see them and write you all particulars.'

Wendy brought paper and he jotted down addresses.

'Could you adopt a baby here?' Brahmanand asked.

'Yes,' I replied in some excitement. 'We wrote some time ago to the Australian High Commission in Delhi asking whether we could, and all the reply stated was that as this had not happened before the matter had been referred to Canberra for our Government's decision on it. We got the second letter about two weeks ago. If we legally adopt two children – I don't know what made them think we wanted two – they will be admitted to Australia as members of our family and after our arrival they will be eligible to obtain Australian citizenship.'

I found the letter and showed it to them. Rup Narayan became even more enthusiastic. 'I promise I will find a baby for you in Delhi,' he said.

But thoughts and hopes on this score were quickly submerged in the events of the rest of the day. We left the house together to join the procession to the village where a public meeting had been arranged to pay tribute to the memory of Gandhi. All along the track our party was joined by villagers. From Sokhodeora a reception committee – the headman, members of the council, and prominent people of Sokhodeora and surrounding villages – advanced to meet Jayaprakash, accompanied by a tumultuous beating of drums.

The two groups met each other with the traditional folded-hands greeting, then merged and moved towards the ruins of the deposed landlord's mansion. Cheer leaders set up a deafening chorus:

'To Mahatma Gandhi...'

'Long live!' responded the crowd at the top of their lungs.

'To Jayaprakash Narayan...'

'Long live!'

'Saint Vinoba...'

'Be immortal!'

'Saint Vinoba...'

'Jayaprakash!'

The drummers achieved a frenzied tempo, the tributes shouted again and again. The steadily growing crowd turned down the lane past the headman's house and the tiny room where the village court held session. Our ears rung with the noise and despite the efforts of some to hold back the crowds from the party of guests we were caught so tightly that it was not possible to move an arm. Wendy smiled encouragingly to Rup Narayan, who responded with a weak grin that suggested the words, 'I'm not used to this kind of thing at all.'

People coming from the other end of the alley were pushed back to let Jayaprakash enter the village library. The room and its verandah filled immediately. At the headman's insistence we allowed ourselves to be pulled through into the room, where we were given stools facing Jayaprakash, and we too had garlands of flowers placed about our necks. Speeches followed, including paeans of most grandiloquent praise for us from the Library Secretary, Shri Dukharan, for the few books and the radio we had been able to provide.

Everyone moved to the landlord's mansion. The rubble from a break in the twenty-foot wall had been dug and tramped into steps. Above these the original stone steps, the surface chipped, the stone banister mostly broken away, the topmost step entirely missing, led to the first-floor level.

Below, the ground-level rooms of the L-shaped building were dark, damp, and rumoured to be full of snakes. The crowd reached the broad cement verandah and began to sit, the official party on wooden beds and cotton mats in front, their white, pressed clothes contrasting sharply with the grey, thin tatters of the audience. On the left were once inhabited rooms with faded murals and palm-frond patterns in pastel colours above the doors. These semicircular designs were now cracked and had patches missing. The landlord's feudal rights had been legally abolished after Independence and he now lived in the city. The poor claimed that he had exploited them cruelly and illegally, interfered with their women, forced them to cramp their houses together to occupy the least tillable soil, and had created the present upper strata of Sokhodeora by his patronage and gifts.

Whether the allegations were true or exaggerated we heard no one regret his going and the passing of an hierarchical pattern of society.

To our right we overlooked the brick-strewn courtyards with their enormous *bel* tree, part earth part brick walls, dilapidated entrance gateway and heaps of earth, once the mud walls of rooms.

Jayaprakash's speech, which came last, continued for two hours. Whether or not he was affected by his present surroundings, he spoke of Gandhi's vision of a non-violent social order in terms of their changing India. Tracing Indian history through the years of the Independence Movement he pleaded for a sense of national unity. (He had not long come from the National Integration Conference, which had sought ways out of India's turmoil of State, caste, language and religious quarrels and fissiparous tendencies).

From the theme of internal peace he proceeded to the destructiveness and immorality of atomic weapons, outlining a role that India might play in securing international disarmament and love between men.

The steadfastness of his humane views have made him a great and loved man in India.

Before he had finished many of his audience were restless and inattentive.

This inability of village audiences to concentrate used to disturb us, but perhaps it is only teachers who demand undivided attention. For during the many speeches of his we heard he only on two occasions broke off his subject to reprimand his audience. Doubtless it was a mark of the magnetism of his gentle personality and the purity of his ethical principles, however, that he could hold an audience captive for as long as he did with his soft, fatherly voice.

The steps were slippery with mud as we descended to the road and Wendy lent her arm to Jayaprakash. 'We're very thrilled,' she said, 'we understood every word. Our Hindi is improving.' He was amused.

Having tea with us the next day Jayaprakash looked up slightly puzzled from the letter of the Australian High Commissioner's Office.

'What's this? Who are these babies?' he asked kindly, seeming to have forgotten Wendy's remarks to him some weeks earlier.

After some explanation she said hesitantly, 'As we are working for you we wanted to consult you because I will not be able to do so much for the village people if we adopt a baby.'

'You didn't have to consult me. You'll be able to do some work I expect,' he replied. 'I'm not worried about that. What I am concerned about is whether you will be able to manage on your allowance. Will you need more money?'

We refused his offer. He then asked, 'What if you have a baby of your own afterwards?'

'They will both be ours,' I smiled. 'That wouldn't make any difference to our feelings about the baby we adopted.'

Early in March a letter from Rup Narayan called us hopefully to Delhi. He met us at the station and had us accommodated at the Gandhi Memorial Trust and Peace Foundation and took us to the Daryaganj Foundlings' Home. There we found we had to have permission to see the children, so after a trip by motorcycle rickshaw he introduced us to Dr Kulanday, the Deputy Health Officer in the Maternity and Child Welfare Section of the Delhi Municipal Corporation.

She was a plump, motherly South Indian Christian.

'I am hoping to persuade my husband to adopt a child from one of the thirty-five homes I administer,' she said. 'Our babies don't grow because they lack the love of a mother and father. I know you would love and care for a child.' And accepting us on face value she excitedly hurried us to another office in the Town Hall building to obtain immediate permission from her superior officer, a Sikh colonel.

After her warmth we felt crushed by his guarded manner. At his request we produced the character references, medical certificates and affidavits prepared by friends in Patna for us according to Rup Narayan's instructions on what the Delhi Municipal Corporation required. Then we were queried on the White Australian policy, and in reply presented the letter we had from the High Commissioner's Office. We felt quite despairing after he had requested further character references and a statement of our motives before he could proceed in the matter.

Dr Kulanday farewelled us with an optimism that was not reflected in our long faces. 'The only thing you really have to worry about,' she said, 'is getting the Magistrate's permission.'

The next morning we presented the additional papers to the colonel, who closed the interview by indicating no more than that he would put our case before a higher authority. We were even more depressed than we had been the previous day and could not see how Rup Narayan could feel such determined confidence about the outcome.

'You leave it to me,' he said. 'I know how to arrange these matters. You should not worry for it.'

That evening we dined with friends, Mr and Mrs J.J. Singh, who promised to introduce us to one of Delhi's leading paediatricians to examine the baby we selected. Next morning Rup Narayan called on us. We shifted our gloomy gazes from each other on to him and asked him dispiritedly what had happened.

'I am bringing you the authorisation from the Municipal Corporation,' he said.

We were astonished. Then in our delight we hugged him.

'I took some friends with me, you know,' he continued proudly, 'and I said, "Here I have invited my Australian friends to Delhi to adopt a baby and you push them from post to pillar and back to post again", and so you know, they expedited the matter.'

He hurried away on his own business while we returned to the Daryaganj Home. There were seventeen small children of whom Vidya seemed to be the favourite, for she was bright, alert and attractive. She looked at us with a puzzled frown that was appealing and we were enchanted. We were informed that she was three months old and had been left here five days after birth and were encouraged to select her, if that had been necessary, with the information that boys were more often adopted than girls.

Then, with a woman from the home carrying Vidya, we went to meet the paediatrician. Dr Seeta Lal was a friendly businesslike woman, who, although single, had adopted twin sons herself against some opposition. She complimented us, 'What a nice thing for you to decide to do.' And added, examining Vidya, 'She's a lovely baby and obviously comes from a good family. She is very thin, but normal and healthy and well developed for three months. She weighs nine pounds and one ounce.' The nurse from the home presented the brief record card and none of us noticed at that time that Vidya was actually six months old.

Having returned Vidya to the home and already feeling fond of her, we suddenly became prey to apprehensions that the Magistrate might give an unfavourable decision. In our anxiety we set out to meet Jayaprakash, who had just arrived in Delhi. We found him in the office of the Association of Voluntary Agencies for Rural Development where he wrote us a character reference in case this might be required by the Magistrate, and promised affectionately, 'If it would help you I could speak to the Chief Commissioner.'

Tis Hazari Court, where we next went, occupied a small room on the first floor of a huge, newly constructed building, in and out of which people moved like ants. The Lady Magistrate told us how adoptions were arranged between Hindus but regretted that we would not be able to adopt Vidya because we would not be allowed to take her outside the court's jurisdiction to Australia. She explained the law as it related to non-Hindus, but then, reacting to the stricken look on our faces, promised to discuss our case with the Deputy Commissioner of the Delhi Administration.

Seeing a faint hope we asked if she felt any objection to us inquiring of the Chief Commissioner. She willingly agreed and we hurried away to search Delhi for Jayaprakash, who telephoned the Chief Commissioner and arranged an appointment for us the following morning.

Next morning, we were interviewed with great kindness, not by the Chief Commissioner, but by his Chief Secretary, Shri L.O. Joshi. He showed us that the *Children Act 1960* gave the Court the right to place a child under the care of a fit person under any conditions it felt fit to impose.

We had no time to savour our profound sense of relief, for in the afternoon we were called to the Court Chambers where another magistrate checked our references, sternly outlined our responsibilities, and fixed our appearance before the Court for the following morning. Immediately we had to hurry, tired but joyful, to the shops to buy clothes for the appellant in the impending case of the State versus Miss Vidya. However, her outfit was not quite all that might be desired, for nappies were not available in Delhi and we had to do with pieces of towelling.

The Foundling Home nurse sat with Vidya at the back of the courtroom while we nervously stood in turn before the Lady Magistrate, observing that the longest part of the proceedings was the typing of documents. Finally I signed a bond of Rs.2000 to reappear before the Court in a year's time and not to take Vidya out of India without the Court's consent. Naturally from this moment on an anxiety was always with us for we did not want to live permanently in India under our present conditions, but just then we felt only relieved.

The Magistrate's seeming severity changed to smiling congratulation, whereupon we observed the custom of presenting sweets to her, the typist and to the onlookers in the Court. Everyone smiled happily. Proud, self-conscious, elated, Wendy carried Vidya into the street. We had become parents, with all a parent's sense of wonder and absorption in a new life.

Returning to present sweets to the staff at the Daryaganj Home we were so depressed by the sight of the other sixteen children that we hastened through the last details and hurried away. Soon afterwards, to our pleasure but also embarrassment, for our room was in a state of complete confusion, the Chief Secretary, Shri Joshi, and his wife arrived to bless Vidya and congratulate us. They only saw her once again and Rup Narayan, who was out of Delhi, only ever saw her photograph.

In the afternoon Mrs Singh called with presents, Dr Seeta Lal vaccinated Vidya and after a whirl of Gandhian Movement visitors we left Delhi.

A doctor friend in Patna asked, 'Why did you go to Delhi? You could have got a baby here,' to which I replied, 'We will next time, if there is one as gorgeous.'

Vidya slept in her basket most of the jolting jeep trip back to Sokhodeora where the members of the ashram family echoed similar thoughts to those of the ashram overseer, Shri Ramraksha Sharma: 'She has a very fortunate Karma. Look at the wonderfulness of it that she was there just when you came along. What might her fate have been? And now she will go to Australia and be educated and loved.' Village people, known and unknown, thronged our house to see this wonder and were shocked to hear that there were foundlings in the cities.

'Did you buy her?' they asked so frequently that, having no conception of Children's Homes, I mischievously said yes, elaborating on the shop and Vidya's being medium priced. That, of course, drew queries about the price. There were even debates. On the dilapidated Kawakol bus one morning the sister of our teacher, Boddh Narayan, contended heartily with the conductor that Vidya had been bought in a shop, while I refrained from settling the dispute by feigning not to follow their village dialect.

Western ways with a baby were found amazing, but what might have been passed off as Western idiosyncrasies were pondered over because Vidya was not Western. Babies wore a shirt and no nappy but Vidya wore nappy and no shirt. 'She sleeps separately from them,' was observed. 'She doesn't cry when you bath her, she likes it. You bath her in *warm* water? She eats solid food? But how can she chew without any teeth? How will she survive unless she is breastfed?'

It was a matter of general concern in the ashram that we were not giving her Worthington's Gripe Mixture or massaging her with mustard oil. 'You must. Mustard oil dries out the water from the body and bones and makes the baby strong. If you do not she will be weak from being full of water.'

When Wendy made Vidya's bottle I had to stand by to keep away the ubiquitous flies. But when labourer Mahavir's wife, sitting on the ground, fed her baby out of a bowl of rice, her fingers as they extracted another mouthful disturbed only some of the flies settled on the food.

There were even requests for us to act as foster-parents to children and one Harijan woman who used to cheerfully offer to sell us her baby for Rs.200.

By the end of April Vidya was recognising us and the temperature was 102ºF inside the house. That year Dr Shrimali had arranged for me to teach for the summer months at the Tibetan Refugee School in Mussoorie. This was situated in the foothills of the Himalayas and as we passed through Delhi on our way there Dr Seeta Lal was very pleased with Vidya's gain of over four pounds. But she still refused to accept fees, saying, 'Do something with it for the poor people you are working amongst.'

There was much to be done for the health of the Tibetan children and we shortly discovered that while we lived in one of the school buildings Vidya was exposed to active cases of tuberculosis. So we found a spartan flat in the town costing us Rs.800 of our savings for the period of two and a half months – the 'season'. Our separate incomes of Rs.200 a month, although most irregularly paid, were double what Indian teachers or ashram workers received, so we could not consider Jayaprakash's earlier offer of a higher income. But as our work would continue to lead us into similar situations we were forced to realise that with Vidya we could no longer accept Jayaprakash's invitation to undertake a second three-year term of work for him. The decision added to our concern about being able to take Vidya out of India.

By August we had returned to Sokhodeora. There, Shri Nawal Kishore, a Government economic investigator with whom we cooperated in kindergarten and women's centre work, surprised us by remarking, 'Shermaji, the Block Development Officer, asked me about you. He has to submit quarterly reports on you to the Delhi Magistrate. I told him if I sold all my lands I could not care for Vidya as well as you do.'

After this, when we heard the rare vehicle on the earth road in the distance, as it could only be the ashram jeep or the Block Development Officer's, Wendy quickly put Vidya into her best dress. We used to smile at our little device. But we also felt concern, for we were reminded of how difficult it was to get prompt medical attention for Vidya if it happened to be necessary.

One morning we forgot to put up one of the lanterns. It had an improvised paper stopper instead of a cap on its tank and Wendy found Vidya sitting in a pool of kerosene sucking the impregnated paper. Dr Spock's justly famous book on childcare advised that a doctor be found immediately.

As luck had it, a friend, who happened to be the Deputy Development Commissioner for Bihar, was visiting the ashram and gladly lent us his jeep. Our panic had not subsided when we reached the Block and scurried into Dr Surendra Sinha's house. He was a young, enthusiastic man with a taste for poetry but no experience of kerosene poisoning. He turned up his medical book, which instructed him to induce vomiting. But Dr Spock was equally firm that this should not be done in case kerosene got into the lungs and since he gave a reason he won the day.

Surendra then put her on his bed and felt her stomach, his eyes growing wider every moment. 'How much did she drink?' he asked in some alarm.

'I don't know,' Wendy replied, 'but that's not all kerosene. She's just had her morning bottle of milk.' He was noticeably relieved and asked, 'Has she shown any symptoms of poisoning?'

'No.'

The only course which then suggested itself was for us all to have a cup of coffee and see if any symptoms of poisoning would appear. Having regained our calm we set off for the ashram and got bogged and dug the jeep out for a couple of hours. Happily for our peace of mind it happened on the return journey.

The incident provided subject for conversation far and wide for a few days, the general feeling being that as kerosene was not poisonous we were on occasion somewhat peculiar.

11

MEALS FOR MILLIONS

Hungry people will not eat any food, but only the foods to which they are accustomed. We had no difficulty in giving tomato seedlings or carrot seeds to village people or in growing half a dozen varieties of vegetables in the schoolchildren's garden, but no one would accept lettuces. They were 'goat food', as Shimada San had also found in his agriculture school. No one, that is, except Mahadev, because he had grown accustomed to eggs, toast and other unusual foods for breakfast. (Indian people eat on an average two eggs a year.)

Mahadev would pluck a leaf or two of 'salad' from our garden and munch unenthusiastically but turn us a virtuous expression as if to say, 'Look at me eating this stuff – won't I be healthy!'

Sokhodeora people were accustomed to so little that contained iron – a handful of a miniature spinach for a few weeks of the monsoon, a tiny pea grown in the rice crop. At one time the Ashram Management Committee, for the sake of getting the Maternity Hospital open again, employed a midwife, Shrimati Medulsa, when no doctors answered the advertisements in the Patna papers. This brisk, dynamic tireless woman, supporting her husband while he underwent leprosy treatment, used to take Wendy on her lightning progresses through the village, regaling her with a stream of impatient comments:

'Look at these women, Wendy sister. They're pregnant and they won't eat any green vegetables. They'll all be anaemic. I tell them to eat green vegetables and they don't take any notice of me. They're so stupid. What can you do with them?'

What could be done? Their monotonous diet of rice, dal and spices, twice each day, was responsible for so many casualties: adults with no resistance to disease, children going blind for lack of Vitamin A, children deprived of protein during their growing period becoming spindly of body and inactive of mind, toddlers catching dysentery and developing rickets when weaned straight on to the family diet. We wrote many long letters of appeal for foodstuffs but only one was rewarded. It was to the Director of the Meals for Millions Foundation in Los Angeles and he granted us a free gift of a thousand pounds of Multi-Purpose Food, the 'Wonder Food'.

The non-profit Meals for Millions Foundation was formed in the USA in 1946 to pioneer a practical action programme for the solution of the world hunger afflicting 80 per cent of mankind. It developed a three-cent meal using protein that was wasted or fed to animals and in fifteen years had distributed over 65 million meals. In 1955 an Indian Meals for Millions Association was formed, with the Minister of Agriculture as president, and a pilot plant was set up in Mysore State to produce Indian Multi-Purpose Food from peanut meal and Bengal gram.

The Mysore Multi-Purpose Food took a year to arrive within thirty miles of us. It appeared at Nawada railway station shortly after our return from our second summer in the hills and we had it brought to the ashram by bullock cart.

We had such a file of letters, information and food recipes that wild with curiosity we reached the bullock cart before it had come to a stop. The consignment had come in thirty-five-pound tins in a wooden framework. Our pleasure was marred by our indignation at finding two tins broken with a third of the food gone, and the remainder in these two covered with a thick layer of rat droppings.

The food was a fine powder, the unspiced variety having a sweet peanut smell and the spiced kind being redolent mostly of ginger. Stacked in a corner of our workroom it attracted the rats at night and we had to keep heavy covers on top of it.

The rats were no mean adversaries. During our absence in the hills they had chewed through the metal tops on sauce and jam bottles and having forced their way inside our suitcases had chewed blankets and linen to pieces. But to cap all this they had chewed a hole through the bottom of an aluminium saucepan, perhaps as a sharpening exercise for their teeth, since there was nothing edible in it.

The Multi-Purpose Food was to be used as an additional protein ingredient in customary foods like chapatis, dal and potato cakes. We tried it out first on Kesurwa and Mahadev.

As it was obviously better for the experiment to be done under village conditions instead of in our kitchen, we provided flour, Mahadev lit a wood fire in a small brazier, and Kesurwa, squatting on the verandah of one of the ashram houses, cooked a number of chapatis. They nibbled them tentatively, then ate appreciatively, and some of the village labourers in the ashram fields were called to finish them off.

Encouraged by this success we set to work to organise a demonstration party. We bought about ten rupees' worth of rice, flour, unrefined sugar (*gur*) and pulse, collected an assortment of brass cauldrons, pots, platters, ladles and iron frying-plates, and with a tin of Multi-Purpose Food set up kitchen in the tiny square in the centre of the

Harijan sector of Sokhodeora. We swept away rubbish and goat manure from the hard earth between the tiny straw-thatched houses, Mahadev dug a pit beside a mud wall, and his brawny but slow-thinking friend, Mahavir, helped him collect scraps of wood, bamboo and palm leaves to light the fire. The three of them squatted to cook six varieties of food, closely watched by an expectant group of grubby, barefoot Harijan children, girls in shorts and bangles, boys in long shirts with no pants or naked save for a caste cord around their waists.

As time passed mothers came out of their houses to watch, bringing small, battered brass or aluminium bowls and the men came in from work. They made a sad sight, the poorest, most illclad people on earth, and we felt, with a tightening of the throat, proud to be able to help them but oppressed by the knowledge that we could help so little.

Not that there was much peace for such reflections, for the square was packed and in uproar, tumult becoming worse at intervals as someone drove his cow home through this widening of alleys and children leapt or were hauled out of the way of the oncoming horns. After considerable shouting, I restored enough order to speak to the crowd about what protein was, how much they needed daily but did not get, the value of Multi-Purpose Food and how it should be added to their dal. I ended with Mahadev's and Kesurwa's testimonial that the food was tasty.

Night was drawing in as we invited them to eat. The adults shook their heads, took a step back smiling apologetically, or bowed over folded hands in a courteous gesture of gratitude but refusal. The children kept up their hubbub, drawing attention to themselves until it occurred to someone to try the food on them first. Sighs of relief followed this shouted decision, while I laughingly teased the men about their cowardice, and some 120 ragged, ill-fed 'naughtinesses' were scoldingly pushed or roared into orderly lines on the ground. They ate greedily.

Then they were chased away and the men came forward sheepishly into the space, many swapping remarks with me but most taking only small portions.

The women in their turn jostled each other vociferously, quick to snatch whatever remained.

To complete the proceedings I distributed a couple of handfuls of the Multi-Purpose Food to those who wanted it. It was carried away in bowls, wrapped in the end of cotton scarves or folded into sheets of the *Australian Women's Weekly.* This distribution became a regular activity. To the best of our knowledge the food was eaten as intended, for there was only one report that a child had eaten all the powder neat and two tales told against someone who had wasted it, the accused hotly denying the allegations. Nothing much could be kept private in such a congested community.

*

One morning after the party a stooped old man padded on to our verandah. He waited until Wendy went to the door to see what he wanted, rose, touched his forehead and gave her a small bow. Then, squatting, he proceeded to unwrap with great care from several squares of cotton cloth an X-ray photograph of the lungs.

'Memsahib,' he asked slowly, indicating the picture, 'what is this? I went to Patna. It cost me thirty rupees but I do not know what it is.'

Wendy did not know how he had found so much money, whether he had earned it or borrowed it, but she realised that this expense must have been a worry to him.

'I cannot read the picture,' she told him. 'It is a doctor's photo and you must take it to Kawakol to the Government doctor there.'

He inclined his head patiently, wrapped the picture lovingly and with another bow edged down the verandah steps on his bowed legs.

'If you wait a minute,' she recalled him, 'I'll give you a letter for the doctor.'

She prepared a brief note for Surendra, saying that if the old man had tuberculosis we could supply milk and MultiPurpose Food to help him.

Several days later when she was sitting with Vidya in the sunshine on the grass square outside our house, the old man returned. He bowed politely and handed her Surendra's reply.

'The doctor says you have a sickness of the lungs which needs milk and extra food,' she told him.

He followed her to the house while she made a couple of paper cones, filling one with milk powder and the other with multipurpose flour.

She told him how to add the Multi-Purpose Food to his chapatis, rice or dal or how to mix it with the milk into a porridge.

He thanked her courteously and went quietly away. Each week after this he came with his polite little bow for more of the food. He gained weight and said he was now able to do light work. She grew to look for him, remembering with affection and some sadness his childlike pride in an X-ray photograph, for which he had paid so much and about which he understood nothing.

Meanwhile, every morning Kesurwa made porridge for the children from the Multi-Purpose Food and powdered milk.

'We need sugar for it, Wendy sister,' she said. 'The children do not find it tasty.'

'We haven't enough money for sugar,' Wendy replied. 'You'll have to use salt instead. I'll give you a few annas to buy it.'

After that the children accepted and ate a bowl each day and at the end of the first week all malnutrition sores had disappeared from the new year's batch of children. Having the food and being short of money we discontinued the shark-liver oil doses for this new group.

At first Kesurwa herself lit a tiny charcoal fire and coaxed the porridge to cook some time before the children were fed, then I persuaded the ashram kitchen staff to make it each morning and Kesurwa had only to collect it and serve the children.

One morning I was there to help her ladle the porridge from the brass cauldron into the brass bowls we used for the children's milk or food. Boddh Narayan came up with the new Government teacher allotted to us for the school.

'What is this food, Allan brother, might I try it?' the new teacher asked.

I inclined my head and went to assist Kesurwa who balanced the pot of warm porridge cautiously on a padded cloth on her head. Together the two of us lifted it to the ground near where the children squatted in a half circle.

Kesurwa took a bronze ladle and spooned some of the mixture into the bowls placed on the ground in front of the children while they fanned away the flies with their hands.

Then Kesurwa, at my request, ladled a portion into a clean bowl and handed it to the new teacher. Under my expectant eye he slowly took the bowl and looked at the food. The consistency was smooth, the porridge not burnt or unappetising to smell or look at. Kesurwa and I waited.

But he merely held the bowl. At last he lamely commented: 'I do not eat milk and salt together. It is not my custom.'

I frowned and Kesurwa lowered her eyes but did not disguise the sullen set to her mouth.

'He's not telling the truth, Allan brother,' Boddh Narayan burst out excitedly. 'It's because she's an Harijan – an untouchable.'

'But she hasn't cooked it,' I replied. 'She has carried it from the kitchen. Just carried it,' I repeated in amazed disgust.

Exposed, the teacher angrily dropped the bowl beside the cauldron and walked away.

'If a dog had licked his food,' I added angrily, 'he could not have shown more distaste. And what are we to do if we can't obtain a teacher for our new school who has even the rudiments of humanity?'

Then Kesurwa gave an embarrassed laugh. 'It doesn't matter, Allan brother,' and she gently herded the children to the well so that they might wash their plates clean.

This had been on Saturday morning. On Monday Kesurwa came to our house on her way to school as she usually did. Wendy looked at her in astonishment. Her right eye was half closed and surrounded by purple discolouration and across her cheek was a long scratch.

'What happened?' Wendy cried.

Mahadev who was cleaning the glass of a lantern looked up and smirked.

Kesurwa looked sullen, then furtive, then embarrassed. 'Did you have an accident? What happened?' Wendy repeated, glancing from Mahadev's smile to her face.

She hung her head. 'There was a fight, Wendy sister.' Her discomfiture was so obvious that Wendy could not question her further. Explaining that she would attend the kindergarten shortly, Wendy sent her off with some new soap and half a new tin of Multi-Purpose Food.

When Kesurwa was gone, she turned to Mahadev.

'Well Mahadev, what happened?'

'Kesurwa and a friend went to watch the food being prepared for a wedding in another caste sector of the village,' he explained.

'Yes,' she prompted.

'The woman of the house told Kesurwa and her friend to go away and Kesurwa refused. They had a fight and then she hit Kesurwa and Kesurwa tore her blouse.'

Mahadev was amused. Such bouts of irritation and violence were frequent in the village and Wendy well knew the type of abuse that the women would have hurled at each other. Doubtless they poured out on each other's families the venom they felt at the time by imputing low sexual morals to each member in turn, with screams, shaking fists, and participation by the bystanders, all in the fitful light of a small charcoal or dung fire.

'The headman told the woman to apologise and Kesurwa to replace the woman's blouse,' Mahadev ended.

Actually the Harijan caste council met and called Ugra Narayan Mahto, the night-class teacher, to write a letter of complaint from Kesurwa to the Sokhodeora Council. Kurian and others from the ashram acted as mediators and the headman instructed Kesurwa not only to replace the blouse but also to apologise for interfering in another caste.

'Poor Kesurwa,' Wendy murmured, remembering the Multi-Purpose Food incident which had preceded this and realising how ill-timed and impotent had been her protest about being a Harijan. Untouchability had been legally abolished, but in a village so insecure, so custom bound, and so ignorant, the passing of caste prejudices would take a long, long time.

One of the Meals for Millions association pamphlets had contained photographs of the dramatic effects of treating starving Korean orphans with the food, but up to this time no thought of doing such work had entered our minds.

A year previously we had bullied Shrimati Pandit, the wife of a potter, into taking her emaciated baby, who was dying of malnutrition as her previous child had done, to the doctor. We had seen that she gave him the prescribed medicine, and supplemented his diet with powdered milk. The news of this had spread evidently and now, coinciding with the coming of the Multi-Purpose Food, we were brought more than thirty young children in a pitiful condition. Some of them had had dysentery for four or five months and that life had persisted in their wasted frames seemed almost miraculous.

Most of the children were about two years old, the most frequent illness being rickets, the result of Vitamin D deficiency, and we decided to try the Multi-Purpose Food on them.

On the mornings when the doctor for the Kapasia leprosy centre came to the ashram and opened the maternity hospital for a few hours I made a tour of the village and brought the mothers to have their babies examined. It was much nearer for them than going to the Government hospital at Kawakol. I spent time with at least two sick children each day for weeks, trying to teach mothers that a sick person should be examined by a qualified doctor, not a quack, and that they should use the medicine as directed, which they usually did not, and observe the results carefully and report back to the doctor – which they also failed to do. The need for such elementary education about health was desperate and receiving no one else's attention.

One morning, as I led my procession of fourteen to the hospital, Shri Ramashray Singh was doing his office work in the sun on his verandah.

'Look, Ramashray brother,' I said, wishing I could interest other people in the helping of such children. The sight of the withered children turned Ramashray's stomach.

'There you are, a foreigner,' he exclaimed, 'and you are caring for these poor things. We should be doing this ourselves. I can't bear to look at them.'

Then one morning we found we had a helper. A woman brought her child from Bhorambag, six miles away, on the advice of Shrimati Mundodrie, who was employed by the ashram as a midwife for the villagers.

Next, Mundodrie elatedly called me down an alley: 'Come and look, Allan brother. Twins. I delivered them last night and they are both surviving. It will be wonderful if we can keep them. Twins usually die.'

The mother had one at her breast and the other lying on straw. Perhaps each weighed four pounds. After a few days, when she said she did not have enough milk for them, I asked, 'What do you eat?'

'Rice in the morning and rice and dal at night.'

I gave her the mixture of powdered milk and MultiPurpose Food to add to her diet, but she was suspicious and would not eat it and it had to be given to another family. But the twins stoutly gained weight nevertheless.

We encountered a case that involved most of the problems of village health work and health education when we cared for the grandson of our egg man. Our most regular egg man was an ageing Muslim with sunken cheeks, heavy lips, grizzled beard and querulous voice. The eggs cost six Australian cents each but were less than half the size of English or Australian eggs. We were obliged to buy them because our poultry co-operative with Mahadev and another lad dismally failed, despite the fortress we had built for our expensive, carefully transported, Governmentbred white leghorns. Dogs, cats, foxes, jackals and finally a mongoose killed them all.

One morning he brought his wife carrying the baby. It was in a critical condition. To begin with they did not tell us what we learned later from Dr Surendra Sinha, that the baby had previously fallen into a coma after months of dysentery and Surendra's injections had rallied the boy for a while.

As the grandmother would not allow the mother to walk to Kawakol alone with me, since that would have been immoral, both women came. At the hospital Dr Surendra prescribed sulphaguanidine tablets, entering the case as one of the 15 per cent he was permitted to allow free. Otherwise consultations cost an anna. Every day after this I went to their house to check that the right dose had been given.

A day or two later the grandfather watched my visit with a shifty, ill-at-ease expression until I succeeded in getting him to confess what he had done: 'I went to the grocer's shop in Kawakol and the shopkeeper sold me some medicine for the child.'

'Did he see the boy?'

'No.'

'You wanted something you had to pay for, did you?' I was too annoyed to disguise my feelings. 'Please show me what he sold you.'

He brought out a bottle of cascara.

I explained, with some heat, why he should trust the doctor, until he agreed not to use the cascara.

But the sulphaguanidine did not stop the dysentery and we became suspicious. We had provided powdered milk, with the usual careful instructions on the consistency the child would be able to digest, and we again went over this ground inquiring carefully if the milk was too strong. But the grandmother avoided our queries and assumed more and more the triumphant expression of the stupid person who exalts in her own supposed cleverness

when she is certain she is deceiving someone.

Finally I saw the trouble. Not only was the child being given the usual coarse mixture of rice and dal, but one afternoon I saw the little boy sitting on the ground and eating, from it, a toasted maize cob. It was the habit to let this monsoon crop reach full maturity until the maize was yellow, full and hard, and then roast the cob on an open fire. The resultant charred food was quite unsuitable for a baby.

The mother and grandmother repeatedly promised to stop feeding him maize and repeatedly lied that they had ceased, but the grandfather's reports on the child's condition, when he brought us eggs, was proof enough of their dishonesty.

In the end we fell back reluctantly on exploiting the inferior status of women, and made the grandfather bully the lesser orders in his house. After that the child began to make progress and when he had had regular meals of Multi-Purpose Food for some weeks he began to look like a normal child again.

From the Harijan sector was 'Tilri's' boy: my use of her nickname caused great mirth. On an occasion when the doctor was absent the headman injected Vitamin D with an unsterilised needle and badly infected the baby's buttock. From the shopkeeper's sector came a baby girl whose older sister was blind. The grandmother obeyed our instructions to the letter: the result was quick and we were humbly repaid with cheap cigarettes. Ajdhodia's four-year-old girl looked two, and her feet were buckled sideways because Ajdhodia kept standing her from a pathetic desire to convince herself that the child could stand and walk normally. She blamed the child's bronchitis – a side effect of the rickets – on the Multi-Purpose Food and would not use it. It hurt us each time we passed the poor little creature, sitting with her buckled limbs outside the door of her house. Ajdhodia's neighbour's boy had a defective heart but we were unable to get help to hospitalise him. A baby on the post office side of Sokhodeora went blind because his mother would not seek the doctor's help, and half the children of the Muslim hamlet on the western side of Sokhodeora were ill.

Mahommed Sherfu Din, the master builder, got typhoid fever and sold his hens and his wife's brass pots to pay a quack who did not visit him. When we found out we brought Dr Surendra and Multi-Purpose Food to him. But the strangest request was for us to help a girl who had turns of looking into space. We were told that she was doubtless possessed by a 'Satan'.

Meanwhile, Wendy visited the Bhorambag village kindergarten to see how her daily timetable and syllabus programme were being put into practice by Mataji. Some time earlier a female inspector had come from the Social

Welfare Board in Delhi to see Mataji's work and how we were utilising our grant. She had found Wendy and Kesurwa conducting the kindergarten instead and Mataji in our school. Consequently Mataji had been transferred. Now she was working very happily at Bhorambag, and we had provided her kindergarten with toys, powdered milk, Multi-Purpose Food, financial aid and a story-book picture Wendy had painted on masonite.

Farmers using the wind to remove the chaff from the wheat grains.

Sokhodeora farmers threshing the wheat crop with the help of their cows (the village is in the background).

Potters casting roofing tiles. One potter turning his wheel with a stick. Newly cast cylinders are cut down the side; in the background, the cylinders stacked for firing, after being parted into halves.

Shri M.P. Kurian taking the parts for the lavatories at our night-class building out of his kiln in the ashram (in the background, Shri Yogendra holding Vidya).

In the afternoons Mataji conducted a Women's Centre, which Wendy officially opened and for which she prepared a series of lectures on childcare.

Both of these institutions had come about through a peculiar revolt. Spurred by the efforts of Shri Nawal Kishore, the Bhorambag Council adopted and moved on a village development plan that included the forming of poultry co-operatives and the installation of a pump for clean water. The women of the village however refused to co-operate in any way in the men's Bhorambag plan unless they could have a Women's Centre. So the village had built the hall that accommodated the kindergarten, Women's Centre and Mataji's living quarters.

Nawal Kishore had been the prime mover also in the matter of the child-care lectures. 'Explain in your lectures, Wendy sister,' he requested, 'how to wean babies early like they do in your country. Here women suckle their babies far too long and it is extremely bad for the health of the mother.'

'I would like to be able to offer some useful suggestions,' she replied, 'but I don't dare interfere in such cultural patterns. I don't know enough about this to know if the mother's gain would outweigh the baby's loss. The mothers don't understand about sterilising utensils, they don't know how to introduce a baby gradually to solid foods, the usual village diet is completely unsuitable for small babies' digestive systems and they don't know how to deal with diarrhoea, and once the babies are weaned they get next to no protein. Let the lectures explain and demonstrate all these things for the present anyhow, without saying anything about when to wean babies.'

Then we ran into an epidemic of whooping cough and realised its seriousness much too slowly. Until she settled into a new daily routine with our baby, Vidya, Wendy did not attend the kindergarten and left Kesurwa to manage on her own.

'I'm sorry, Kesurwa,' she apologised, 'I didn't realise there would be so much for me to do.'

'Babies are a lot of work, Wendy sister,' she replied, looking at Vidya in her basket, and then asked very shyly, 'How much did she cost you and Allan brother? Do you think I could buy one?'

Wendy sadly explained something of our experiences and bond, unable to see any hope of Kesurwa being able to get a baby in a similar way.

'How are the children at the kindergarten?' she asked, escaping to the only children it seemed Kesurwa could have.

'Some of them have coughs, Wendy sister. I send them home like you say, so they won't give it to the others.'

A week later Bassanti's mother appeared on our doorstep carrying her daughter, who was far too heavy for her but too weak from the constant bouts of vomiting and croup to walk herself. The listless, heavy-eyed little girl was a great change from the restless, merry Bassanti who led most of the naughty tricks in the kindergarten. Wendy remembered how not long ago she had seen Bassanti's mother whacking her with a length of hand-woven rope. She had been screaming, Bassanti had been weeping, and now they both looked so helpless. Bhagia, the eldest daughter, followed her mother, carrying the youngest baby. This was usually Bassanti's work and we frequently sent home kindergarten children who arrived with a baby sister or brother straddled on their hip.

'Give me some medicine, Wendy sister. Bassanti is so ill. She can't eat anything and see how thin she has grown.'

Bassanti had certainly lost a great deal of weight. But it was not unusual for village people to ask us for medicine for any complaint.

'I can't give you medicine. I'm not a doctor,' Wendy replied, as always.

'Do you know how many other children have also got this sort of cough?'

She seemed to think a great many and in fear for the number of very small babies who might not survive this attack Wendy accompanied her to Sokhodeora to see for herself.

On the way Wendy consoled her as best she could with assurances that we would seek help from the Government doctor. It was useless to ask her to isolate Bassanti from the other four children in her family because it was one of the poorest in Sokhodeora. She and her husband, Akloo, had neither land nor house but depended on the hospitality of other Harijans almost as poor as themselves for a corner of a room or an end of a verandah. In the time we knew them they moved four times with their few cooking utensils and scraps of cotton. At the moment all seven of them lived, ate and slept in one room which had been built by the ashram as part of a spinning and weaving centre in the village. Their beds consisted of a pile of straw on the floor and their stove, situated in the middle of the chimneyless room, was a small mud structure open at the base for sticks or cow-dung cakes and with a hole at the top on which pans could be placed.

It was a terrible April day. The searing wind gave the landscape a sort of white desolation and although it was only mid-afternoon

Wendy always had the impression afterwards that she had visited Sokhodeora that day in the early evening when night was falling. The heat in the restricted alleyways was stifling and as she went from house to house asking if their children had contracted whooping cough, pieces of straw and pulverised filth whipped into her face, burning in her nose and gritting between her teeth.

She could only find one unaffected family and that was Mahadev's, as their house was larger and built around an open courtyard in which a small child might be confined. She explained carefully the need to isolate the babies. Disease came from God, the village people always believed, and she did not seek to question this. She merely explained that this disease could be caught and if children who did not have it were isolated straightaway they might escape.

A large group gathered while she explained and they listened in silence. 'Give us medicine, Wendy sister,' Chotun Mochi's mother requested.

'Come and look at my baby,' Tilri wept.

'My little boy hasn't eaten for three days, Wendy sister,' another cried. Wendy went with each in turn, followed by the small crowd of anxious parents who pathetically waited for her to pronounce some sort of judgement, which they hoped would solve their worries. There was, of course, nothing she could say save that we would bring the Government doctor to them. Knowing that whooping cough took such a long time to run its course she was afraid for these undernourished children and hoped almost as illogically as the village people that Dr Surendra might produce some miraculous cure.

We sent Mahadev with a note for Surendra as soon as Wendy reached home but it was after eight that evening when we saw the lights of the Government medical jeep swing out of the village on to the ashram road. Surendra was very tired. After a morning of cholera cases he had just returned from a journey to Nawada where he had gone with a small boy who had driven an object inside his nose. It had been necessary that he go to the Nawada hospital to have it removed.

We drew chairs on to the front verandah and placed our Petromax lantern on a stand beside us. Wendy brought cold coffee for the doctor and his compounder who had accompanied him.

We explained, and I went with Surendra to the village. Wendy could see the brilliant beam of the Petromax until we turned into the alleyway between the houses in the Harijan sector, and then there was just a soft glow, a slight added brightness which followed the direction we took.

In the alley outside Mahadev's house the Harijan mothers crowded around the lantern, holding their sick children forward, crying, 'Look at my child. Look at mine,' and it took some moments to make them stand back enough so that Surendra could get his stethoscope out of the bag in the compounder's hand.

He listened to the lungs of a couple of the nearest children to satisfy himself that he was dealing with whooping cough as we claimed, and then said to me in a whisper, 'There's really nothing I can give to arrest or cure the whooping cough. All I've got is some medicine to prevent complications arising, but I only have enough of that at my hospital for three or four children.'

Turning back to the mothers he shouted, 'Only the sickest ones, only bring me the worst ones!' There was a moment's urge for everyone to hold her child out again, then they held back and six young children were selected by unanimous agreement. Bassanti was one.

Surendra completed his inspection and insisted briskly that someone come to his hospital for the medicine for the six in the morning. 'I haven't got enough medicine for you all,' he announced. 'I'll try to get more supplies from Patna. If your sick child becomes very much worse bring him to me at once. Keep sick children isolated from healthy ones if you can.'

'That's all I can do,' he told me as we came away. 'You could keep an eye on them and advise about feeding, but they'll just have to ride out the six weeks.'

12

SHOVA

There were always waterbirds around our house in the monsoon. In the early morning they poised, grey and white and delicate on the edges of pools, on the bunds criss-crossing the rice fields, on the edges of the stretch of dam water that lay between Sokhodeora village and the arc of the built-up road to Kawakol. To us they represented the delicacy and freshness of early morning, the respite we were always grateful for, before the oppressive humidity of day set the dark-green grass steaming.

It was on such a morning, after Wendy had prepared our breakfast of boiled eggs, home-made whole-wheat bread and tea, fed Vidya and done the day's washing in buckets that Shova's mother arrived.

She walked up the steps of the verandah with the lithe, hip-swinging movement usual in young village women but curiously at odds with her timid expression. Her face had a madonna-like quality; it could almost have been painted with a blue cowl on an Italian church wall of the Renaissance period. The forehead was high and rounded, the face oval, the nose slightly elongated so that it seemed to droop a little towards the mouth which turned down delicately and sadly at the corners. She was nervous and hesitated at the top of the steps by the verandah pillar. Her elderly mother, who had a deeply lined face of dejected expression, paused by her shoulder.

As Wendy looked questioningly at the bundle hidden beneath her sari she drew the cloth aside.

'Look, Memsahib,' she said, and then at Wendy's exclamation of pity, horror and accusation she drew a piece of the tattered cloth of her sari across her face and sobbed.

The baby she had exposed was barely human. It was a sight to which we had become accustomed but never inured. The backbone protruded from the taut leathery skin, the flesh on the buttocks and thighs had fallen away to nothing leaving sags of loose skin, the legs were spines of bone. The head bones were so softened that her weight while sleeping had flattened them and all her hair had fallen out. It was the worse case of rickets we had yet seen.

'Allan, come here quickly,' Wendy called anxiously.

As I appeared the two women retreated.

'Let me see,' I asked quietly and the baby was uncovered again. We exchanged shocked glances. 'Can you come to Kawakol at once? I'll take you to the doctor there.'

They stood irresolute.

'Can you walk that far?'

They nodded but still hesitated.

'Never mind that I am a man. Come with me now. Your baby needs immediate attention.' They nodded again, silent in their desperation and distress.

While I put on my heavy boots to cope with the quagmire of village streets, Wendy prepared and brought a weak solution of boiled milk, water and sugar.

'What is your baby's name?' she asked gently.

'Shova, Memsahib.'

She spooned a few drops into the baby's mouth. Almost immediately the child turned to her mother's breast, making instinctive but feeble sucking movements.

'Are you able to feed Shova?'

'No Memsahib, there is some milk...' she began, and stopped, confused between her constant hope that she might have enough milk and her knowledge that this was not so. Many village women suckled their children until they were as much as three years old and this was certainly to the child's benefit because after they were weaned they rarely tasted milk. A baby that could not be breast-fed had little chance of survival, for there was no knowledge of the preparation of milk for babies nor of the necessity for cleanliness in such preparation. Of course it was possible that Shova's state was the result of a long period of unattended dysentery – often the forerunner of rickets.

'Has Shova had dysentery?' Wendy asked.

The reply, related only to present symptoms, was quite illogical. 'She has such a bad cough, Memsahib,' and she lifted her distressed face to Wendy's, for she had crouched to hold Shova and give her the milk. Wendy was used to such illogical answers because village people rarely thought in terms of cause and effect as she had been trained to do. There was no connection in the woman's mind between the past and the immediate and she did not press the matter.

While they waited for me, Wendy made soothing comments about the kindness of the Government doctor and about how she need have no worries about the cost because we would see to that.

The two women followed silently at a proper distance behind me. They had already walked three miles and came slowly. From time to time they passed the baby to each other and rested by the roadside.

Dr Surendra sat behind a cheap table in the Kawakol hospital. Facing him from a bench along one wall of the tiny room were two families in discoloured clothes that showed the skin of chest or leg through the holes. He wrote a prescription for the woman standing on the opposite side of the table and handed it to his compounder, who was obliged to squeeze sideways to leave the room.

'*Namaste,* Allan brother,' Surendra said warmly, 'what service can I do for you?'

'*Namaste,* Surendraji. Would you have a look at this sick baby?'

'You see how kind this man is,' he said to the women, 'bringing you here to my hospital.'

'It's nothing, Surendraji,' I protested in embarrassment.

'Sit down. I'll see you after these people if' – he turned to me – 'that is all right.' I nodded. The women sat humbly on the floor until the other patients had gone.

'What's the trouble, Allan brother?' Surendra asked.

'They saw a quack and he gave them cough mixture and sulphaguanidine. Fortunately they called at our house on their way home because I'm sure that's not what the child needs.'

He made his examination with a detachment all the more remarkable after our own surge of shock and pity. Shova's mother answered his questions monosyllabically, her eyes cast down to the floor.

'What's the matter?'

'Dried up.'

It was the village term for such emaciated babies: strikingly appropriate, the loose folds of the skin looking like the wrinkled neck of a lizard. He took the sulpha tablets from her, explaining that they were no use.

'Why did you let the child get in this state?' he demanded and both women burst into tears. Turning to me he whispered sympathetically, 'I'd only give her another twenty-four hours to live unless you can get Vitamin D injections.'

'Have you got any?' I asked anxiously.

'No, you'd have to get it from Nawada. Could your Mahadev be sent?'

'The bus has gone. Nobody could get there until tomorrow.'

'You could try in the medicine shops here, but I don't think they will have it. If you do get it and I'm gone by the time you get back, the compounder can give the injection.'

The two women followed me to the other end of Kawakol and sat on the concrete steps of the shop. The owner searched through the bottles and boxes on his shelves and shrugged his shoulders.

'I could get them in for you.'

'I want them immediately,' I insisted anxiously.

'You could go to Nawada tomorrow.'

I shook my head.

He brought out a dusty box with ampoules higgedlypiggedly in it and put it on the counter.

'You can have a look through these if you like. But I'm certain I haven't got Vitamin D. Colloidal calcium wouldn't do?'

'No,' I replied, obliged nevertheless to look at the ampoule which was put into my hand.

I stared at the label incredulously – *Colloidal calcium and Vitamin D. 10,000 units.* The shopkeeper shared my surprise. There were five ampoules. They cost 30 naya paisas each.

Shova's mother asked for a bottle and received a discoloured one the size of a thumb. She filled it with water from a well and tried to get some of it into the baby's sucking mouth.

'Where are you going now?' the grandmother querulously demanded.

'Back to the hospital to have the injection.'

'I can't go any farther,' she told her daughter.

'I've got to go with him.'

The old lady inclined her head. 'I'll wait here for you.'

When we reached the hospital again it was after midday and the door was closed. Unable to find the compounder we crossed the shallow river at the east end of Kawakol, followed the road to the Block gate, and went through the compound to Surendra's house. To begin with he was irritated at being disturbed during his leisure and spoke sharply to the woman.

'I couldn't find the compounder,' I insisted.

'Someone can go for him,' he said vaguely. He told the woman to wait in a room and getting over his mood drew me companionably into his bedroom, where he proudly showed me his things. He had a quilt for his bed, a black box of medicines and instruments, three books and a small suitcase containing two spare shirts.

The two of us sat on the bed.

'She's got severe rickets,' Surendra said, 'I've just been looking up all about it.' He brought his medical book and enthusiastically showed me the passage. Shova's symptoms were described in full – the flattened skull bones, the loss of hair, the bronchitis. Then he talked about the other common illnesses he met at the hospital, his annual budget of Rs.2700 for hospital and medicines, which was equivalent to 4 naya paisas per year per person in the area, and we looked together at other pages of the book.

My attention was divided between my anxiety for the woman and her baby waiting alone in the other room and my understanding of Surendra's loneliness.

'That baby could have died, you know, Allan brother, if they had trusted the quack and gone home instead of coming to you. It would have been murder but they're too poor to be able to do anything about it. I'm trying to get an inspector here to do something about the unlicensed medicine shops in Kawakol. They're illegal. The Government should try to stamp out quackery too. They tell lies about the hospital and frighten people away.

'I'll show you my medical box. I carry it everywhere with me. These are all samples. This medicine is for cases of tetanus,' he said and indicated other drugs and their uses.

'This is my hypodermic.' I judged the time now ripe for my appeal, when Surendra was feeling so proud of his work. 'Couldn't you give Shova the injection?' I pleaded and Surendra relented.

We returned to the other room as the grandmother wearily appeared. Surendra vainly felt Shova's arms, buttocks and thighs for any flesh into which he could inject.

'There's no place to put it,' he mumbled. 'Completely dried up. I'll just have to try here.' He puckered up the hanging skin above one knee. Shova began to cry weakly.

I could watch no longer. It was not the sight of the injection but the state of the baby that made my stomach heave. I went outside.

The women could not face the return to our house in the heat to get the powdered milk they would need for the baby and they returned to their village, Jerawadi. By the time they had reached there they would have walked about eleven miles.

That evening Shova's mother came again to our house. Jerawadi was three miles away but she still carried the baby with her and her face had that stoical weariness which deadens all expression. She crouched once more on the verandah, shifting her weight so that her back rested against the pillar and the baby's weight rested across her knees and thence on the flat of her feet. It was a posture peculiar to village people, especially women who did most of their cooking and household chores in this position.

Wendy made two cones of paper, poured powdered milk into one and Multi-Purpose Food into the other, and handed them to her. She wrapped them in her sari, tying the cloth around the parcels. She made no comment on the day's events but when Wendy offered a few words of encouragement, replied in a voice thin with fatigue, 'Memsahib, she is so weak,' and rocked the baby, alternately placing the cloth of her sari over the baby's face and then removing it.

Wendy told her how to prepare the milk, in what strength to mix the powder with the water, how to sterilise the container from which she fed the baby, how to cover the milk against flies and dust. The Multi-Purpose Food Wendy explained, was for herself. Later the baby might have some but now she was not strong enough. Then she told her kindly to go home since she seemed almost too weary to make the decision herself.

She returned every week for the Vitamin D injections, the milk powder and the Multi-Purpose Food.

At first we had to seek her out to remind her and sent Mahadev two afternoons after her visit to tell her that the baby's second injection was due.

Mahadev naturally wanted to know her full name, for the village was not his own. We unfortunately knew her only as Shova's mother and Mahadev, at last, resignedly set out to find a woman and child about whom he only knew the baby's name, the fact that she was ill and the fact that her mother had come to us for help. But such small affairs were of vital interest in a village from which people rarely travelled more than ten miles in their lifetime and Mahadev found her without much trouble.

It was very necessary that we watch to see she did not fall a victim to another quack, for she and her family had no education. However, we need not have worried, for she had determined to abide by Surendra's instructions and she persisted regularly with Shova's treatment for six months.

Four weeks or so after the treatment had begun Shova began to show more interest in the things around her. She began to reach for objects and she would follow other people and their movements with her eyes, but her progress was still unsatisfactory.

'How often do you feed Shova?' Wendy asked one afternoon. 'Twice a day,' she replied. Then as Wendy frowned, and she caught her disapproval, she shifted helplessly.

'What can I do? I have to work in the fields and I must take Shova with me. I feed her before I go out to work and when I return in the evening.' She added needlessly, 'We are very poor, Memsahib.'

Wendy knew it was very difficult for her but begged her to try to feed the baby at least four times a day. She understood that Shova could still only take small quantities of food at a time and she must have managed something, perhaps a small brass or earthenware pot which contained the prepared milk was carried to the fields and left somewhere in the shade under a cloth – because Shova progressed more rapidly after this.

Her mother grew happier and more vital each time we met and she excitedly showed us Shova's increasingly rounded limbs. Soon the little girl was able to eat a porridge of Multi-Purpose Food and milk powder. She was still being massaged with shark-liver oil and taking vitamin tablets or drops and occasionally we gave eggs and oranges for her.

'What do you feed your baby girl, Memsahib?' Shova's mother asked one morning, smiling and nodding at Vidya whose little fat face peeped over the barricades we had erected in the doorway. Wendy hesitated, miserable with sorrow, for it seemed only cruelty to list all the foods – oranges, eggs, bananas, vegetables, meat, milk – which she could never afford to give Shova. She hesitantly mentioned some and watched the woman's face become closed and resigned.

'We are very poor, Memsahib,' she said again needlessly.

Six or seven months after her first appearance Shova was fat as a toddler should be, and we were delighted. Her mother's face having lost its anxiety had even more a Madonna quality than before.

We never dreamed that she would thank us in the way she did. Taking me unawares and embarrassing me utterly she cast herself flat on our verandah and touched my feet with her forehead, insisting, 'You are God. You have saved my baby. You are God.'

'No, I'm not,' I replied hastily, 'and get up, do please get up. It was the doctor who saved your baby, not us.' 'No, it was you,' she replied doggedly, 'you are God.'

13

PEACE THROUGH THE AGES: A VILLAGE ENTERTAINMENT

Except for celebrations in honour of religious or political leaders the keeping of birthdays and the giving of presents is not an Indian custom. But the celebrations for leaders commonly took the form of processions between four and six o'clock in the morning chanting songs and shouting 'Long live', meetings with hours of speeches, and some form of social-service working bee. The ashram family's tribute to its founder, Jayaprakash, on his sixtieth birthday was the most memorable of any such celebration we experienced.

To begin with, when Kurian came to invite me to the casting meeting for his pageant he and Wendy disputed vociferously on whether it was

Jayaprakashji's sixtieth or his sixty-first birthday. It was Kurian's energetic contention that as Jayaprakashji would be beginning his sixty-first year it must be accounted his sixty-first birthday, which led to the dispute as to whether a baby is zero or one when he is born. The dispute was good-humoured but the confusion was as if prophetic of the chaos to come.

That evening the men met in the ashram library. The lantern inside cast light through the door on to the clutter of sandals on the earth verandah and upwards on to the murals inside depicting the incidents of the life of Buddha, painted by the artist Shantiranjan.

They sat cross-legged on the blue cotton floor covering, Shri Goswami, the Superintendent of the Bihar State Village Industries Training Centre, taking pride of place since he had written the pageant. It was entitled 'Peace Through The Ages'. He was a big man, always immaculately dressed, quietly spoken, gentle and kind, and we had willingly helped him get recruits for his Centre at the expense of losing our Literacy

Class Room to it. At present he was infusing everyone with his cheerfulness and was clearly an admirable person to have in charge of the coming celebrations.

Kurian came late and, growing irritated at the ribbing he got, insisted on awaiting the arrival of the ashram manager, Shri Ramraksha Sharma, whom he took to task much more severely than his one hour late deserved.

Kurian's enthusiasms tended to be tremendous but not necessarily long-lived, and rightly or wrongly he was just passing through a phase of believing that he could manage the ashram better than Ramraksha. This was because he had built a new lavatory for Jayaprakash with sliding window shutters like he had seen in Japan – behind, it must be admitted, a quite satisfactory lavatory already there. Then he had gone on to create a large brick urinal between the eastern and western colonies of houses, and was annoyed that the Ashram Management Committee had not only stopped his building because of lack of funds, but had finally demolished it.

However, overcoming all this friction, Goswami goodhumouredly cast the parts and all left excitedly, I having been allotted the various roles of Pontius Pilate, Woodrow Wilson and the Viceroy who jailed Gandhi.

The first rehearsal took place the next night and when it ended at about eleven o'clock I issued a fateful invitation to all to drink tea. Our only guests were Goswami and Kurian, but talking, drinking tea, brewing more tea and consulting photographs to see whether Wendy could play Mira Behn (Gandhi's famous English disciple, Miss Madeleine Slade) we were all surprised to see the sun getting up. We caught an hour's sleep before Vidya awoke for her six o'clock bottle, but Kurian apparently only got half an hour.

Then he was called to set up the stage in the ashram hall.

He employed workers from the village and they were busily and happily constructing and decorating when Ramraksha arrived. Insisting that the ashram had no money to pay the men he dismissed them. Kurian was livid at what he considered the disrespect of Jayaprakashji's ashram to its founder's birthday. Had he had more sleep the problem might have been solved, but as it was he went and hid himself in the jungle. Goswami and company had to find him, pacify him and bring him back.

Plump Ramashray Singh, full of sympathy for Kurian, put the facilities of his semi-government department at Kurian's disposal and construction of a stage began in the quadrangle inside the Village Industries building. He was a man made of three roughly equal measures: efficiency, humour and temper. In leisure, at home, he often waxed grandiloquent with resounding Urdu vocabulary and wild fantasy, saying: 'Make way for the great ruler Maharajah Allan Sahib', and creating a picture of court and populace abasing themselves – which might have been a description, for all we knew, of the time of the Muslim rule of India. Or else he would passionately quote long passages from the Mahabharata. He and I usually exchanged the courtly Muslim greeting instead of the usual Hindi *namaste* and he never seemed to tire of laughing at a play on words between 'thank you' and a similar-sounding expression meaning to throw oneself on one's face at the feet of one's revered teacher.

There was no longer any doubt that there would be a stage but there must have been other frustrations, because it was asserted that Kurian had to be soothed and brought back from the jungle four times that day. I visited him in the early evening to see if I could sympathise with or cheer him and found him hunched on a table on his verandah so morose and miserable that he was incapable of speech.

That evening's rehearsal dragged pitifully, for co-author and co-producer Kurian was exhausted, and in any case had become more interested in decorating the stage beautifully. It failed to hold my attention too: I dozed off in mid-stage, awoke at midnight and retired to bed. But the rehearsal and attendant arrangements moved to Ramashray's house where it was disputed until after two o'clock that the pageant must have a director, who should be Ramashray since he had provided the stage.

Next day was Jayaprakash's birthday. In other parts of the State a purse was collected for him. The ashram mounted a procession for him at 4am. I joined in the chanting and cheering through Sokhodeora, and in the general cleaning of ashram paths and the continuing work on the stage.

The third or dress rehearsal was held that afternoon in Goswami's office at one corner of the Village Industries building. New leadership had clearly been assumed by Ramashray who monopolised one of the four chairs and much of the heated discussion, and did not look in the least tired. Goswami, beside him in another of the chairs, sat patiently but obviously no longer participating or wishing to tread in the corridors of power.

Out through the door Kurian in a green hat could be seen bustling about the stage and efforts to bring him to the rehearsal met only with his enraged bellow: 'I'm having nothing to do with it. I'm going to do the make-up and that's all. I dust my hands of it!'

In this tense atmosphere surrounding the pacific pageant it was all too easy for me to offend against the peace of the ages. I altered my lines without consulting the others, simply because I felt sure that Pontius Pilate had not exactly said: 'Kill that man.' This was just too much for the young artist Shri Roni who immediately stopped being crucified and flung tempestuously out of the room. Apologies, of course, followed.

But I, on chair number four, went one naive step better. Having some experience of producing plays and feeling that the quick succession of scenes of a pageant necessitates an able stage manager, I strongly recommended this and said the pageant would thus be well over in half an hour. For lack of Hindi vocabulary, however, I used the word 'director' instead of the term for 'stage manager'. And that was petrol to a flame that had warmed the ashram family since we had begun missing our regular bedtimes. The rehearsal gave way to a chaos of shouting, reproaches and recriminations.

At seven the sun was down and, arrayed in Roman sheeting but carrying Vidya, I was surveying the delicate beauty of hundreds of tiny wicks burning on the brick tree-guards and along the verandahs facing the stage. Kurian had arranged for our school and kindergarten and the other ashram departments to give the pottery oil-holders both for Jayaprakash's birthday and to celebrate the annual festival of the lights.

Village people already sat under the canopy between banana fronds planted for decoration. Invited guests from the Block Development Scheme were taking up their chairs on the verandah of the carpentry department, rather too far left to get a full view of the stage.

By eight the quadrangle was packed with hundreds of villagers, most sitting cross-legged on the grass, women and children separate from men. Here was all the entertainment they knew, the homemade kind, and they brought to it an inexhaustible patience.

Goswami's verandah and office behind the stage had become dressing-rooms where Kurian, while the political speeches were made about Jayaprakash's heroism during the 1940S Quit India Movement, was meticulously creating the faces of the Gods who began the pageant by debating who would undertake the frightful responsibility of creating and overseeing man. The very long delay after the speeches dismayed neither him nor the noisy audience.

When the Gods had decided and left the stage and it was time for the cavemen, the borrowed microphone made insane noises and expired despite the efforts of the technicians dashing about the stage. Goswami determinedly went on with commentary to the end, although audience noise drowned him out even to the actors. But it had no more serious consequence than Wendy later on taking for a carousal scene what was intended for the collapse of Ashokha's Empire.

Of course the cavemen scene did not begin immediately the Gods withdrew. That was the cue for a messenger to be sent into the audience to round up the village-people-cavemen and when they had assembled before

Kurian's fastidious eye another messenger had to find their leaves. As they dressed the audience chatted. The hiatus of perhaps half an hour was just about to end as they entered the back of the stage when Kurian insisted they must return to the dressing-room and remove their singlets. And thus, bare-chested but Forest of Dunsinane legged, the cavemen enacted man's first war. In the audience Mahadev fancied their violent deaths might have come about through quarrelling over a girl of the wrong caste, but we assured him the next morning that it had been merely over a bone.

While Kurian prepared Lord Buddha for the third scene the stage was almost empty but for negotiations going on with some village musicians, who, unaware of the enormity of interrupting so sophisticated a pageant, thereupon announced their items and played them. One pumped and plinked the harmonium, one played drums and the third sang.

Meanwhile in the dressing-room the actors from neighbouring Bhorambag village were hotly insisting that they be allowed to stage their play. With so many aspects of courtesy to be considered the debate was by no means a short one. Kurian could not give his whole attention to the issue since he was slowly, painstakingly, painting Buddha's face. Having been a dynamic mass of readiness, I was beginning to lose my belief that I would be on, in Scene Four, at any instant. And this was just as well for, with Goswami's closing word on the issue, the Bhorambag players were politely given the stage.

Their drama, music, dancing and poetry reading ran almost without interruption for an hour or more. Then 'Peace Through The Ages' started at the beginning again.

By this time someone had removed and secreted Pontius Pilate's small sledgehammer, but the scene could be managed without it, for it was only a brief scene. All the scenes took up perhaps half a minute each; the waits in between perhaps each a quarter of an hour.

At this juncture Pilate, leaving Hitler and Tojo in Kurian's capable if unhurrying hands, took his sleeping daughter Vidya home to her cot. He and his wife made tea and drank it. Then after some time the agricultural student who was playing Prime Minister Nehru came urgently calling Woodrow Wilson for his scene.

The urgency was fictitious, as the League of Nations could not make its appearance until the name of each member country had been carefully pinned on to a backdrop. About this time one of the crackers for the atom bombing of Hiroshima went off in the dressing-room. Woodrow Wilson made an impassioned plea to the League of Nations – in English – and the scene dissolved.

Interestingly enough, Mahadev sympathised with Wendy next morning that Allan brother must have been in a temper, having spoken to all those people at the meeting and not one of them being polite enough to answer him.

There were so many other scenes of man's efforts to achieve peace to be shown before my next appearance as Viceroy of India that I had time to persuade Shri Roni to add this wicked role to his success as Christ. And as I surreptitiously departed for bed the remainder of the Hiroshima sound effects exploded. What happened when that scene was acted I never learned.

We had been asleep for at least two hours when we were wakened by a violent shouting: 'Long live independent India!' which was the explosion of righteous indignation of the nation at the arrest of Gandhi. In the morning Mahadev confessed that it was 3am before the scenes about Jayaprakash and Vinoba Bhave's work for non-violence in the world brought the pageant to an end and the village people went home.

It should be in fairness admitted that Ramashray did not see the pageant in the same light as we did, and who is to say whether as a witness he was less reliable than we were. His account of the celebration was typed and read before Jayaprakash at the next annual general meeting of the ashram. Perhaps we were unjust in finding his wording a shade grandiloquent, a trifle pompous.

In any case there was no mistaking its deadly earnestness.

14

THE GIFT

'I will see if I can buy some land,' Mahadev told us. 'I will not say it is for you I am looking because if I do they will put the price up. I will let them think it is just my father wants to get some more land for his family.'

'Very well, you try. And can you work out an estimate of how much it will cost?' I said.

'I will discuss it with some people in my quarter,' he replied confidently.

'We have the Rs.500 worth of windows that were made for the Experimental Rural School and if the Ashram Management Committee won't decide to let us start building the school we'll use the money we have from Australia for your night class. We won't be here very much longer and we want to use it before we go.'

During our stay we had received a total of AU$1400 from Australia. It had been sent to us from family, friends and the Quakers, from the students and staff of McKinnon High School where Wendy had taught, and from Elwood High School where a friend was teaching. But about AU$540 of this total had been sent from the pupils' Social Service Fund of Brighton High School (where I had taught), thanks to the sympathetic interest of the headmaster, George Stirling, and the affection of staff and students.

Their first AU$260 had been used on the windows, the projector, books and medicines for the school and free textbooks for fatherless pupils. Now we had received a second gift of AU$280 and could see no better way of using it than to provide the villagers with something they felt they needed.

Mahadev's estimate came back scrawled clumsily on a grimy scrap of paper. He had begun arithmetic lessons with me from a Grade 7 textbook, but his struggle with it was ample reason to have the figures for the building checked. The difficulty proved to be that each person who made me an estimate, as well as remembering materials Mahadev had forgotten, arrived at a different total.

Two months later we had to give up the idea of buying land. Cheap plots were too far from the village; near the village they were too dear. When Mahadev found the ideal situation, the farmer, wanting to keep a piece large enough for his bullocks to plough, would only sell a portion at least four times bigger than we needed.

'That's too dear,' snorted our plump, smallpox-scarred friend, Ramashray Singh, about the land prices I quoted him. 'You leave everything to me. I'll get your land for you.' He set off to the village at once.

Ramashray was employed by the Central Government Khadi and Village Industries Board as the organiser of the Kawakol Intensive Area Scheme. His offices, training workshops, and staff living quarters occupied the larger part of the ashram and since the scheme was the offspring of the Management Board of the ashram, he played something of a dual role as a public servant and member of the Gandhian Movement. It was the not uncommon co-operation of a government and a voluntary agency.

He was devoted to the betterment of his country. In his mid-thirties he drew, by his own choice, Rs.130 a month wages to support his wife and children, but lived a bachelor life in the ashram.

He was a dignified, intelligent and far-seeing man, extremely efficient and practical, with a cyclonic temper for poor or dishonest work. Of all our friends he gave us most help with our work and most encouragement when we were feeling frustrated.

'Land is very dear around this village,' he admitted. 'It's remarkable how it has gone up in Sokhodeora. Why in...' he made comparisons with land values in other neighbouring villages. 'Why don't you ask the headman to let you have some common land? You shouldn't have to use the money sent from Australia. I'll talk to him and see if I can arrange it for you.'

Two mornings later the headman, Goverdan Sau, Ramashray and I (in a state of suppressed excitement) went to see the land. We walked along the track from the ashram to where it crossed the creek and broke into a Y around the east and west side of Sokhodeora. At the junction was an irrigation well beside a huge *mahua* tree in the shade of which cows, buffaloes and goats rested on their way to and from the village and jungle. The right-hand leg was the way to Kawakol.

'You could have this bit here,' Goverdan Sau indicated a triangular widening in the left track just before it was joined by another track which led to the post office, the school and a temple under a *peepul* tree. After this junction the disused remainder of the left leg of the Y was overgrown with weeds.

'It is near the Harijan quarter and it is high ground.'

'Is that a tenth of an acre?' Ramashray asked.

'About that. This bramble fence should go back a bit,' he replied. 'These farmers have encroached on it here, but come along farther. There is a much better site along here.'

He stopped at a low, swampy site much larger in area.

'There are eight-tenths of an acre here,' he said. 'You would have plenty of room and could have a flower garden here in front. This is where we are going to build our new village library. We are looking forward to receiving your kind help with that, too, because you have been so helpful to our library.'

'Yes, we would be quite happy to do that,' I replied. And I asked, knowing the answer. 'Have you the plans made out for it yet?'

'No, that still has to be arranged.' He changed the subject, pointing along a foot track which led to his part of the village. 'This would be the better site. It is nearer the other sectors of the village and other castes could attend too. They would not want to come if it was as far as the other site.'

'Goodness, it's only a stone's throw between them. Surely they could walk that far.' I protested, sensing an antagonism and wanting to counter its arguments. 'This is a swampy spot, and we wouldn't want to upset things for your library.'

'They could both be built here. One there and one there.' 'Yes, but the other place has those two trees. I rather like them.'

'If you have it near the Harijan quarter only the Harijans will attend. It's not only for Harijans is it? Will members of other castes be allowed to attend?' His voice had grown sharper.

I thought cautiously before replying, remembering Mahadev's anguished cry when he heard about the common land – 'The other castes will take the night class from us when you have gone. They'll get in and then push the Harijans all out. That's what they're always doing to us.'

'I don't see why other castes can't come,' I said somewhat vaguely. 'Everybody is entitled to learn to read and write.'

'Aren't you going to call it the Harijan night class?' the headman demanded. 'If that is the name no one else will be prepared to attend.'

'That's just the first name that came to mind. We could change it. I don't mind what it is called,' I replied to conciliate him, adding half shrewdly and half sincerely, 'How could anybody refuse to let other castes come if they help to build it too?'

I knew that it would take decades of education to do away with caste prejudices, and it did not seem worthwhile to jeopardise the existence of the night class for an effort to solve in Sokhodeora a fundamental social problem. We saw no hope during our stay for unity and unselfish co-operation between the caste groups.

'Yes, I am sure everyone will help,' Goverdan Sau replied airily.

As we had expected, Mahadev favoured the location near his own caste's quarter. I told the headman.

'It's the wrong site,' he still insisted. 'The other place is much better. You've got no room for anything with the one you have chosen. You won't be able to have a garden or trees or anything.'

'I fancy the goats would eat it all anyway,' I said with a wry smile.

'You could have a brick fence around it.'

'Well, it's the place Mahadev would prefer.'

'What does Mahadev know about anything?' he retorted angrily, and then added disgruntledly, 'You can have whichever place you like.'

I thanked him.

Immediately we consulted Ramashray and other friends, drew up a constitution, and formed a committee for the night class with some of Mahadev's family as members.

The Public Meeting called by the headman took place in one of the rooms on the first floor of the disused landlord's mansion. The headman, Boddh Narayan, Dukharan and I sat just inside the door facing the audience. On the left were men from the upper castes, sharply differentiated from the Harijans on the right by their certainty of manner and the appearance of their clothes. The Harijans had sleeveless working singlets, skimpy *dhoti*s – the others wore long-sleeved shirts and ample *dhoti*s. Their clothes were white, those of the Harijans an unbleachable grey.

Goverdan Sau explained the request for a tenth of an acre of common land and recommended that the meeting should agree to this. A number of speakers followed, among them Dukharan, who protested violently against the choice of land near the

Harijan sector and worsened the conflict over this side issue. The Harijans were too timid to speak but their faces and hands showed their anxiety and their sense that they were struggling against the upper castes. Mahadev mulishly interjected that the land they had chosen was the better place.

The village nature-cure doctor quietly asked leave to speak and stood up in the back corner. Having intuitively chosen the moment when emotions were running high, when whatever he said would have greatest effect, he applauded the desire and efforts for literacy, praised the work that had been done by Allan brother and Wendy sister and then launched into a blistering attack, the more incredible because on the few occasions he had met us he had always been amiable.

'I am shocked and appalled at Allan brother encouraging caste divisions in this village that has always been so happy, and where we have all lived so harmoniously together and co-operated so fully together. It may not be known to Allan brother that our Government has abolished untouchability. We are all equals, as it should be in a democratic society. This village should not give common land for the establishment of a Harijan night class. It would be a reactionary step; setting one caste against another. Possibly Allan brother does not properly understand our society. We mix together. We must go forward uniting the castes in every way, treating one another as brothers.'

It was a long, impassioned speech and it won the upper castes of the meeting. The Harijans squirmed and muttered impotently.

Goverdan Sau asked what any of them had to say. Only one youth stood, his jaw set with the fighting spirit of despair, but he mumbled incoherently, fell over words and became abruptly silent.

Feeling ill at their plight I rose to defend them but I had been hoist with my own principles, with things I had said throughout the village, with attacks I had made on caste prejudice, with my democratic behaviour in relation to all people in the village.

My opponent I knew had an allegedly dishonest past. He played the contradictory roles of organiser for the Communist Party in the village and astute businessman, proprietor of an unlicensed and so illegal chemist shop in Kawakol. He was also a nature-cure doctor who would prescribe medicines and charge high fees without necessarily going to see the patient.

'I agree with you with all my being that men should be equal,' I said, 'but wherein are you equal here? You have bigger houses than the Harijans; you have more land than the Harijans; you can read because you can afford to go to school but the Harijans cannot. Look at the difference in the way you are dressed.' The words of a speech of JP's I had heard three years earlier came to mind and I continued:

'All men have equal need for food, shelter, clothing, medicine and education. This is the significance of Ganhiji's teaching and Christ's in the parable of the vineyard.

'Yes, you should be equal, but can you tell me you treat each other as equals? Do you know what I saw a man do only some days ago? He refused to eat some food because a Harijan had carried the pot it had been cooked in – merely carried the pot. (I was remembering the incident between Kesurwa and our Government teacher.) As if the touch of a Harijan was as disgusting as a dog licking your plate. That is your equality and co-operation. Get away dog, don't lick my plate, don't touch – Untouchable.'

There was a silence. I felt I had lost my temper, had been insulting and offensive to half my audience, had said things which had humiliated everyone.

My opponent replied that I had exaggerated things, not knowing the many ways in which castes had co-operated here. He said that he knew the person concerned in the incident and that it was not a resident of Sokhodeora but a man who had come there from another village. (This was true.) He demanded that the name Harijan Night Class be dropped and won general assent for his own choice of 'Jug Jeevan Ram Night School'.

'If you want it to be associated with Harijans then why not have the name of an inspiring national leader. He is a Harijan and he is now Minister for

Transport in the Central Government, but he's not just a Harijan. He belongs to us all. Nobody else will attend the class if it is called Harijan.'

I reflected sadly to myself that 'Harijan' meant 'known to God'.

He insisted that there should be non-Harijans on the committee and was prepared to be a member of the committee himself. Debate flowed briskly but confusedly in the educated half of the room on a variety of matters.

In an effort to conclude matters, I said: 'Very well, then, let's end discussion and put the giving of common land to the vote. Those in favour.'

No hand stirred.

'Those against.'

Goverdan Sau patted me on the shoulder: 'We don't do things like that here.'

'What then?' I asked in some bewilderment.

'We just keep on discussing a matter until everyone is agreed.'

Everyone's agreement was reached very simply. Someone I did not know, who was said to be a teacher, an MA graduate and a learned man, quietly said to the meeting: 'Let's give it to them. It's only one-tenth of an acre. It's so little.'

'Before you go, sign your name on this agreement,' Goverdan Sau called, and a paper I had prepared was passed about. 'Allan brother will fill in the plot number later.'

I followed the Harijans out on to the verandah, smiled at Mahadev and grabbed a cigarette. I offered one to my opponent, the doctor, and we made conciliatory remarks to each other.

'He was just being naughty. He wouldn't have spoken like that if his elder brother had been there,' someone later sympathised with me.

The headman must have been swayed by the arguments into a change of mind for we noticed next day that he had failed to sign the agreement. Ramashray had worded it very neatly to the effect that the signers had no objection to the giving of land, nor would raise any objections in the future.

But it only took some a few hours to forget that they had signed to the latter promise. The following morning

Dukharan argued against me that the site was wrong.

The morning after that, accompanied by Boddh Narayan, he again sought me out, this time at the kindergarten, and we sat on the step to argue.

Making no progress over the site he then demanded: 'Why have you got to build it and make two? We are going to build a big library and community centre for the village. It's unnecessary duplication. We could have one really fine centre for the whole village.'

It was a better plan, but I could not believe in its practicality in the months left of our assignment. Impatient of arguments that stemmed at least partially from envy, I asked callously, 'Dukharan, hundreds of rupees have been collected from the people of Sokhodeora, wrung out of their poverty, for the building of your new village library. Why hasn't it started? People say the money has taken wings? Has it? Is the money still there or isn't it?'

He did not reply.

A third time he approached me in the ashram garden when I was buying cabbage seedlings.

'Don't make a building for the Harijans. It's a mistake. They won't look after it properly. They'll keep the pigs in there.'

I turned on him angrily. 'That's all. I've heard the last words from you about it. Keep your superiority to yourself. Don't speak to me about the night class again.'

The Government's village social worker was a young cheerful, perky person, uncomfortably thin with a bony, triangular face. His office was one of the first-floor rooms of the landlord's mansion but I had not known this and had walked to the Block Development Offices in Kawakol and back to find him. He obligingly tugged out a Lands Department map, jerkily spread it on the floor and pored over it with me, searching for the plot and its number. When we had found it he unearthed a length of surveyor's chain and I departed to establish the boundaries of the plot and how much encroachment had taken place.

Mahadev we released from the household chores for two or three days to take the petition round the village for the signatures of as many heads of families as he could. The head of the family signed for any sons or women in his home.

The night-class committee was enlarged. It was insisted that I be president. Three non-Harijans were appointed – Wendy, Ramashray and Nawal Kishore – so that the committee was, in appearance, not one caste but had outsiders who would, if necessary, ward off take-over bids.

Mahadev returned exultant at the end of the first day. He had kept signatures on one side and thumbprints on the other. We had to paste another length of paper on to the original sheet.

'Some said, "What's this?",' he reported. 'Some of them said they would sign because all the others had signed.'

He was enjoying his importance immensely. We waited for the second day when the list was long before sending him for the headman's signature and those of the village council. In all, he collected a hundred and twenty signatures.

Then we filed notice with the Lands Department at the Kawakol Block Development Office that the village had given common land for the building.

We were ready to begin.

I pegged out the building helped by some boys who happened to come along. Most of the men who passed by looked at me and objected, 'It's not square on the block.'

'How else can you put it?' I countered, which was unanswerable.

When I had talked over the project one evening, sitting outside Mahadev's house in the moonlight, the Harijans and their caste leader, Tiloh Manjhi, a carpenter, had enthusiastically agreed to provide voluntary labour. On Mahadev's estimate there were a hundred and fifty Harijan homes and two days' labour from a member of each would be sufficient.

He appointed an overseer who was to keep a roll and round up the workforce each morning. To have continuity the overseer was to work every day and be paid after his two voluntary days. Stumps were grubbed out and the foundations dug, while the passers-by objected that the building was going to protrude too far into the road. Our overseer, who was about Mahadev's age, began to fail to bring workmen, to arrive late, to absent himself, until Mahadev quarrelled with him and he took another job. From then on, Mahadev, in the evening and before he came to work at our house in the morning, rounded up the day's team.

A little way along, on the opposite side of the road, was an irrigation well from which a channel was dug to fill the foundation trench with water. The earth was then thrown back in again and the workers walked up and down in this, sinking thigh deep as they kneaded the mud with their feet. After two or three days of winter sunshine the foundations were dry and solid.

Often we had to wait our turn at the well. Occasionally women drew water from it for their homes and around lunchtime farmers came there for their daily bath. The fields stretching away from the road had been ploughed and were now irrigated for the wheat seeds. Beside the well a Y-shaped post was bedded solidly into the ground.

Across its fork balanced a long pole weighted at one end with a heavy lump of tree trunk. To the other end two women tied a rope and bucket, and by this see-saw arrangement drew water all day. The bucket was made of riveted plates and was pointed at the bottom, looking something like a Viking's helmet upside-down. When it came up full of water it readily overbalanced on the side of the well because of this pointed base, spilling the water into a channel that led to the fields. Other women and children of their families directed the flow of the water in shallow channels across the soil, splashing the now muddy water across the dry areas between them with pieces of broken pottery. It was a slow and laborious method of irrigation.

While we built, the wheat was planted. The farmer drove furrows through his soil with a one-share wooden plough pulled by two bullocks. His wife followed behind with a bag of wheat tied at her waist, dropping the seed by hand into the furrows. Then he drove round again so that the plough covered the seeds with earth.

A farmer with his field across the road donated his topsoil for our building as he wanted the field deepened so that it would hold the monsoon rain for rice growing. Dug with mattocks, it was carried in baskets on the top of the head and thrown in a heap inside the foundations. Buckets of water were tipped into it and it was barefoot-tramped into a thick plastic mud. In balls as big as one's head it was carried to the wall-shapers.

The wall was made about three feet thick but at any one work session it could only go 'one hand' high or else the mud flopped over. A hand was a measure from fingertips to elbow, or about eighteen inches. I quickly learned how to throw the mud on and shape the sides straight by scraping the fingers along, removing bulges and filling dents. Throughout I was architect, foreman and labourer. Even the Harijans had something of the attitude that an educated man does not use his hands, saying, 'Don't you do that. You just watch and we'll do it.'

Building the mud walls of the night-class building. Mahavir is seated above the verandah pier; the boy with the mud for him is Manjhu son of Bunwari Manjhi

The completed night-class building.

Shri Jayaprakash Narayan holding Vidya at his home.

When the walls were low and soft they were damaged by passing cows scratching themselves against them.

Each 'hand' of wall had to dry before the next level could be added but we watched its upward growth with excitement, sure now that we had been correct in believing that the project would be an important one in social experience for the Harijans, educational in that learning to co-operate with each other they could set their ability to achieve things against their frequent feelings of hopelessness. We hoped too, ever so faintly, that the experience would lead to their trying other community development projects in future years.

Soon the barred windows were being set in bricks in the walls – eight of them for ample light and air. We decided not to employ the Muslim bricklayers of Sokhodeora but to keep the wages in the Harijan quarter. So one of Mahadev's elder brothers, Meghu, who was unemployed during the absence of Shimada San, and his slow friend, Mahavir, learnt bricklaying by doing it. The bricks were joined with mud and not always perfectly in line with the walls but the work was sound enough.

Ramashray Singh, continuing to help, sold us the bricks cheaply, and they were transported in hired bullock carts. Bricks were made by hand, shaped in wooden boxes and piled, interspersed with pieces of black coal, into huge mounds of 100,000 bricks or more. These 'kilns', or more accurately, brick stacks, were covered with a thin layer of mud and manure and fired. The result was termed 'third grade' bricks, for they were too absorbent to have cement binding between them.

Ramashray sold us the remnants of two old 'kilns' in the ashram. Pulling them out of the stack, I found the hardest of all building jobs.

One night, to our annoyance, someone from another caste pulled a newly set window and its bricks out of the wall. Meghu and Mahavir determined to act alternately as night watchmen, but as they had no blanket and the nights were cold we had to buy one for them. Still, no further damage was done.

When the brick wall was laid to hold the earth filling of the verandah it protruded on to the land that had been encroached. Meghu and Mahavir shifted back the bramble fence, carelessly trampling on half a dozen lily-like vegetables. Though the farmers had agreed to give back the sixfoot or so wide strip their wives were not so amiable about it, coming to shout violently about the fence and demanding compensation for the plants lost.

Meghu and Mahavir then built brick piers spaced along back and front verandahs to support the verandah roofs. For two of the front piers I sent my labourers to bring a bullock cartload of two hundred and fifty bricks but they returned fifty short. I stacked enough to complete one pier near the place where it was to be built, and the remainder where the other was to be. But Meghu and Mahavir started next morning before I arrived to see their part of the work. To my amazement they had spent their time shifting the bricks from the pier where there was enough to the pier where they were short.

This was one of several such pieces of unnecessary work. It was surprising that ill-fed people who could not afford to waste effort did not think of starting where the least amount of effort was involved, did not search out the easier way. Our Bengali friend, Pranhari Chakravarty, used to claim that the village people 'messed up things to prolong the job so they could be employed longer'. Here, since they were working on something of their own, it seemed to us to be a symptom of the peasant mind, which had never been trained in the division of labour or the industrial processes. We were reminded of the somewhat lone battles of a friend, Shri Tekumala, in the Central Government's Khadi and Village Industries Board, to introduce time-method-and-motion studies into official fact-finding researches into agriculture and handicrafts.

At first we thought to buy a tree for the wood we needed.

One Sunday afternoon two forest guards in khaki shirts and shorts and military boots went into the jungle with us. I carried Vidya on my hip. Just behind the ashram back fence huge rafts of bamboo, the grey solid not the green hollow kind, were stacked against a tree awaiting a contractor's truck to carry them to town. Here, too, prickly bushes grew in profusion: the village people used the branches of these to make bramble fences to keep the goats out of their crops.

For cities and towns the jungle provided timber, bamboo scaffolding and baskets, leaf plates and leaves for wrapping betel-nut and for the cheap, cigar-tasting cigarettes – *bidis;* for the village people it gave, in addition, grazing for cows and buffaloes, firewood, leaves for tanning leather, palm juice for home-brew toddy, edible berries and blackcurrants – a necessity in the diet of the poorest families. The Harijans hunted rabbits or porcupines for food with iron-tipped bamboo poles.

Seeing two villagers in loin cloths carrying light axes, the senior guard yelled at them, 'Hey you! What are you doing?' He grumbled suspiciously at their explanation and on we went.

There was a running battle between villagers and forest guards over wood, which once issued in a round of conferences which even Jayaprakash attended. The guards' preservation of the wildlife was also a grievance to the villagers, for the deer and wild pig did great damage to their crops.

'We know how to deal with the pigs,' Tiloh Manjhi once told me, laughing confidently. 'We make up a ball this big of such and such and leave it in the crop. The pigs gulp it down and *boom!* over they go. But we can't do it because they'd catch us and fine us at the Nawadah court.'

Shaded by the trees, we followed the foot tracks till we reached a giant *mahua* blown down by the wind. It was cheap, but with their light saw blades hung across the middle of a thin, wooden frame with plaited tight strings at either end to hold the frame together, Tiloh Manjhi and his employees would have worked at it for weeks. Because it would be so slow we decided against becoming owners of a tree. So planks for the doors, lintels, and window shutters were bought in the surrounding villages after long haggling and longer walks, and Tiloh Manjhi began making the doors.

Next we had to buy a palm tree of fair price to split into roof beams. Distinct from the squat toddy palms these towered gracefully up to sixty feet, adding beauty to the landscape. But most of those in the fields were owned by the Government, the Block Development Officer Shri Sharma explained, and could not be cut.

Half-a-dozen agents and I found privately owned palms and argued prices from village to village. In the end Mahadev said he had 'okayed' one owned by a Harijan family in Sokhodeora and had badgered them into a low price because it was for their own caste's night school.

When I wormed like a rabbit into their house yard and gazed up at the straight towering trunk, I was struck not only by the tree's bigness but the probable impossibility of felling it. Except for one narrow gap it was surrounded by houses only a few feet away. Moreover the owner had not 'okayed' it and was furious about the deal from a surprising number of angles.

'Why shouldn't I get over a rupee a hand for it? When it falls down it could crush that house and that one and their owners will attack me and I'll have to pay for the repairing of their houses and where am I to get the money from to fix their houses if he doesn't pay me for the tree?'

I promised to be responsible for any damage and a few days and conversations later the deal had been concluded.

Tiloh Manjhi agreed to fell it and split it. 'Twenty rupees', was all he said. His assistant, whom he had to pay at the carpenter's rate of two-and-a-half rupees a day, said nothing.

'No,' I replied, 'it's too much,' and I walked away. But no one else wanted the job.

'He is being naughty,' Mahadev commented. He and his friends worked on Tiloh's conscience that the night class was for their community until he took the job for twelve rupees. Four men shared it.

First a toddy tapper was employed for 50 naya paisas. With a short rope looped across his ankles he caterpillared up the palm and lopped off its foliage. This fell without doing any damage, leaving a trunk that the wind could not catch and deflect as it dropped.

Tiloh had demanded coconut-fibre rope but it was not to be had. Instead he used thick ropes of plaited rice-straw tied to the now dead-looking trunk and gripped by his helpers. He chopped.

It thumped down in the gap, its top end gouging a mark down a house wall but not doing any harm. They split it in halves with wooden wedges driven by wooden clubs.

While all that was being arranged I bought some heavy poles from the Forestry Department at Kawakol and asked permission to cut one-hundred-and-fifty light poles from the jungle.

'Certainly,' the Range Officer said helpfully. 'But you will need to get the permit signed by the Sokhodeora headman.'

I ran across him in one of the other Block Development offices and persuaded him to go back to the Range Officer's room.

'He can cut one-hundred-and-fifty poles from the jungle for his night-class building. You can sign the permit for him,' the Range Officer told him.

'I won't know what to do,' Goverdan Sau protested.

'You just sign on the day they cut them.'

'I haven't got a book of forms.'

The Range Officer had a clerk find one for him.

Mahadev collected his voluntary workers for Sunday. I saw the headman to see if Sunday suited him and asked three times whether there was anything else that should be arranged.

'No. Everything's OK,' he replied. 'You don't have to do anything. Just send Mahadev and I will sign.'

On Sunday morning, seventy-four Harijan men assembled and went into the jungle, forgoing a day's labour that could have earned their families a rupee. But the headman refused to sign the permit unless a forest guard went with them. Mahadev ran half a mile to tell us, then three miles to the Forestry Department Office to bring a guard. They told him they had to go somewhere else for the day, so he brought the men back from the jungle empty-handed.

We waited until their anger had ebbed and made arrangements for another Sunday. Forty men assembled. By some ill fate on that day a contractor working on the Kawakol Nawadah road was offering Rs.2.50 for a day's work, more than double the normal wage, and the men passed up this opportunity.

Mahadev went to the headman's house. He again refused to write out a warrant unless the forest guards were present. Mahadev told him they were coming, but when they arrived the headman could not be found. And again the men's day was wasted.

Bitterly angry and suspecting him of obstructing our efforts from caste motives, I visited him and watched him for some time remove ampoules of cholera vaccine supplied by the Government from cardboard packets and stack them in a cupboard in his room where he had proudly hung photographs of both of us. The ampoules were stamped 'Keep between 0 and 4 degrees Fahrenheit'. I reflected that if he kept them through the heat of May and June they would be useless.

Finally I raised the question of poles and reproached Goverdan Sau for the loss of 114 man days and for the employment the Harijans had missed.

'It's Mahadev's fault,' the headman persisted angrily. 'Well, will you sign the permit for us if we organise another day?'

'I'm not going to say anything. I'm not allowed to write out permits unless two forest guards are there. I give the permit to them. I'm not writing it out for that Mahadev.'

We learned after the event that our friends Ramashray, Kurian and Yogendra went to meet him one night subsequently to ask him to help the night class. Whatever was said to him he replied: 'Allan is a clown,' upon which Kurian lost his temper and they all parted angrily.

But one day the two forest guards walked up to the building (thirteen feet wide and thirty-two feet long inside) and admired it. 'It's a real hall.'

Finally one of them asked, 'You still want to cut 150 poles from the jungle?'

'Yes, but I don't see how,' I said dispiritedly.

'We'll take it on our own responsibility.'

I collected whomever I could and went immediately, although we would only get about half a day's cutting. Our team had to walk a couple of miles before we entered the jungle.

'This is the Sokhodeora coup this year,' the guard explained, pointing to stone markers. 'Along there will be next year. We have the forest allotted into forty coups, one a year for the next forty years so that it will grow fully.

The trouble is, these village people will steal wood from anywhere. We have to watch them all the time.'

As we climbed up a precipitous foot track through rocks, trees and brambles four men in loin cloths appeared carrying huge barked and white logs on their heads.

'Hey you!' shouted the guard. 'Where are these from? Where are you taking them? Give me a look at the end.' As soon as he saw the Government seal imprinted at the end of the logs he let them go.

I was amazed at their endurance; they had brought logs heavier than I could carry for miles up and down hills on broken paths and over the top of the range 1700 feet high, on an inadequate diet.

Our poles, too, were stamped before they could leave the jungle. I returned happily with the first one.

Over Christmas we went to the Quaker International Seminar in Madras. When we returned we found that Mahadev had organised wonders. Palm beams straddled the room holding up the ridge pole. The jungle poles had been tied on with straw rope over half the roof and a bed of thin saplings had been laid on them.

His caste had done more than they had promised, having given 500 days of free labour when their income was three rupees a week per person. To help them for their loss of wages we distributed the remaining tins of Multi-Purpose Food after each day's work. But no other caste had helped despite invitations. Mahadev had underestimated the work involved but we had enough money to pay for most of the remainder.

For the roof a potter cast 10,000 tiles, at Rs.9 a thousand, on a heavy stone hand-spun wheel, and fired them. Harijan women, including Mahadev's two sisters-in-law, brought them in baskets on their heads and took them up the ladder after reaching an agreement with Mahadev for the payment of 75 naya paisas per day.

Now it was time for Akloo's two days' free labour as he was a skilled tile layer. Akloo was a semi-cripple who was employed as a casual labourer in the ashram garden and orchard for a rupee a day. One leg was much thinner than the other and his foot was twisted outwards. He had five children, the oldest of whom was Bhagia who had learned so quickly at Wendy's now extinct women's night class. His wife was taking their new baby with her to work on the building of a new ashram dairy. The baby lay there near her with a thin scrap of cotton over him to keep off the flies, and slept unaware of the cows around him.

Their security could not have been at a lower ebb than at this time. Neither his wife nor Bhagia, who both usually carried bricks eight at a time on their heads for one rupee a day, could find employment. Bimul, aged seven, was earning a few naya paisas a month as a cowherd, but Akloo too was unemployed. He was washing the pots in the ashram kitchen in return for the food left over after the community meals.

Despite all that, he did his two days' free labour, roofing the night-class building with his habitual cheerfulness, but it was more than we could accept.

'They are one of the poorest families in your quarter, aren't they Mahadev?' I asked him at our house. 'Then let's pay him skilled labourer's wages – it's only two rupees a day – on the quiet so the others who gave labour won't object.' As Akloo laid the tiles I sat on the uncovered roof poles between jobs and watched him work.

'Allan brother,' he said tentatively, 'I have a pain here in my chest.'

'Akloo brother, I am not a doctor. You should go to the Government doctor at Kawakol.'

'I have been to him, but I thought you might be able to help me.'

'What did he say?' I asked.

'That it would cost fifteen rupees to cure me.' He paused for some minutes. 'How could I save fifteen rupees?'

I could find no reply. If you have TB or something fatal, I thought, that will be the price of your life!

Akloo went on working.

15

THE HOUSE WITH THE POMEGRANATE TREE

'Before you leave India I would like you to see my house,' Jayaprakash said to us in his library in Patna. 'It is about fifty miles from Patna and we will travel by jeep until we reach the Ganges and then we will have to continue on elephants.

'We live between two rivers which mark the boundaries of Uttar Pradesh and Bihar. Every so often the rivers flood so badly that they change their course. For years our house was shifted from one side of the river to the other being rebuilt each time. We've used what we could of the initial wood and materials but now our home is only a quarter of its original size. The whole village stretches over an area of some thirty square miles. You will find it enjoyable, if,' he added with a little hesitancy, 'it is not too difficult for you with the baby.'

He picked Vidya up and placed her astride a long log-like pillow, which served as a back-rest since with Jayaprakash we usually sat on the floor in traditional style.

'Now you are on a gee-gee.' Vidya slipped sideways and he caught her as they both chuckled.

We happily accepted his invitation and left Patna excitedly one bright cold winter morning early in February. Jayaprakash travelled with us in the back seat of the station wagon while his other guest, Ganga 'Babu', the leader of the Indian Peoples' Socialist Party, travelled in the front. He was a short, plump, genial man who suffered from blood pressure, but this did not inhibit his flow of witty reminiscences and stories.

Conversation was desultory.

'S.K. Dey, the Minister, made a lightning tour of the Community Development Projects – unannounced,' Ganga Babu remarked as the jeep driver, blasting the horn, slipped between a rambling bullock cart and a careering bicycle. 'He says the country is going to the dogs.'

Vidya was restless. I let her stand a minute on the floor of the car then Jayaprakash lifted her to his knee.

'She is very nice,' he said and turned her so that she might look out the window. It was not long before she was asleep, Jayaprakash holding her in a position that was obviously awkward for him.

'Do shift her,' Wendy told him but he continued to hold her this way in case she awoke.

Soon the uneven bitumen of the congested Patna streets gave way to an earth road in the process of construction. We shut the windows against dust and occasionally clutched for support as the station wagon veered off the road down a slope along a secondary track indicated by a detour notice.

'This is the worst road in Bihar and the Chief Justice of the Union lives here. They have been repairing it for months,' Ganga Babu said, and chuckled at the irony of it.

Our destination was the banks of the Ganges, across which we had to travel by boat.

At this season of the year the Ganges was one main stream flowing through a mile of sandy waste. In the monsoon this waste became an ocean of swirling, rushing muddy water.

The station wagon swung into a tiny village that crouched on the edge of the low scrub area backing the sand. The jeep in which Prabhavati had travelled to the village the day before was waiting there. Everyone climbed out to discuss whether or not we should plod the half mile or so to the river on foot or attempt to take the jeep some of the way. While they all talked, Wendy made Vidya a bottle of milk and gave her some mashed banana and cereal under the curious eyes of a number of small village boys and girls who watched with still, intent faces through the windows.

Jayaprakash returned and stood by the window: 'I suppose Allan can carry Vidya. We will have to walk.'

However there was suddenly a change of plan. Our party returned to the station wagon and the driver swung the car on to a narrow uneven track following the jeep. Our way was finally barred by a high earth bank running across the track. The jeep had bumped across it but the station wagon balked and this time we all climbed out. A few steps and we reached the blindingly white expanse of sand. The porters laden with trunks and bags on their heads and suspended from the crooks of their bent arms set off for the river at a jog. In the distance two camels swung along the sand.

'Let Wendy take Vidya,' Jayaprakash suddenly told me, 'and we'll see if the jeep can make it.'

He urged her in, climbed up beside her and they reached the broad green expanse of water long before anyone else. It reminded Wendy incredibly of what she had always imagined Kipling's great grey-green, greasy Limpopo River would look like, but it lacked the fairytale quality. Although the Ganges was always thought of in India in the feminine gender it never seemed to her a feminine river. It had the huge, slow magnificence of the Rhine at Cologne and seemed eminently masculine in its strength.

A cumbersome flat-bottomed barge some thirty feet or more in length awaited us. Balanced across the thwarts were low wooden beds.

We sat on one of these in the middle of the craft and the riverman at the head of the punt slowly poled us away from the edge. The barge swung at an angle into the main current which sluggishly carried us downstream. The punters pushed their poles deeper and deeper as we gradually approached the opposite bank and at last abandoned them and took up the oars. The farther bank sloped steeply to the water and we scrambled ashore on stones and clambered up the uneven track. At the top two elephants lazily rocked and shifted their huge feet restlessly while they waited. A young mahout sat on the head of each and placed upon each broad grey back was a padded sack. Under the trunk, around each side of the elephant and under the tail, was a thick rope and this was all the support offered.

'You, Allan, and the baby ride on one elephant and we'll take the other,' Jayaprakash said, indicating himself and Ganga Babu.

Nervously Wendy watched the huge beast lumber down on to his knees.

'I'd rather walk, JP. Is it far?'

'Three miles about. You can't walk, come along. Give the boys your shoes. Hold on to the tail.' Wendy eyed the flat expanse of the elephant's rump and stopped.

'Get up, Wendy,' Jayaprakash said shortly.

'I don't have to ride the elephant if I don't want to,' she replied with childish asperity.

He did not bother to reply and she managed to scramble in a thoroughly undignified manner on to the sacking, where she sat rigid with fear and clutching the rope. I clambered up after her and Jayaprakash handed Vidya to me.

'You'll get used to it shortly,' Jayaprakash spoke reassuringly.

The mahout, sitting astride the elephant's neck, called in a staccato voice and beneath us the grey back heaved as the creature lunged to his feet and set off with a rhythmic, swinging roll.

For the first few yards Wendy clung to the rope, then suddenly the padded sacking seemed quite secure and comfortable and she relaxed enough to look about her. I had a more difficult time because Vidya would jump about in my arms and as I struggled to hold her we both slipped farther and farther down the elephant's flank. However the three of us enjoyed our ride.

The elephant enjoyed himself also. Our path was a narrow track through acres of pea fields and every few steps his questing trunk collected a few pea bushes and he munched contentedly.

Jayaprakash, a short distance in front of us, suddenly called out.

'See those animals? They are half horse, half cow, a terrible nuisance to the crops, but the Hindus and Muslims won't kill them and the Christians daren't for fear of riots so they eat and eat.'

We curiously watched one of these creatures lift an alert, delicate head on a long graceful neck. But the rest of the body had the heavy ungainliness of a cow. Jayaprakash did not know what they would be called in English and none of our friends on our return to Australia ever quite believed this story. They requested photos as evidence, but we did not get near enough for that.

At last we swung into the alleys of Jayaprakash's village. It was far more scattered and open than Sokhodeora, and Jayaprakash's home itself lay in an open space completely clear of the surrounding houses.

The house had been built some height above street and flood level. Half a dozen steps led to a small walled front garden and from there another short flight of steps ascended to the marble-inlaid verandah on which easy cane chairs and a wooden bed covered with a brilliant khadi cloth had been placed. Across the verandah from the steps was an enormous pair of heavy-studded wooden doors. They were so massive that we joked immediately about whether or not there were *dacoits* (bands of armed thieves) in the area.

Across the narrow roadway was Jayaprakash's vegetable and flower garden and the well from which servants carried water to the house.

It was a home built around two courtyards. The rooms around the first courtyard, which we entered through the massive doors, were the family's living quarters with extra rooms for guests. The open section of the courtyard was of stamped earth, cemented in the customary manner with a fine crust of cow-dung and water. The verandah, which ran around four sides of the yard, was a step up and from this the rooms opened. At one end of the verandah was an open recess with a low table from which we all ate after seating ourselves on reed mats. At two corners of the courtyard were concrete concave sinks with outlets under the house walls, and above these sinks there were small tanks with taps so that anyone wishing to might wash their hands. The verandah pillars were painted a soft blue and the rest of the walls were whitewashed, glinting bright and clean in the clear winter sun. The roof, for there were no ceilings, was of a delicate close thatch. So uniform, slender and closely placed were the thin lathes upon which the thatch was placed and then the tiles that the roof from underneath gave the appearance of a one-piece structure. It sloped steeply inside in an almost Norman manner and toned in colour and texture with the floor and walls.

Our room was oblong with four windows that overlooked the village and both house courtyards. The upper and the lower courtyard were joined by a passage, the latter being reached by a steep flight of steps dropping to street level. Off this lower courtyard were the kitchen and the servants' quarters and here a pomegranate tree grew in a corner.

It was a beautiful house, not beautiful in the modern sense of having streamlined furniture, pastel walls, correct tone prints and the atmosphere of months spent over careful interior decoration, but beautiful in that sense of being part of an established order of things. It was almost as if here William Butler Yeats might have written: 'O, what if gardens where the peacock strays/With delicate feet upon old terraces', and then asked: 'How but in custom and in ceremony/Are innocence and beauty born?'

But there were no peacocks in the garden, only the somewhat bare pomegranate tree in the lower courtyard. Yet that pomegranate tree has always symbolised to Wendy the richness of the house. Perhaps because the pomegranate in India is so succulent, such a lush crimson-fleshed fruit, perhaps because it grows where the sun is always prodigal, perhaps because it is associated in her mind with Persephone and the Greek legend of spring and renewal.

We were all dusty and tired after the trip. Prabhavati was cross because she had prepared a midday meal for us and we were late by some three hours. However, in a few minutes she was cheerful again and brewing us tea on the Primus stove. We sank into chairs on the verandah and were introduced to two other house guests, Shri and Shrimati Saudani. He was a carpet manufacturer, a big-boned gentleman whom Vidya took to immediately.

His wife had a dry sense of humour and a fanatical love of chillies, which caused us much amusement. She responded to our quips with a slow smile and a twinkle from behind her heavily tinted glasses.

With the tea we ate Indian sweets, a lovely, treacly flavoured crisp flaky cake, which we loved, and fruit cake which had doubtless been brought for us since Jayaprakash constantly worried about whether or not we would like their food.

Then everyone retired to bath and we gave Vidya her evening meal and prepared her for bed. A servant had brought Wendy a small bucket of creamy milk.

'Take what you need for the baby and he'll bring the rest to me,' Prabhavati said.

A lad brought us two lanterns, one a hurricane lantern, the other a heavy, round glass shade containing a strong kerosene flame. He placed them on the stand outside our door.

At last we tucked Vidya into her basket, drew over it the mosquito netting and went to join the others. A barefoot girl in a dark-blue sari was placing shiny steel platters and matching containers for water on the polished table. The mats were placed around. A lantern set in the wall recess threw a soft yellow light over her movements and the table. The courtyard and verandah were in darkness but from the outer verandah came the fitful murmur of voices.

Jayaprakash, Ganga Babu and some friends from the village were there. We joined them but sat quietly on the wooden bed, losing ourselves in the outskirts of the gloom which deepened to a padded blackness where the garden disappeared into the street. Very faintly the smell of village fires, the slightly acrid odour of burning cow dung, reached us and the sharpness of the smell emphasised the softness of the night. Voices murmuring lost themselves in the darkness and seemed unrelated to individuals, moods, emotions and thoughts.

Prabhavati's call to us to come for the evening meal broke the spell. The village men remained sitting on the verandah. We were to notice in the next few days that there were always several village people on the verandah, waiting to see Jayaprakash to discuss with him village or personal problems. Frequently men came requesting Jayaprakash to help them get a job or to write a reference for them. It was part of a paternalistic way of life, the whole village looking to him for guidance.

He rose quickly, drawing his long soft woollen *chudda* (a type of long stole) about him: 'Well, Wendy and Allan, shall we eat?'

We followed him.

On the platters small quantities of spiced vegetables had been placed. Prabhavati brought hot, soft chapatis, which had been cooked pancake-fashion from wholewheat flour, bowls of dal made in the form of a light spiced soup, jars of chutney and lastly a large earthenware pot of curd.

It was usually eaten with the spiced vegetables and rice but we each consumed a large bowl with sugar. It was delicious.

Jayaprakash plied our plates with more until we had to laughingly protest at his anxiety that we might not be taking sufficient.

'Our village is famous for its curd,' Prabhavati remarked proudly as she served the rich creamy food. 'We always take some to Patna with us for Rajendra Babu.' (Rajendra Babu was Rajendra Prasad who had been India's first president. Now he was retired and living quietly in a gracious house built for him in the grounds of Sadaquat Ashram on the outskirts of Patna.)

Ganga Babu suddenly gave a deep rumble of laughter.

'Do you remember how we all used to meet at Sadaquat Ashram during the days of the Quit India Movement?' he began. 'Rajendra Babu had a servant who had all sorts of strange ideas about food. He was convinced that pumice stone was edible and he determined to serve it up with the meal.' Here he stopped to chortle again.

'My servant came to me in great anxiety, "Sahib do not eat all the dishes tonight, just take of the ones I offer you."

'Rajendra Babu wondered why none of the rest of us was served this dish. The other servants made themselves appear obviously busy and we were all very puzzled. Suddenly Rajendra Babu dipped his fingers into the dish of stones, took a large mouthful and bit.'

A spasm of laughter all but choked him ... 'There was a great crunching noise and all at once his false teeth shot straight out of his mouth.'

We all dissolved into peals of laughter.

'What became of the servant?' Shri Saudani chuckled.

'He left in a great hurry,' Ganga Babu replied, wiping his streaming eyes with his large khadi handkerchief.

Still laughing, we all rose from the table to wash our fingers, for there had been no cutlery with the meal, except for the spoons we were given to help us eat the curd.

We opened the barred window that looked over the village, turned our lantern very low and climbed into bed to sleep between hand-spun hand-woven sheets on firm, narrow cotton mattresses in the silence that crept in from the sleeping village.

Jayaprakash usually came to his home at this time of year. It gave him a rest from the turmoil of his political life and enabled him to lead ceremonies held on 14 February in memory of the day, according to Hindu ritual, on which Gandhi's soul departed from this earth.

Because the spinning wheel had been used by Gandhi to symbolise an independent India and a non-violent social order, spinning sessions were organised by the village council and also a meeting at which Jayaprakash was to be guest speaker. He himself intended to spend a quiet time spinning a certain number of hanks of cotton.

After accompanying me on a walk two days later, Wendy returned to the house ahead, leaving me to carry Vidya and talk with some of the young men at the small Gandhian ashram built next to Jayaprakash's garden on land donated by him.

Jayaprakash was spinning in a corner of the verandah. The whir of the machine reminded her of the soft, rhythmic snores of a sleeping man. He was seated cross-legged on a reed mat using a hand *charkha,* or spinning wheel, which operated on two wheels controlled by a belt and a spindle.

He caught the pencil-like screw of teased cotton on the end of the spindle and holding the cotton deftly in his fingers drew out a slender even thread. Then he reversed the process and wound the spun thread backwards around the spindle. Beside him was a small, four-spoked wooden frame, which turned on a centre pivot. When the spindle was full, he unravelled the thread around the four sides of the spoked frame; so many revolutions produced a hank, which was then twisted into a skein. Jayaprakash had vowed to spin a certain quota for that day, and was trying to complete his self-imposed tribute of remembrance.

'May I sit and watch?' Wendy asked tentatively, 'Or will it disturb you?'

'No, sit down, Wendy.'

She pulled an unused mat against a pillar and sat down with her back against it.

'Shall I ask Daniel to bring you a chair?' Wendy smiled at Daniel who was Jayaprakash's temporary secretary and a friend of ours from the days in Delhi when we had been adopting Vidya.

'No, thank you, I am quite comfortable.'

'How many hanks have I there, Daniel?'

'You need five more.'

'I can see I shall be here until midnight,' Jayaprakash said, between amusement at himself and consternation. 'I should have begun earlier.'

'I came to sit in here because I do not spin regularly and it didn't seem—' he hesitated, almost as if even his apology might sound presumptuous '—right that people should think I do.'

'Gandhi would forgive you, I'm sure,' Wendy smiled.

'Well, I'm five hanks short and I couldn't cheat him,' he returned the smile. The thread broke and he twisted it so skilfully that there was barely a thickening at the join. After that he worked in silence for some time and Wendy was content to sit peacefully watching.

'Tell me about the Independence Movement, JP.' She had not meant to ask the question, for we had always felt that there had been so much suffering for the people involved in those years that they were not to be questioned lightly. But he did not seem to mind.

Because the Sokhodeora ashram had been built in the area through which Jayaprakash had made his escape from Hazaribhag jail, Wendy asked him about it.

'I wasn't there as long as they intended,' he chuckled. 'I absconded over the wall. We tied our *dhoti*s together, then I made my way over the hill track at the back of the ashram.'

'Sometimes it was worse than others,' he continued reminiscently. 'At one time in the Red Fort in Delhi they questioned me for fifty days and wouldn't let me sleep. They kept changing my questioners. They even changed the style of interrogation – a couple of fellows tried to appeal to my better nature by begging me to give the information and so save them from losing their jobs.' He shook his head in an amused way at the fellows' stupidity.

'As soon as I started to go to sleep they would shake me awake. It was very difficult. They wanted me to promise not to escape and when I refused they put chains on my feet. They even expected me to take my daily exercise bound like this.' There was indignation in his voice. 'Of course I refused and they had to carry me. Eventually they took them off.'

The images were desultory but Wendy needed little imagination to fill in the rest of the picture. She now understood Jayaprakash's fanatical hatred of all forms of political persecution.

She was shocked that a man of such sensitivity should have been subjected to these indignities and realised with humility that these conflicts had left Jayaprakash not bitter but with a greater humanity. But she could find nothing appropriate to say and so remained silent.

'So you are thinking of adopting another baby, Wendy,' Jayaprakash changed the subject. 'What will you and Allan do with all these children?'

'Another will only make two,' she protested with a laugh. 'We may as well be busy with two as with one.' Daniel, who had slipped away, suddenly reappeared and bending down told

Jayaprakash something quietly. 'I have a visitor,' Jayaprakash apologised to Wendy and rose quickly.

At that moment I returned with a tired Vidya and we went to bathe her in the small bathroom where a charcoal burner sputtered and crackled as it warmed the water. We all bathed by crouching on the concrete floor and dippering containers of warm water over ourselves. All our friends bathed in the morning but we chose to do so at night. Vidya's bare grubby feet, for she never wore shoes inside the courtyard, made such a mess of our clothes when we picked her up that we felt the need to change for the evening meal.

This evening was to be special, for a puppet show was coming to the village and Jayaprakash and Prabhavati had invited the performers to set up the stage in the courtyard. As the showmen erected the stage, fitted the curtains and organised their dolls the servants and their families and children slipped in to sit on rows of mats before the stage. There was much excitement and noisy jostling and laughing.

The puppet play, unfortunately, chose to depict the Chinese encroachments on the Indian border. It would have been more fitting had a fairytale been chosen, for the depiction was crude and unpleasant. Jayaprakash shifted restlessly a couple of times then eventually told the performers that we had all had enough and must have our evening meal. He was irritable throughout the meal, but it was understandable. As a believer in non-violence and non-violent resistance, and at the same time a man who loved his country above anything else, he had been deeply distressed by the Indo–Chinese conflict and the personal choice he must make about the type of resistance to be offered.

We had never seen him so vulnerable and worried as we had on the night in November when he had addressed the ashram family about the conflict.

Even now the question of whether or not he should advocate the national use of non-violent resistance over this dispute still weighed with him and the crudity of the puppeteers' performance had left him disgusted.

He finished his spinning late that night and the next morning Prabhavati called us early, for we were returning to Patna. We fumbled around in the gloom, packing, feeding Vidya, preparing boiled water for her for the journey and were late in joining the rest of the party. All the household goods Prabhavati had brought and the personal luggage went with the porters. In addition, a small rough-haired pony clopped along with a laden back. Jayaprakash had ordered an elephant for us from the village, for in this village several families owned them. A few days earlier we had come upon the mound where a young elephant had been buried on the spot where it had died. The task of shifting his huge bulk had been too difficult.

The sky was just lightening as we hurried to the front of the house.

'Your elephant isn't here,' Daniel said, 'will you wait? The rest of the party has just left.'

'Let's walk,' Wendy said to me. I agreed and placed Vidya comfortably on my hip.

Several people took it in turns to carry Vidya but nobody talked much. Shri Saudani carried her astride his shoulders for the last part of the journey and she eventually fell asleep, her little head with its bronze-tipped curls nodding against his.

Once we all halted by a large black swamp with muddy approaches on both sides. We crept out to a decrepit old boat, which sagged with the depth of water in its bottom. However, a few at a time, we safely crossed in it and straggled out in small groups on the other side.

Sections of the path led between tall plants of mustard seed and dal so high that we could not see over the top and walked blind along an earth track. Suddenly the crops opened to a clear space and there was the river and the heavy barge swinging against the bank with the swish of the waves. We waited while the luggage was placed on board and the porters climbed in, then we also clambered aboard, sitting in the bows where a narrow wooden seat ran round the inside edge of the barge.

Last of all the horse was manoeuvred on. The punt was already laden. Shri Saudani looked in amused horror at the riverman shuffling the pony into the centre of the boat.

'Look, brother, what are you doing there? We have such a crowd already.'

His consternation, the typical nature of the whole situation in a country where transport had to be made because it was not always provided by power, and yet the essentially odd collection of things which faced us across the barge, brought tears of laughter to our eyes.

The sun, which had risen with a brilliant burst of yellow warmth over the horizon, sent arrows of light along the curve of the swell as the punt swung away from the shore. Prabhavati handed around our breakfast of hard-boiled eggs and biscuits cooked on top of her oven stove. Lastly we drank coffee from earthenware cups, which we then flung into the river. It was all very lighthearted.

Then the barge ran into the mud on the opposite bank, a wooden plank was placed so that we could reach the sand, the porters were laden, the horse, resisting and nervous, cajoled ashore.

Everyone stood about waiting while Prabhavati, as usual, organised the luggage with indefatigable energy. Suddenly the party felt subdued.

The tranquillity of the last few days was ended. In Patna air-raid sirens would be screaming at all hours of the day. For us it had been an incident in which we had experienced a world that was passing even from India. As Jayaprakash had said:

'When we were children there was always the excitement of waiting for those expected, unexpected guests. With the slowness and difficulties of transport no one quite knew when they would arrive, then suddenly they were there.'

It was a gentle order of things.

We thanked him as we walked towards the jeep.

16

WORK AND WORRIES

When the decree of adoption and permission to take Vidya out of India were made final without our having to reappear before Tis Hazari Court in Delhi, we began to consider adopting another baby if we could do it in the time remaining before we left India. Jayaprakash, overhearing our conversation about this with Brahmanand, leaned over the balcony outside his library in Patna, gave us a startled look and said: 'My God, Wendy, you are still talking about this, but what will you do with all these babies? I'm not going to encourage you in this. You have enough to cope with.'

Nevertheless he introduced us next morning by telephone to the District Magistrate who, in about a minute after we had reached his office, had signed our written application, scrawled a note to the Superintendent of the Patna

Medical College Hospital to give us a baby, and had agreed to allow us to take the baby out of India in April.

We decided on a boy who had been left at the hospital at about two weeks old. He was a long baby with large brown eyes and a mop of black hair. We decided to call him David.

In addition, Jayaprakash introduced us to Dr Lala Surajnandan Prasad, the hospital paediatrician, a kindly man but extremely hard to catch. He examined David for us and, to our surprise, happened to be acquainted with Dr Seeta Lal in Delhi who had helped us so much with Vidya.

'He's got an awfully long nose for a baby,' I commented to him with a laugh.

'Babies with strongly defined features often turn out to be very handsome,' he replied in amusement, and his prediction proved to be correct.

In David's case the adoption procedure was the reverse of that which we had had to follow in Delhi for Vidya. We had to receive him from the hospital before we could proceed to court. So, nursing him protectively against the bumps, I brought him in a bicycle rickshaw to our temporary home in Jayaprakash's flat on the day of the death of Shri Rajendra Prasad, the ex-president of India.

David was now a month old and weighed six pounds. We were excited and happy but a little apprehensive about having a frail baby in such a remote place as Sokhodeora now that the ashram jeep had been sold and it would be so slow for us to reach a doctor in an emergency.

Vidya was agog with curiosity. Friends and acquaintances came to see him and all was cheerful confusion. Our dearest friend, gentle Bengali Shrimati Shova Chakravati, who conducted a kindergarten but had no children herself, held him tenderly and, sensitive to our anxiety, said: 'He will soon grow fat under your care, Wendy sister.' Brahmanand, who was unused to small babies, retreated hastily from David's basket and gave his attention to Vidya.

The next day was one of even greater confusion. Jayaprakash flew from Delhi to Patna to attend the funeral of the ex-president, to whom he was related, so Brahmanand had us pack everything and moved us in case Jayaprakash wanted to stay in his own flat overnight. In the evening, as this was not going to be so, he moved us back again.

None of us had to appear in court on this occasion. The adoption papers were signed in David's absence in the rooms of a Magistrate, Shri Sharan, behind the courtroom. Shri Sharan explained his procedure with the comment: 'I do not like children to come to court. They might see a criminal in handcuffs and what might be the impression on their minds?'

Having posted the documents to Mr Smith at the Australian High Commissioner's Office in Delhi for the necessary entries to be made in Wendy's passport, we returned to Sokhodeora. There smallpox seemed to have broken out.

One of the twins had caught it but, like everyone else, Mahadev was not sure whether the illness was 'big sores' (smallpox) or 'little sores' (chickenpox) as the doctor had not been called.

At our request the Block Development Officer sent a vaccinator, who arrived inconveniently in the middle of the ashram's Annual General Meeting. But I accompanied him to the village, where he vaccinated about fifty youths and children at random in the Harijan sector. All the women hid in their homes and some of the men refused: 'You don't clean that thing after you do each person.'

Obviously he should have made arrangements with the village council to move from house to house until every person had been vaccinated, but although he agreed to my suggestion that he do this he did not fulfil his promise to return and carry it out.

Dr Surendra refused to have David vaccinated because he was too young, merely advising us to keep flies away from him as they could carry smallpox. The same day, on the road through the village, I met a sad procession. One of the twins had died from the sores. The mother was carrying the body in white cotton behind the postmaster who had a crowbar and a boy who had a mattock. It seemed impossible to us for the other twin to survive now and we recalled all the pride and care that Shrimati Mundodrie, the ashram-employed midwife, had taken over the twins. The village maxim 'Twins don't live' had been proved.

Then a woman, accompanied by her mother and carrying her sick baby under her sari, came tentatively and humbly on to our verandah. Wendy understood her to say that her other baby had died recently and jumped to the conclusion that this was the other twin. What particularly worried her was that there were flies everywhere, and in a panic she ordered the woman to go away. Having relied on our help the woman, shocked and distressed, began to return home.

Just then I came in and cleared up the misunderstanding. We found that the baby had rickets and got her medical attention. The incident, however, made us very aware of how the women's attitudes towards us had changed from aggressive suspicion to trust and willingness to accept help.

We remembered how in our first weeks there a woman from Seepur hamlet had come to us hectoringly demanding a banana for her grandson who had smallpox. Her crude attitude had quickly destroyed any sympathy for her individually but we had given her the banana after a lecture she did not like, or take, on going to the doctor. Mahadev had waited until she had gone to confide, somewhat reproachfully, that hers was one of the wealthiest families. Unfortunately the result of banana and no doctor had been a child blind in one eye, a cruel punishment for ignorance.

David slept most of the time, but when he cried Vidya became most upset, caught Wendy by the dress to pull her to him and by hand signs and noises insisted that he be fed and burped. Otherwise her affection for him took the form of giving him presents – dropping shoes or saucepan lids on him.

The night-class building neared completion. The walls had been surfaced with a sand-earth-manure plaster; limestone brought from the jungle had been fired with coal in an oven to produce whitewash for the inside walls; coloured earth ochres had been applied outside; the floor had been filled with earth, stamped level and cow-manure solution had been applied; a cupboard had been installed for library books. To our delight the unfinished work had been completed by Kurian while we had been away at Jayaprakash's home.

But we wanted one last refinement for our public building. Two lavatories.

For over a year we had vainly sent orders to Lucknow for the moulds of Mr Eckersley's World Health Organization village latrines. We had aroused interest in Sokhodeora people and had grown acquainted with some of the problems of installation. Mahadev's family, for instance, had a tiny room suitable for a lavatory at the back of their house with vacant land behind. The pipe could have come through the mud wall into the sealed pit outside, but the land was not theirs. Their land ended on the line of tiny holes the rain had made as it dripped off the edge of their roof.

Turning in another direction, we persuaded Kurian to make the pit lids and lavatory parts in his pottery centre in the ashram out of local red clay. To make the pan and pipes waterproof he gave them a blue glaze in his oven since its temperature was too low to fire a white glaze.

He and I installed them. The water seal worked and the pans flushed by means of a small bucket of water thrown sharply. We were very proud of our small achievement, for Jayaprakash had once remarked to us: 'If you install toilets in a village that will be a revolution.'

On the other hand, we were full of regret that these would be our first and last village lavatories. It seemed that one could spend a useful lifetime introducing lavatories into villages and village schools. Not that they were what people felt they most needed. The Harijans would listen politely to our talk about lavatories and then bring the conversation round until they could ask, without appearing to contradict or be ungrateful: 'If you want to do something for us build us more wells. We can pull the buckets to irrigate our crops. We want more food in our stomachs.' And they would take us to look at sites and talk about Government grants, for hunger dominated their thoughts to the exclusion of concern about environmental sanitation, which would have prevented so many of their illnesses.

Mahadev insisted on an opening ceremony for the nightclass building. So coloured paper and some precious magazine pictures were hung, we provided food and he engaged a local Hindu priest to dedicate the building. The two of them made a small altar within a canopy of banana leaves in the centre of the floor, keeping a fire burning on it into which tiny portions of food were dropped. Mahadev had to earn his right to participate in this ceremony by fasting from food and drink all the preceding day.

There were no cotton carpets, white clothes, rules of conduct of meeting or formal speeches such as the educated group would arrange for Jayaprakash's village meetings. The unkempt Harijan men sat together at one end of the room that they themselves had built, singing to the beat of drum and brass cymbals. There were no women present despite our past lectures to Mahadev. Lantern light streamed through the big, barred windows into the darkness around, conjuring up memories for us of open-windowed Australian country halls. Nearby jackals barked.

For us it was more than an opening ceremony. It was also the presentation of our gift to them. The following days would be empty without the sweat and haggling and organising. We looked back on the unexpected hitches, the sixty-odd miles walked to and from the Block offices to obtain a Government subsidy for kerosene and running expenses, the document a mistaken official prepared for us by which we would have made our hard-won land over to the State Government.

And it represented the climax of our work. For two-and-a-half years we had planned and interviewed and worked to bring Jayaprakash's Experimental Rural School into being. We had filled four bulging files, written reports and articles and typed two hundred pages of syllabuses. We had even had the foundations dug, but it had all ended with a letter from the Indian Government informing us that all building grants had been cancelled because of the national emergency –

the military clash with China along the border.

Jayaprakash wrote to us sadly: 'About the experimental school ... like so many of one's dreams I have to see it buried deep ... If ever I happen to come across the right sort of person who would be prepared to give, say, ten years of his life to building up such a school, I might take up the idea again, but I am afraid I would be dead by then. As for you and Allan, Wendy, if I could help it I would not let you go at all...'

In the days that followed mothers brought more sick babies to us and Dr Surendra and the Block Development Officer brought others. But the powdered milk and Multi-Purpose Food were finished and as we had been unable to obtain further supplies we had to turn them away. The last case we were to help with was Shri Bunwari Manjhi's.

He was a landless Harijan labourer, tall and thin, with angular cheekbones, heavy lips and a haunted expression in his eyes. His family of four lived along the alley from Mahadev's home in two straw-thatched rooms, which together with his house yard would have fitted into many a Western sitting-room. Sometimes they ate meat when he caught a rabbit or porcupine in the jungle. Angni, his daughter, had come to our school for a time but had left partly to earn a few naya paisas herding goats and partly out of fear because we wanted to treat her trachoma.

One morning I was going to a shop to buy nails for the nightclass roof when his wife, Shrimati Chinta Devi, pleaded, 'Allan brother, come and look at him.' She was a tiny woman looking, like most village women, aged far beyond her years, with a habit of rocking her head sideways in a gesture of utter hopelessness.

Bunwari was lying in the open on a string-strung bed, pitifully emaciated and almost too weak to sit up.

'What's the matter with him?'

'Cough.' Then she added, weeping: 'He couldn't work, just lie down. We haven't had any food for three weeks.'

'Who are your relations – to help you?' I asked, for they had no welfare state to turn to.

'None.'

I took her to the shop and bought her rice and dal and for about three weeks she came to our house for food, sitting herself on the verandah, rocking her head and weeping.

We employed their son, Manjhu, perhaps fourteen years old, on the night-class building for Rs.1.25 daily – as high a rate as any other paid labourers would tolerate – but to begin with regular hours were too much for his boyish nature and he would run away in the afternoons to play with other youths or to go fishing with them.

One evening we had Bunwari carried to a corner of the road where Dr Surendra would pass in his jeep. Our suspicions that he had tuberculosis were confirmed. Mahadev walked to the Kawakol hospital for the ampoules next morning and Chinta Devi seemed to be finding someone to give the necessary injections.

We had taken the responsibility of doing what was needed, but it was at the time of our departure. The outcome depended on whether the family could take the initiative for themselves.

Bunwari Manjhi may still be alive, for he was entitled to more years than he had seen, and Angni may not yet be blind, Manjhu may even have permanent employment and Chinta Devi may be earning something rice-pounding in other women's homes; but we are not hopeful.

Our last activity was a piece of salvage work. When we had told Jayaprakash that we could not accept his offer of a second term of three years he had decided to close the ashram school. His decision both saddened us and left us concerned for Boddh Narayan whose employment had ended and who had not passed the examinations, despite our tutoring, which would have admitted him to a teachers' college.

Our Government teachers returned to the Sokhodeora school, which the State Government planned to rebuild. All our pupils had to find other schools and anyone above third grade at a Government school would now have to pay fees. It was a source of extreme worry to Mundodrie, for her husband was dead and she received only about Rs.35 a month as ashram midwife. Her whole life was in her son and her work, and we had seen her weeping bitterly over the callous remarks of a Muslim eye doctor about the white spot on one of her lad's eyes. They lived in one small room and whenever the boy was ill she was tormented by the fear that he too would die. But if she was able to send him to Kawakol Middle School it was only because Jayaprakash paid the fees for her.

The only child we were able to substantially help was Chotun Mochi, one of the most talented children. His father was a thickset cheerful and dignified Harijan who had no land but share-farmed on another's fields and mended shoes. We used to share our shoe repairs between him and Mahadev's father, and when they were returned we had a standard argument about the price.

'How much do you want?'

'It's not for me to say. Anything you decide.'

'Twenty-five naya paisas?'

'Whatever you give.'

'Look, take a rupee then, I haven't any change.'

His father adored Chotun and was the only parent who expressed to us a determination that his son should have a better life than his, but he would not send his daughter to school. Perhaps that was partly the mother's influence. She was a tired, worried-looking woman with a series of hard lumps under her skin up to three inches long and broader than a finger. The skin over them was discoloured and itched, but the family would never have the money to send her to Patna for the pathology tests that the local doctor recommended.

Chotun's father simply hammered us with arguments for education until we found some money and I walked with father and son to Kawakol Middle School to pay the six rupees enrolment fee. His books and khaki uniform cost another ten rupees. We were thanked in a voice hoarse with emotion and, after harvest, with some handfuls of peanuts. Food was the most precious thing he had that he could give.

Selecting a few peanuts I insisted: 'We'll take this many. It's not our custom to eat peanuts' – both of us knew that was a lie – 'and you give the rest to Chotun Mochi to keep up his strength for his studies.'

Our last week in the ashram began with a fright, which we thanked fate for not engineering during our first week. For as it was, we wore sandals or shoes at night and walked carefully enough about the house, having been stung by wasp and scorpion and having found a centipede on a door, the creature being as long as a man's hand and as broad as a thumb. Snakes we had killed in plenty near our back steps in the monsoon; their presence was advertised by the squeals of frogs as the snakes slowly swallowed them, but this was not the season for such intruders.

With the slowness of one Primus burner to cook on, our house seemed to have become a day-and-night cafeteria where meals or their preparations were ceaseless. In addition to ours and Vidya's meals, there were

David's six feeds a day, the last being at two in the morning. One night, exhausted, we fell asleep at nine o'clock leaving the lantern turned to its lowest. I woke at eleven, an hour late for David's supper, and as I dazedly put my feet out of the mosquito net there was a snake.

Not quite knowing why I had missed standing on it, I snatched one of Wendy's golf shoes from a shelf as the vague shadow slithered towards Vidya's low cot. I hit it and it turned back towards Wendy's bed. The blows angered it. It turned, reared to retaliate, and made a succession of strikes.

Since the rubber-soled shoe was useless I seized the shoe brush. Dodging the head I broke its back. It was a kind we had not seen before. Trembling now from shock I threw it outside.

'Krait' was Mahadev's first word when he arrived next morning. 'Deadly poisonous.'

The news got about speedily bringing us several visitors and snake stories, but no one's feelings remotely approached Kurian's obvious affection for cobras:

'Cobras are very sensitive fellows,' he maintained. 'They are most brave and very intelligent. If you disturb a cobra he will get up like this' – he bent his elbow and cupped his hand like the snake's hood – 'and say to you: "Don't meddle with me, brother, I am a very dangerous fellow. If you want to fight me I am ready for you but I advise you to creep off".'

17

MAHADEV'S WEDDING

Mahadev looked ill. We asked him what the problem was and found it was what the surveys unemotionally call 'pre-harvest hunger'.

'There's no food in the house, our crop isn't ripe yet. Bindeswar hasn't been paid his 20 rupees stipend from the Government Handicraft Training Centre and it is past the end of the month. My wages and Meghu's are two months overdue. My father goes to Kawakol and sits on the side of the road but he's not getting any work.'

'What are you eating then?' we asked anxiously.

'We cut some of the rice green. It's not good.'

'That's disastrous, Mahadev. You won't have enough later on.'

'Other people are cutting their crop green too. It happens most years.'

'What else are you eating?'

'Mahua bread,' he replied, laughing in embarrassment.

I protested: 'That's not food, Mahadev.' I knew it was the poorest of foods and likely to cause diarrhoea.

At the beginning of the summer the *mahua* trees dropped thousands of rosebud-shaped flowers, which became for months of the year the food of the poorest families. The flowers were fleshy, yellow and bitter-sweet in smell and taste. Some people owned *mahua* trees, some had collection rights to individual trees on common land, but the flowers of *mahua* trees in the jungle were free to all. The flowers were dried on mats, stored and later eaten in a thick pancake – Mahadev's *mahua* bread.

Giving him what food we could, we also arranged for him to receive some rice as part payment of his overdue wages, all too aware that this was only a stop-gap expedient that helped one family on one occasion.

'We've worked out that it costs our family five rupees a day for food,' Mahadev explained. 'Two meals a day for thirteen people – my father and mother, Meghu and his wife and their baby, Bindeswar and his wife and their two little girls, Surju, Chamilwa, Kesurwa and me. The trouble is we don't earn five rupees a day all year round.'

They lived according to the joint family system, which is typical of at least three-quarters of India's village families, a self-protecting economic unit whose property is held by the father to whom all owe respect and obedience. On his death the family responsibilities pass to the eldest son. If anyone is unemployed, as Mahadev was for the two years after we left, the others support him.

The father, Paro Mochi, worked their scattered plots of land, one of which was four miles from their house, bought skins of cows that had died and tanned them with jungle leaves, and repaired, made and sold shoes. He had spent years in Calcutta as a shoemaker. The eldest son, Bindeswar, who had not long returned from Calcutta, was attending Shri Goswami's Handicraft Centre. In his spare time he helped on their land and made shoes. Meghu and Mahadev worked in the ashram as servants to Shimada San and ourselves, earning together Rs.85 a month and occasionally getting time off to help carry home the sheaves of wheat or rice. The children Surju, Chamilwa and Kesurwa cared for the cow, buffalo and goat.

The two young wives who were both plump, round-faced and cheerful, did much of the farm work – harvesting with a sickle, planting rice seedlings in flooded fields, irrigating from a well, dropping wheat seed by hand behind the buffalo-drawn single-furrow plough, and cutting grass to carry home for the family cow. They drew water from the well and carried it to the house, helped prepare meals, cut and carried wood from the jungle, collected dung and made the fuel cakes, cared for their babies, and shared the mother's worry of making the budget support the family with rice at 25 naya paisas a pound and dal at 40 naya paisas a pound.

Their most arduous household chore was pounding the husks from their rice and wheat, which they did just inside the house door in the sort of antechamber in which their cow was housed at night. For balance one of them gripped a piece of rope that was attached to the low roof poles and stepped on and off one end of a thick wooden pole, making it rise and fall like a see-saw. She usually held her baby astraddle on her hip with one hand. At the striking end of the pole a wooden head had been inserted vertically and this head continually fell on to a heap of rice, which one of the other females of the family kept pushing back into place.

The work of all these people from dawn until dusk every day of the week provided five rupees' worth of food a day. So when we heard that Mahadev was going to be married we were concerned as well as delighted.

He was about eighteen when his 'second marriage' was arranged by his father.

'My first marriage would have been when I was about ten years old,' he said. 'The girl lives in Pukri Brawan. My father took me to her house and they gave me sweets and made a fuss of me for a while. Then they chased me out in the street to play so that I wouldn't see the girl.'

'What is her name, Mahadev?' we asked.

'I don't know yet. In any case I won't ever use her name. It is not our custom to say each other's name. Bindeswar and Meghu never say their wives' names. We can make up our own private nicknames for each other but we wouldn't say our real names.'

'Then how do you speak to your sister-in-law, Mahadev?'

'I'm not allowed to talk to my sister-in-law and she won't talk to me. It is our custom,' he repeated with dignity. 'How much dowry are you worth, Mahadev?' we joked. He laughed in return but his answer was serious. 'There isn't any dowry. The girl's family is too poor.'

Instead his father borrowed about twenty rupees, out of which he bought her some trinkets and a fourteen-rupee sari to be married in. The girl, however, was exceedingly rude and offended his pride, for she said she did not like the sari and refused to accept it. Perhaps she had dreamed her dreams of a husband's family wealthier than this or perhaps the girl's mother had prompted her to acquisitiveness, but her father's anger did not budge her. He did what he could do to excuse the discourtesy, but Paro Mochi replied that if the sari was not good enough for her then neither was his son. He walked the fourteen miles back home and some weeks passed.

When the girl had given in her father sent a message with a male caste member that if Paro still wanted to arrange the marriage he must let him know his intentions within a day or so as they were too poor to continue feeding and keeping their daughter and would have to arrange her marriage with someone else. Early winter, December, the season for marriages, was at hand. Paro had expected this appeal, for there could be nothing but ill-luck from breaking the betrothal, but even so it touched his sympathies for he was a gentle, compassionate man. Squatting on his haunches on the ground before his house door for hours he discussed what he should do with family and caste members, one of whom took his reply.

From a sympathetic shopkeeper Paro again borrowed money – perhaps as much as Rs.100 – and bought food: wheat and rice, yellow lentils and red lentils and clarified butter fat, and Mahadev and the men of his caste had the first wedding feast. Then he walked the fourteen miles to Pukri Brawan to the tremendous beat of his friend Mahavir's drum. It was the trunk of a tree, half as high as a man, hollowed out with deft care. The ends were taut pigskin and hundreds of peacock feathers were embedded in a thick ocean richness encircling the middle and the ends. There was no such drum for miles around.

In Pukri Brawan, a Hindu priest, known as *saddhu,* officiating, Mahadev was married and his small brother, Surju, was betrothed to the bride's younger sister. One interesting difference between northern and southern Indian villages is that in the north the boys are married outside their village, usually with a girl from a village not less than four miles away, and girls of the same family are married to boys from another third village; in the south there is a preference for marriage with certain near relatives.

Again the men feasted and on the following day the marriage party set out for Sokhodeora. Through the warm afternoon on the dirt road half a dozen youths straggled along, each with something of his garments yellow, and Mahadev and Surju with new yellow *dhoti*s. A hundred yards behind them trailed the sixteen-year-old wife and behind her some paces her sister came. Their new saris were pulled over their hair covering their faces, their heads hung and they only saw the dust of the track as it squirted between their toes.

About six miles from their new home they lagged farther and farther behind. Betrayed from his proper male role by sympathy, Mahadev let the youths go on and encouraged the girl whose name he did not know and would never speak. He even demeaned himself so far as to carry her little parcel of all her belongings. The way was uneven over the irrigation banks of small rice plots. She was slow and he spoke angrily to her. She cried and her sister too. They were frightened about their new home. Mahadev felt angrier and confused and sorry and miserable. They arrived long after dark.

He returned to work at our house next morning in a doleful mood, resentful against the unexpectedly painful feelings he had been plunged into by the arrangements and expectations of the members of his society.

For a month the two brides slept with their mother-in-law and their two sisters-in-law and then walked back alone to their father's house. After they had been gone about three weeks Mahadev took leave to bring his wife back, saying she would not come until he went for her. After her return she kept within the house and hid her face from strangers while her sisters-in-law giggled at her shyness. One day she was sent to the well for water, another day to the fields to gather cow-dung for fuel and to cut grass for the cow, until she stopped hiding her pretty face with its thickly moulded lips beneath her sari and became one of the female community of Sokhodeora. It was about two months after the wedding when Mahadev began to concern himself about having a bed made. It was a system of courtship after marriage.

She had come to a mud-walled house roofed with potter's tiles, the low, windowless rooms forming a closed rectangle around a tiny open, inner courtyard where a hen clucked her chickens after her and smoke rose from the small mud stove on the ground, where rules for her behaviour in the family were strict and most comprehensive.

As the time for our departure approached Mahadev became increasingly gloomy. 'What can I do?' he asked, 'because my father won't try to find me some other job.'

I walked to the Block and asked the Block Development Officer whether there might be employment there for him. On my return I came across Paro Mochi making a pair of moccasins on the ground outside his house and tried to stir him into some sort of action to help allay Mahadev's fears.

'*Namaste*, Allan *bhai*,' he said courteously.

'*Namaste*, Paro Mochi. I have just been trying to find work for your Mahadev with the Government. Nothing came of it. What are you going to do about it?'

'I will pray to God,' he replied simply.

'Have you asked anyone who might employ him?'

'I will ask God's help, Allan brother,' he replied.

'You don't think that you ought to give God a helping hand?' I asked between resignation and exasperation at his unconcern. 'There is Mahadev's wife to be supported now. One day she will have children. Mahadev is very worried about being unemployed.'

'It is in God's hands. I will pray,' Paro repeated, and went on stitching the leather imperturbably.

18

DEPARTURE

Our assignment had ended. Young men we could not remember meeting told us that they would ask Jayaprakash to keep us and not let us go to our own country. Perhaps we represented to them what a social worker should represent, a certain kind of security, a sureness of judgement about what is possible, a kind of hope. The old had become hopeless and embittered because they could not see any way out of their problems, so they were fatalistic in their outlook. The young men were still prepared to struggle and dream.

Sokhodeora was a problem village, disunited by caste loyalties, inequalities of sex and conflicts of leading families. Its traditional social structure relegated a section of the people to congenital inferiority. Its leaders were members of an upper caste and the headman was a compromise between two quarrelling families, but he lacked the vision to unite the elements in a common endeavour. A change of attitude was needed. Community development could only proceed when the privileged sections of the village acknowledged the importance of their fellow beings even at the risk of forgoing their own advantages.

Culturally and economically this was one of the most backward areas of India, the dances, songs and statues at festivals being graceless, inartistic and unrestrained, the average income being only half of the all-India average of Rs.330 a year per person. The skills of planning and organising development had still largely to be learnt. They had to learn how to produce more. The breakdowns in the social fabric had to be repaired or a new fabric created. Over and over when we had found a need we had been able, because we were foreign, to make the temporary struggle against defeat, getting children to school although there was no certainty of their being employed, calling a doctor to an epidemic to find he had insufficient medicines.

In many ways Sokhodeora could progress no faster than the State and the whole nation. It had to await Bihar State's greater expenditure on electricity, roads, railways, water supply, health, agriculture, family planning and education, and it had to share this development with forty million other Biharis.

On the national education scene there were now 43 million Indian children attending school, compelled up to Grade 3 and during the current Five Year Plan an attempt was being made to raise this number to 69 million and to lengthen the years of compulsory education so that all children would have to attend school to Grade 6.

Obviously educational progress could be stepped up if the West would more heavily commit itself to help educate the world's people as well as its own citizens, as part of the United Nations' Decade of Development. We are all responsible for the human condition and those who are educated are responsible to those who are not.

The West could provide thousands of technical schools complete with equipment and lend teachers for them if so requested. It could create hundreds of Teachers' Colleges and help frame teacher-training programmes. It could assist with building schools of the latest design, complete with plumbing, sanitation, blackboards, libraries, science equipment.

The West could finance writers' committees jointly set up by developing and assisting countries to prepare school textbooks and translate them where necessary. Millions of books are urgently needed and the West could pay for printing them. Much could be achieved by daily co-operation between teachers' unions if Western teachers would rise to the challenge of removing one of the greatest social injustices, illiteracy, from the world. Most interesting pioneering work could be done to assist scheduled tribes and social minorities: Mr Dhebar, ex-president of the Congress Party, told us on one occasion that India has many millions of tribal people for whom no written language exists at present. There is the double problem of providing primary school textbooks for them in their own regional language as well as in the national language.

All development depends on highly trained personnel and an increasing level of general education in the entire population. But in addition to this the speedy development of education is essential in India to create a sense of national unity strong enough to lift people above regional, religious and caste divisions.

We felt most unhappy to be leaving the ranks of those helping in the developing countries and very envious of those who were going on. The movement Gandhi began for the uplift of all would continue, its workers striving to improve agriculture and animal husbandry; promote handicrafts and voluntary co-operative farming; collect donations of land for distribution to the landless; revitalise village self-governing institutions and establish co-operatives; usher in equality of rights and status for men and women; correlate education with environment and development.

We had a sense, too, of all those young people in United Nations teams, in the American Peace Corps, and working as Australian Volunteers in Indonesia, and wondered how many of them had gone abroad feeling that the motive springs of their lives were out of harmony with those of their nation. We wondered how many would return after living with poor people to become uneasy members of Western society, whose code is wealth, property and the pursuit of affluence. For such workers measure achievement by width of sympathy and imagination, by how much responsibility one will take for others.

Our farewells were deeply affectionate, regretful and memorable. In much the same way as visitors had come to Jayaprakash's front verandah at his home, so people came and went for two days, paying respects and sitting chatting on wooden beds we had put at the front of our house.

The Harijans held a farewell meeting at the night-class building. They had built an arch of leaves over the road and lined the track to greet us with folded hands – Tiloh Manjhi, Luttan, Paro Mochi, Saudigar Manjhi, Akloo and so many others we knew. Ramashray Singh and Goswami accompanied me. Unfortunately it was so hot that Wendy had decided to stay at home with Vidya and David. Mahavir had made another drum and decorated it also with sheaves of peacock feathers, and the two drummers wore decorative grass skirts over their *dhoti*s and cotton headpieces like halos tied under the chin. They pounded the drums while others shouted: 'Long live Wendy sister! Long live Allan brother!'

On the road in front of the night-class building a dance was performed to music from brass cymbals and a rough instrument Bindeswar and Mahavir had made with wire strings played with a bow. One of the night-class youths was dressed as a woman with a sari fastened around his head, and he danced with clumsy movements. Mahadev's thin younger brother, Surju, however, did look like a girl in his sister-in-law's blouse and sari with reddened lips, black *kejul* around his eyes, white beauty spots in a circle on both cheeks and in a line across his forehead. His hair was combed down the middle with vermilion colour along the parting. A third dancer of Surju's age wore a cap and liberal black strokes all over his face.

On the back verandah Kurian and Yogendra had helped them arrange a cloth to sit on, two chairs and a table for the guests, a tablecloth and a vase of flowers. A few of the audience sat on the mat but the majority sat on the ground in the fallow fields of the two farmers whose encroachments we had taken back for the building. Garlands of flowers were presented and hung about my neck and this was followed by the speeches customary on such occasions. I promised to provide a radio for the night class and expressed a hope that each time they went past the night-class building they would think of it as symbolising education, their way to a better life.

For throughout our work we had aimed at showing how education could achieve the maximum development of children and adults in literacy, initiative, creativity, skills and happiness. We had tried to demonstrate how a democratic atmosphere might be achieved in school, how a teacher should show affection, kindness and understanding towards all pupils, should become responsible for their health, should understand how children learn and how to stimulate them to learn, and how teachers should have a social conscience and desire to improve their society. We had hoped, too, to form a Teachers' Association to improve teachers' status and conditions, to influence parents to send children to school, to attract women teachers to win girls to school, to run working bees to make lavatories, fences, wells, and to press for the building of more middle schools and high schools and for free education in them.

Then there was another meeting of youths and children to address in the centre of the Harijan sector and finally a meeting arranged by the headman and village council on the flat roof of the landlord's mansion overlooking the village roofs as the sun sank behind the mountain range.

I returned home to another meeting on the grass before our house with the ashram family. Despite the danger of bears the Block Development Officer,

Shri Sharma, and his staff had walked the three miles from the Block to wish us goodbye. 'They are fortunate children,' they said of Vidya and David, and knowing the affluence of most countries in the West, we thought sadly of Shova from Jerawadi, of the children we had taught and fed, bathed and de-loused, of all village children.

Brahamand held his own private farewell in Patna and managed to be the only one not tearful when our train drew out of Patna. Three days later we reached Bombay, filthy and exhausted, having left behind our kindred in the poor, the sick, the uneducated, the unfortunate.

'We don't know whether we will ever see you again,' we said sadly on the dock as we parted from Jayaprakash.

'I could never imagine', he wrote in a subsequent letter, 'that it could affect me so deeply – leaving you all behind at the pier. I dared not even look back, but it was an experience worth having – it did something to you that, though it hurt, yet made you feel a better living being.'

Our ship drew down the harbour, past the island of the rock caves of Elephanta and their huge statue of the three faces of God.

We looked at each other, sharing a hope that Vidya and David would someday return to experience the frangipani and bougainvillaea of Bombay and discover an India whose present aspirations had come to be.

EPILOGUE

In 1964, with Vidya now two-and-a-half and David barely a year, we left Melbourne and Allan's temporary employment to live in the beautiful, seaside regional city of Warrnambool. The Victorian Education Department had agreed to re-instate the promotion Allan lost when we went to India and provide us with an Education Department house at low rental if he would work in a country high school for some years. So began our happy lifetime there of over fifty years.

We missed our Indian friends and they in turn missed us. In reply to our letters Jayaprakash Narayan (known affectionately as 'JP' in India) wrote: 'A few days ago we were in the ashram and looked at your deserted house. We were both very sad and missed you terribly.' And again: 'Your house is locked up and the vegetable garden going to seed. I asked Mahtoji [the gardener] to do something about it but he complained of the goats. Everyone in the ashram is missing you.'

In another letter he requested a copy of the article Allan wrote about building the night school and reported that 'the school is still running and doing well. Mahadev has kept it going'.

We endeavoured to keep in touch with Mahadev and assist him financially. He replied in his halting Hindi that he had managed to get the money we sent him and shared it among the other Harijan families but it was difficult because the bank had queried his identity and he had no means of proving it.

To our questions about how the village people were faring, JP replied that 'communities in this area are slowly moving forward'. However, he was less hopeful in December 1965 when he wrote 'the food grain position in the country is truly frightful but despite the general failure of the monsoon, Sokhodeora and the villages around have not done too badly. Somehow the rain god has been kind to them'.

This was the first intimation of disaster. A second year of monsoon failure plunged the entire state of more than 30 million people into famine. It was Jim Howard the Oxfam field director in India who made it impossible for me to go about my daily life without brooding over the cruelty of starvation and impossible to watch my own children without feeling an anguished sympathy for the mothers of Sokhodeora unable to feed theirs. In November 1966 after an extensive tour of Bihar he wrote 'The wolf is through the door and we are faced with massive disaster. The districts of Gaya, Patna, Hazaribagh ... are having starvation deaths now'. On almost the same day we received a copy of the appeal issued by Jayaprakash Narayan, president of the Bihar Relief Committee.

We did what we could at home. On behalf of the Bihar Relief Committee we launched an appeal. The mayor lent his support and the Warrnambool community donated two thousand dollars. Then it was suggested to us by the director of the Australian relief organisation Community Aid Abroad that while others could raise money we were in a unique position to go to Bihar and report on what was happening there. We could not both go. Our baby Nalini had been born in 1965 and we now had three small children to care for. Allan could not leave his teaching post again. So after much discussion it was decided that we could use the royalties earned from sales of *A Mouthful of Petals* and I should go. My mother agreed to help Allan with the children. JP was enthusiastic with our proposal and offered to make all arrangements for my visit.

I boarded the ship in Melbourne with a large steel trunk full of vitamin pills donated largely through Community Aid Abroad, which had connections with Nicholas Aspro. The A and D capsules would be invaluable as food supplements with milk for children.

*

India and Bombay again after four years absence. I had almost forgotten the light, which gave the sea the smooth sheen of an iridescent pearl. Friends met the ship and we hugged each other. Then I spent most of the first day filling in forms and going from office to office energetically defending my claim that the tablets in the trunk were not drugs but food additives. My friend Kusum, in exasperation, said tartly 'anything from antibiotics to soda pop that comes into this country is drugs'. However at long last I made my point and the trunk was cleared.

I met JP and Prabhavati again that evening and we greeted each other warmly. Two days later I took the train to Patna, travelling in the same carriage as them. During the long journey I was able to have a long talk with JP about the famine and what I might contribute. He was upset and discouraged that his appeals for help had not met more generosity but spoke in detail about the Bihar Relief Committee working in conjunction with the Bihar State Government and the voluntary aid organisations.

Originally it had been their intention to open only ten feeding kitchens in the worst affected areas but by the end of September 1967 they were operating 1400 kitchens each feeding about 500 people a day.

I jotted down sixteen pages of statistics until finally he said to me, 'I can give you these facts and figures,

Wendy, but it will be your job when writing about the famine to tell the personal story and recreate the people.'

We reached Patna about 6am the second morning of travelling. We had to change trains at Allahabad and that had meant a three-hour wait. From Allahabad to Patna I shared a first-class coupe with Prabhavati, but what with the broken night, the hard bunk and my excitement I had slept little. At four o'clock, as was her habit, Prabha had risen and sat cross-legged on her bunk. I got up and joined her and we sat together, talking sporadically in a mixture of English and Hindi.

Occasionally stations burned out of the blackness, a sudden brilliance of light and scurrying porters and people muffled to the ears against the coolness. It had rained from Allahabad onwards and JP had commented bitterly, 'Whoever would have thought of rain in March and now it is likely to damage the wheat crop not yet harvested.'

We drove to JP's flat. The rain concealed much of the dirt of the city but not the congestion of bicycle rickshaws, bullock carts, pony carts, bicycles and pedestrians through which an occasional sedan car or jeep sped with blaring horn. I was to be JP's guest and as their flat had no guest room they had set up a bed with mosquito netting on a partially closed-in section of the veranda. I was comfortable but hoped that I would never wake to find a squirrel skittering across my feet.

That first morning JP called the secretary of the Bihar Relief Committee to meet me. Together they had planned my program, appointments and travel arrangements for the coming weeks. Jaya Narayan Singh, who had recently retired from his employment as District Superintendent of Police and was now giving voluntary help to famine relief work, was to take charge and look after me throughout my 800-mile (1300-kilometre) tour of Bihar. But during those first few days in Patna I had to gather as much background information as I could. So I began by interviewing aid workers who, although stationed in Patna, were in the frontline of aid work.

Father Donahue, head of Catholic Relief Services, summed up the prevalent attitude: 'We are fire-fighting, just fire-fighting. We are a private organisation, this is all we can do. By last October I was telling my people to start planning for they won't be able to bear it when people come crying at their door.

'It was then JP made his public statement that it would shame us all if later we had to admit that those of us who had food had been responsible for allowing others to die of starvation.

'Now we are also faced with a terrible shortage of drinking water and people may thirst to death.'

I found Bert Stringer, one of the Oxfam (Oxford Committee for Famine Relief) team, sitting at his desk with half a typewritten report in his typewriter. There were mauve pouches of weariness under his eyes. He was thirty years old and had studied languages at Christ Church, Oxford. He was addicted to Western movies, Tschaikovsky's violin concerto and Saint-Exupery's novella *The Little Prince,* but now there was no time for these pursuits. He worked from one room at the Loyola Institute and his bed and chairs were covered in books and papers.

'I don't think there will be a sudden catastrophic end to it all,' he commented, 'but just a slow deterioration in health conditions – a gradual decline from deprivation to extreme malnutrition. Our main difficulty in the beginning was to get clear information about what was happening in Bihar so we depended on Father Donahue and JP. It took until January for the information to emerge that some districts were worse than others. Then the second main crop of the year – the spring crop of wheat, barley and vegetables – also failed. So from January we have been struggling to meet the growing need of a workless, moneyless population and by "we" I mean all the relief workers engaged in the fabric of aid.

'In Oxfam we have been obtaining as much Multi-Purpose Food and milk powder as possible and distributing it through the Catholic missions and Bihar Relief Committee.'

Finally, I had an interview with the Deputy Chief Minister of Bihar, Kapoori Thakur, when he came to JP's flat for discussions with him. In response to my questions he began cautiously: 'You understand, Mrs Scarfe, that Government officials have estimated that we need to provide food for 36 million people and we have to try to keep the economy of the State functioning when ninety-two per cent of people live in rural villages.' He spoke slowly and cautiously so I could write down accurately what he said. Occasionally he looked at what I had written and corrected a spelling error. He explained the rationing system that had been put in place and the operation of the Fair Price shops to distribute free grain. Bihar had been divided into areas according to the degree of crop failure and people allotted a ration accordingly. Those suffering total crop failure were allotted eight ounces (225 grams) of grain a day. Those with some food from their crops received less. He spoke of the Food for Work programmes, which were employing people according to the level of their physical ability. Strong young men could be employed building roads and dams, frailer women in spinning cotton. His was a new Government and he determined to put Bihar 'on a war footing'.

But all told I felt it was a frightening picture and I was to set out on my tour of Bihar with apprehension. I left Patna on 25 March. Despite a tiring round of interviews the previous day I woke at 5am to gloomy skies. I ladled water over myself in the bathroom, packed two suitcases and an overnight bag including some Australian dry biscuits, dried fruit and nuts, a thermos flask, an Indian clay water pot, a sleeping bag, an inflatable mattress, a first aid kit and a Primus stove. I laughed when Prabhavati said in all seriousness that I was travelling light. And in comparison with the mound of tin trunks, tiffin carriers and bedrolls she travelled with I suppose I was.

On this morning she confronted me with a huge breakfast of orange juice, corn flakes, *halooa* (a dish prepared from carrots, flour, sugar and ghee), coffee and eggs. In conversation JP echoed Father Donahue's concern: 'The greatest danger now is not food shortage but water storage. This frightens me. People might die of thirst.'

A comfortable Ambassador car with driver arrived promptly at nine o'clock. It already had three passengers: a friend we had known in the ashram, Tripurari Sharan, and two little girls returning home for the festival of Holi. They all squeezed into the front seat with the driver leaving the back seat for Jaya Narayan and me. They refused my offer of room for a child with us. Prabhavati handed in a basket of fruit, some small wrapped packets of bread and two-ounce pats of butter in wax paper. My luggage went on top of the car.

Prabhavati instructed Jaya Narayan to see that I had plenty of cups of tea so I would be able to survive any crisis. Goodness knows what his initial impression of me was but we became good friends and he was a tower of strength throughout the long and often gruelling tour. He had a law degree, a brisk and confident manner, a fund of kindness and a keen interest in seeing for himself how the relief programme was going.

There was no sign of crop failure or the desperate situation in Patna and on the outskirts there was an unexpected surprise. In a normal March the unharvested wheat ripples like pale yellow silk but here on either side of the road were green vegetable crops and hundreds of earth (*kutcha*) wells, spotted across the area, their irrigation poles looking like a host of television antennae. However further along the road the countryside changed and we began to pass through a dead landscape. From now on, day after day through many of Bihar's villages, I saw nothing but barren earth gaping with cracks: a grim mosaic of desolation, drained of colour. The deciduous trees were lifeless skeletons, the riverbeds dried up. Over this forbidding landscape cattle and buffaloes with protruding ribs and backbones searched and nuzzled endlessly for food. I was witnessing the effects of Bihar's worst drought in 200 years.

Our first stop was the shambling town of Nawada where we had often sent Mahadev to purchase food supplies. Then after a short break we stopped at a small hamlet and Father Jacob Kunnakal's mission. It was a large campus enclosed by high white walls. He greeted us warmly and led us into his small office, a bare room with concrete walls and floor. Jaya Narayan and I sat opposite him at a scarred wooden table.

'We are feeding about four thousand people each day,' he said. 'At first we just opened the gate and let them come in but they all rushed in and some were knocked down. Now we issue cards to one member of the family and they come to collect enough for each member.' He took us outside to see how it was done. He chuckled, smiling at us through his spectacles.

'You will see a few people from a neighbouring village have arrived. They don't hurry themselves because they live next door, so to speak, and are always late. Isn't that like people everywhere.'

Since our arrival a group of people had gathered and were waiting outside the gate. They were a sad spectacle:

among them a cripple who dragged himself along by two wooden pieces held in his hands, his bowl for food balanced on his head; an old woman so emaciated that her body took up hardly any space in her skimpy sari. The gate was opened and they came in quietly and squatted on the ground with their food receptacles in front of them Two brawny young men carried out one of the huge cauldrons of porridge, a food made of wheat meal and powdered milk, and began ladling it into the receptacles. Father Kunnakal supervised the distribution, sharing a fond word with each, and reproaching a woman who had only brought a small receptacle. 'That is not large enough to feed your family,' he said, shaking his head at her. 'You must bring a larger one.'

Sokhodeora Ashram was our next stopping place and I felt a mixture of pleasure and apprehension to be returning there. After Nawada I expected a long bumpy ride over dirt roads but was amazed to find that a new bitumen road linked Sokhodeora to the outside world. Where congested tiny mud houses once huddled against a meandering bullock track they were now set back from the wide new road, which was straight, smooth and modern. My second surprise was to see the amount of wheat standing green and healthy for at least eight miles (13 kilometres) on either side of the road. Tripurari, who had been with us the entire day and who was now the ashram's general secretary, chuckled at my surprise and delight. 'Yes,' he said in answer to my question. 'This is our work. We have had an extensive well-building programme.'

Our car stopped just outside the house where Allan and I had lived for almost three years. Mahadev emerged from the kitchen and greeted me shyly but with evident pleasure. He was still skinny, his face was thinner and he still had a nervous manner. He was now employed on a casual basis to cook for and do the chores of visitors to the ashram. Akloo, with his withered leg, limped after him and greeted me with his grin. He was similarly employed. Both asked after Allan and wanted to know why he wasn't with me. After we had unpacked and Mahadev had made us a cup of tea I asked him to sit down and tell me how his family had fared.

His was a story of long struggle. There were now nineteen members of his joint family. They owned four small plots of land dispersed four miles (6.5 kilometres) apart. The two plots near the village had good soils and water but the other two plots farther away were less productive and had scarce water. (I recalled that one of Tripurari's jobs had been to try to organise the consolidation of land plots, a job that had involved endless negotiations between landholders.) On the fertile plots the men dug four earth wells and by hand irrigating saved enough of the rice crop to feed them all for six weeks. They attempted to grow wheat at the same time on the other two plots but lost it because the earth wells dried up. After harvesting their rice they obtained vegetable seeds from the ashram and good seed potatoes. They planted and hand irrigated these and the vegetables sustained them through what remained of the winter months.

The women in the family sold all the small pieces of jewellery they had. At the beginning they received a good price but as more families did likewise the prices dropped to nothing. The men tried to sell some of their land but no one wanted to buy. Mahadev's father and brother were shoemakers and repairers. They walked the three miles (five kilometres) to Kawakol daily and set up shop by the side of the road but no one wanted either new shoes or repairs for old ones.

I asked him what they were eating and he said maize, only maize. And I recalled that while we ate corncob sweet and young the village people often waited until it was fully ripe and although already old they cooked it over the fire and ate it half charred.

Now in March there was no food left and Mahadev's irregular wage from work in the ashram was the only money coming into the family. He and Akloo prepared us a frugal evening meal of scrawny, leathery chicken, and a few tiny potatoes and tomatoes. Jaya Narayan ate his with cheerful resignation but mine tasted like ashes as I thought of Mahadev going home to another meal of maize.

Before he left I gave him the money from my purse asking him to share it with Akloo and the other Harijan families and I felt ashamed to do so little.

The next morning when he returned to help with breakfast he brought the ten rupees he had been unable to give to Chinta Devi the night before. Shortly afterwards she appeared, a desolate emaciated figure. She and her husband and two children had lived in a mud and straw thatch house about eight feet square (six square metres). I remembered that shortly before we left she had appealed for our help. Her husband had been lying on his bed too weak to move.

We had given them milk powder and Multi-Purpose Food and persuaded Dr Surendra to visit him. He had TB and now as she stood and wept on the veranda I learned that he had died and she and her children were destitute. They had no land and landless people were the first and the worst sufferers in the famine. They had no resources and nowhere to turn.

Mahadev gave her her share of the money and she wept even harder, alternately coughing and covering her head with the rag of sari she wore. My Hindi was not sufficient to comfort her so Jaya Narayan spoke with her assuring her the ashram would help. She crept away.

Later that morning Mahadev's pretty young wife came to visit me bringing their two little girls, one a babe in arms the other a toddler. Mahadev hovered between pride and shyness. I asked him to invite them into the house but they would not come and stood on the path outside. I went out to meet them. In her self-effacing way she tried to persuade the toddler to greet me but her little girl hid her face against her skirt only peeping at me occasionally. Mahadev who had followed me asked, 'Do you like their dresses, Wendy sister?' I had not noticed the little cotton frocks but now I noticed how fresh and clean and new they looked. 'Why, yes, Mahadev,' I said. 'They are very beautiful.' He beamed and suddenly

I realised they had been bought for the special occasion of introducing his children to me. My instant reaction was to protest at such a waste of his money but it would have been unforgivable to deprive him and his wife of this moment of happiness and pride.

A little later Tripurari arrived proposing an impossibly energetic programme of visits to relief works. But by lunchtime I had moved no further than the front veranda as a succession of friends from the village came to greet me. They were more tired, more anxious, weaker than I knew them normally to be but their attitude to life was the same. They had always experienced hunger; there had always been distress for them. Now they went on enduring.

That evening Tripurari explained at length how he had managed to keep the people of Sokhodeora alive. He had realised the previous September by just looking about him that there would be more than 'scarcity'. 'All the low-lying ground should have been green with rice crops ... farmers busy cutting between the bunds to let water flow from high fields to low ... fixing bamboo traps across channels to catch small fish. The big catchment dam at the foot of the hills was dry. There was no human activity in the fields and the farmers sat in their doorways anxiously talking about whether it might rain.'

What he had proposed was a massive program of building earth wells. Early in October JP explained his programme to the Chief Minister of Bihar and as a result the Government agreed to help people build 250,000 wells. For this farmers would be paid. However the Government had been slow so when JP visited the ashram in October he agreed to personally guarantee 10,000 rupees for the construction of a thousand wells. He also promised to give two rupees worth of vegetable seed for every well dug. I could see now from Tripurari's story that Mahadev's family had been able to survive because of this scheme. However, Tripurari was unhappy. As a voluntary organisation the ashram could only go so far. 'We could build *kutcha* wells,' he said, 'and we distributed vegetable seeds to between four and five thousand families but we did not have the money to help farmers build concrete wells deep enough for summer. This was a Government task and it was too slow. Now between April and September most of the State will be on direct relief. When the monsoons break farmers will have no capital to plant their rice crop. Their animals are dying now. The village people sell everything – even their agricultural implements. I keep on working,' he said, 'but I do not look too hard.'

We had been talking to each other by electric light. At the minute it was only a globe hanging by a cord but it was possible to envisage that a new road and electricity would make an enormous difference to life in Sokhodeora. But not now.

That night I was very tired. Tripurari had reluctantly answered my questions about Kesurwa. To my horror she had not died in childbirth, as I had assumed, but violently. Her body was found in the well. Overwhelmed by memories of her, the desperation of the people we had known so well and achingly homesick for Allan, our children and for Australia where people did not die of starvation, I succumbed to a bout of weeping. Jaya Narayan watched me anxiously and eventually begged, 'Do stop crying, Wendy. JP told me to look after you because you became easily involved. But he didn't tell what to do about it.' And I managed to smile at his quandary and please him.

The next morning Tripurari arrived to take us to see the dam construction site. He was accompanied by Boddhu and Dukharan the village librarian, both of whom I knew well. The dam was being built by village labourers and their wives who carried the earth dug out in baskets to the retaining wall. When full in the next rain it would irrigate ten acres of land. On its level floor and under the retaining wall of loose earth a cloth had been draped between two bamboo poles. To my delight the sign read *Gift of the people of Warrnambool.* Then I remembered that JP had told me that the donated money I had sent had been used in Sokhodeora. 'I thought you would like that, Wendy,' he had said. In front of the sign a length of coir matting had been laid to form a square and sitting cross-legged on this were the male representatives of most of the families who had joined the co-operative. The meeting had been arranged in my honour.

I was introduced and then the group discussed their affairs for some time. Tripurari, for the Board of Management of the ashram, had sponsored this hard manual labour scheme in combination with the State Government, both parties agreeing to meet the cost of the dam. These Food for Work programmes were set up throughout Bihar.

Tripurari had interested five farmers in getting the work done on the basis of a co-operative rather than employ a private contractor and on their own initiative they had canvassed the village, asking other labourers to join the group. They had succeeded in persuading one hundred and one families to join a co-operative, representing about six hundred people. The members had then drafted a constitution, based on a model constitution published by the State Government. In order to have a working capital and to obtain Government subsidies, on the basis of ten rupees for one, the group had issued each member, on paper only, with ten rupees as share capital and one rupee as their entrance subscription. To do this the ashram had provided Rs.3000 rupees; the donation from Warrnambool had provided another Rs.6000.

The co-operative members were buoyant at their success on the dam and were ambitious to undertake further contracts. They had applied to the Government for a loan to buy electric saws and take up forest-based wood and bamboo industries for making baskets and furniture. And they planned to set up a cardboard manufacturing industry using local woods, bamboo and grasses.

With such fine ambitions for the future of The Forest Workers Co-operative I felt sure this project would please the people of Warrnambool. However, Tripurari was very clear-eyed about the challenges the group would face. They were not used to working together co-operatively as a village and they had no management experience. Some had had no education at all. However, he said,

'They are making progress,' and I could see from the cheer around me that a belief in themselves and planning for a future had given them hope.

Despite the hope of the co-operative it was impossible to leave Sokhodeora without weighing the amount of relief given against the size of the disaster. Before leaving we visited Tripurari's feeding kitchen for the children of Sokhodeora. It was operating out of the Night Class building the Harijans had constructed with Allan's help.

Inside the mud-walled building two cooks prepared the milk powder and Multi-Purpose Food supplied by the Bihar Relief Committee, the Indian Red Cross, Catholic Relief Services and the Bengal Paper Mills. The children filled the room and spilled out onto the ground under the leafless *mahua* tree. They all squatted on the ground holding a tin or metal bowl. I recognised Basanti who had once attended my kindergarten. She was about ten now. Her matted, wispy hair poked out from the sides of her head. Her little legs were spindly and her stomach protruded in ugly distortion. My distress deepened as I looked along the lines and saw how close to death so many of the children were. Tilri's little girl was another whose bloated abdomen hung over her attenuated legs. All were thinner than I had ever seen them. Their bodies had shrunk down onto their rib cage.

I recognised one of the Harijan women who used to work at surfacing floors with cow-manure paste. Her two children hung listlessly at her side and she was pregnant. And I noticed the sad decline in general care. With the wells nearly empty the children were dirty with matted hair. Even if they survived it would be impossible to estimate what long-term damage had been done to their health.

Sadly I set off with Jaya Narayan for Bodh Gaya, the small township that has been a place of devotion and pilgrimage ever since Gautama Buddha is reputed to have ended his spiritual quest there over 2000 years ago. The road to Gaya ran through a cruel landscape of desolation. A few women were scratching at places where a few points of rain had left a film of green on the earth. They were not cutting, but scraping the grass out of the soil. With this they hoped to sustain their scrawny buffaloes and cows.

Jaya Narayan and I lunched by the roadside on the dry biscuits, dried fruit and cheese I had brought from Australia and thermos tea sweetened with condensed milk. We always offered some to our driver but he preferred to find his own Indian food. Sometimes he brought something with him.

Jaya Narayan confirmed my fear that this was one of the worst affected areas of Bihar and to add to the problem the density of population demanded a high concentration of relief workers. Our car entered the gateway of a small Gandhian ashram and we stopped beside a house that overlooked an orchard of guava, mango and paw-paw trees. Dwarko Sundrani, the energetic and intense manager of the ashram, appeared. Immediately, he bustled us back into the car and took us on a whirlwind visit to look at his Food for Work programs. He, too, had labourers working on the construction of a dam and a well. He showed us a light manual work programme where the village women were engaged in weaving palm-frond mats. For each mat he gave the women two kilos of grain, sometimes dal, sometimes wheat, sometimes rice. He varied the food given, he said, 'to help maintain their health'. We did not see them but he spoke of women in another village whom he had encouraged to use wool from their sheep to make blankets. The blankets he could not sell but he kept them in storage.

Because the bamboo makers were hungry he organised a programme for them to make baskets and so far two hundred and fourteen families had been helped. An amazing total of eleven bullock carts of baskets had been dispatched to Delhi and sold. In addition he was running and supervising four free feeding kitchens for children.

In some parts of Bihar the forests, usually strictly controlled in regard to usage of bamboo and wood, were thrown open to the villagers although one District Commissioner forbad the killing of wildlife. I wondered how such an order could be policed, for even in good times the Harijans of Sokhodeora had supplemented their food supplies with an occasional porcupine.

That evening Dwarko visited us with one of his helpers, David Marwood, and they spoke, as others had done, of the ever-present problem of providing and supplying water.

'We have a scheme,' Dwarko said, 'for digging fifty ring wells. We approached the Catholic Relief Services and under this plan they supply us with one-and-a-half kilos of grain for one day's work on the well and David here is my chief helper in well making.'

David Marwood was in his mid-twenties, a young Englishman who had been born in India. In England he had trained as an engineer and for the last four years he had been in India working on community projects. In his last project he had helped Peter Stein, another young Englishman, with well boring.

'Stein,' David explained, 'devised the idea of concrete rings for open wells. First the rings are cast in concrete, the well is partially dug then the rings dropped down on top of each other. This holds the walls apart so that the well can be deepened further and, of course, saves the diggers from fatal cave-ins. The previous summer we managed to get Indian drilling machines that needed repairing. Some Canadians fixed them and we took them with a trained crew to the plateau area. As you probably know the plateau area is desperately short of water. In places water is being hauled in on bullock carts. But with this equipment it took the operators about six weeks to bore one well through the black basalt. Far too long to be practicable. However the idea of drilling for water on the plateau took hold. The organisation, Action for Food Production, took an interest in the idea and flew out a drilling machine, which started a train of events. JP learned of it and asked the Quaker Centre at Rasulia if they could help. Through them John McLeod, the missionary engineer working with the powerful Halco Tiger drills in another state, sent his expert operator Cyrus Gaikward to staff a Halco Tiger Drill, which is now working on the plateau. It is the only machine that can bore through rock to a depth of 200 to 300 feet (60 to 90 metres) to reach water. There are two Americans, two Canadians and five British volunteers helping Cyrus staff the machine. The ring wells were a good idea for future water supplies, particularly in the hot summer months, but the Bihar Relief Committee told us that they wanted water immediately so we must install bores and pumps.

'The Bihar Public Health and Engineering Department had a five-year programme to put in pumps for drinking water and they agreed to give us the material if we could use it to install the bores and pumps where they had planned to place them.'

'But,' Dwarko broke in, 'we needed to install the pumps where the village people would help us.'

'And that brings us to the story of Bill Casey,' David said, with a twinkle in his eyes.

'Bill Casey was an Australian of Scottish descent and had still retained his family's Scottish accent. He was a dynamo of activity. He had been travelling from Australia to Malaysia to work on an oilrig but had stopped off in India for a short spell. As soon as he discovered we were planning to put in hand pumps he was off. He announced to the Bihar Relief Committee that he wanted six drilling sites by the following afternoon. The people allotted to help him threw up their hands and protested that there was hardly enough time to get there and back.

"'Right,' replied Casey, "then you'd better set off at once. This is an emergency," and he rolled the 'r' in emergency around his tongue.

'By three o'clock the next afternoon we were on our way to Nooseri Block, about sixty miles (100 kilometres) from Patna, determined to show the village people how to put in a hand pump, although,' David chuckled, 'we had never put in a hand pump in our lives. And the really funny part about the situation was that digging a bore is common knowledge in most villages. Of course we had a very good theory,' he laughed. 'We worked out that if we put it in a dry well we should reach water. We struggled for a week with that first bore but it was fine sand all the way down and we never reached water. At last Casey gave in or, I should say, temporarily gave in. When he crawled out of that hole he rubbed his hands together merrily and said, "Right. Now we know all about it and we'll be successful next time." And we were. But there were all kinds of problems.

'One day we arrived in a village to start work. We had arranged with the village headman to take all the equipment to a cleared space in front of the mud-and-thatch primary school but when we arrived there was nothing there. A group of people who had watched our arrival conducted us to the headman's house and there we found all the equipment. He claimed that as he had paid for the bullock cart to transport the pipes he should have the pump at his house. There was a great argument. Casey asked some village men to help him shift the pipes to the schoolyard but no one would help so he picked up the pipe himself. Instantly there were protests. "No, no, Sahib. What are you doing? This is a perfectly good place." It was quite obvious that we had met a village faction,' David said, 'and no one wanted to be out of favour with the headman. Casey put the pipe down.'

'"Very well," he said. "You won't put it in the schoolyard and I won't put it here. So we had better put it in the Harijan quarter." There was an enormous hulla – people shouting, protesting, gesturing. And Casey just stood astride the pipe and pump equipment. Grinning. Of course, at last everyone decided that the best place for the pump would be the schoolyard.

'Casey put in eight badly needed pumps before he had an urgent telegram and had to go home. Now the American Peace Corps boys are continuing the programme of hand pumps and I have come up here to help Dwarko.' Later I was told that that first pump in the schoolyard had WILLIAM CASEY written on it but I never saw if this was true.

The four American Peace Corps boys took over the responsibility of installing the bores and pumps. I met two of them when they reported to the Oxfam office. I was talking to Bert Stringer when I heard their voices and asked him eagerly if I could meet them.

'Sure,' he said levering his long body out of his chair. I followed him through the wire door and met a handsome boy with a mop of jet-black hair still damp from the shower. His blue eyes looked at me with mock consternation and amusement as he clutched a towel about his waist. 'I do not usually meet ladies like this,' he remarked and crossed his bare feet and looked at me with simulated bashfulness. Bert Stringer introduced us.

'Mrs Scarfe, Hank Cerasoli.'

'May I talk with you?' I asked.

He grinned. 'Sure, I have never met a lady writer before and a pretty one at that.' I laughed at this piece of charming flattery. 'But,' he added, 'you must speak with Wayne too.' And he disappeared to get dressed.

Wayne Thurston was more sober. He had been in India for three years – 'Mostly in Bengal,' he said, 'doing poultry extension work at the village level and trying to teach better methods of breeding and a confined system of rearing. But,' he said, 'it is very difficult to get the village people to work together in a co-operative.' I sympathised because Allan and I had tried unsuccessfully to rear poultry at Sokhodeora. When we had caged the birds the village people had shaken their heads at our silliness. Hens only like to run free.

'However, when the famine began,' he continued, 'most of the Peace Corps volunteers asked to be shifted onto relief work here. We have an assignment to drill a hundred bores and install pumps. Our aim was to have one man for five wells and have him complete them in five days. But we haven't managed to work at that speed. At the worst it takes us ten days to dig the bore and install the pump. Often we have to file the parts to make them fit. And often we have to maintain the pumps because they frequently break after we have installed them because they have sub-standard fittings. We have put in forty pumps now but we can't leave them because they need constant repairing. Our policy,' he concluded, with a slight smile, 'is not to leave the area until all the pumps are working at one time. We haven't managed that yet.'

The next time I met an American Peace Corps volunteer it was Hank Cerasoli again. He was at the UNICEF (United Nations International Children's Emergency Fund) office in Patna talking with the liaison officer David Henry, a tall young Canadian who had been working as a schoolteacher in India before he accepted his post with UNICEF. Hank Cerasoli was more subdued and there were black smudges of grease ingrained into his hands and forearms. He was a motor mechanic and UNICEF was using him to train Indian Block Education Officers (the Block being the centre of Government Administration for a District) to ride the Suzuki motorcycles UNICEF was supplying to facilitate supervision of the CARE/Oxfam/UNICEF feeding kitchens. UNICEF had imported 255 of these motorcycles, and an engineer from the Suzuki Company in Japan had recently completed running a three-week training course in Patna for mechanics who would assist in the maintenance of the bikes. The Block Education Officers had been trained to ride them by the Bihar Police Department.

'The problem of transport facilities is one which bothers most of the relief organisations,' David said, and added, 'particularly in the plateau area where villages are widely scattered and distant from each other.'

'Although,' Hank cut in with a laugh, 'not all Block Education Officers are grateful to us for giving them a motorcycle. One poor chap in a rather hilly Block begged me quite pitiably to permit him to continue walking. He said he would never survive riding a motorcycle over unmade hill roads with sharp bends and steep drops.'

David continued. 'Apart from the Suzuki motorcycles we have brought in ten jeeps which are being used by the District Education officers for supervising the school feeding programmes. It is Hank's task to help keep all this transport running.'

Later I was to hear JP at a Bihar Relief Committee meeting express his despair at the shortage of transport. 'We are feeding five million and it should be ten million if we only had the transport.'

From Bodh Gaya we began to climb onto the plateau and a short way out of Daltonganj we stopped at a middle school. The village was so widely spread out, the surrounding countryside so barren, that the school seemed to be put down in the middle of nowhere. Our halt there was unscheduled. As we drove past, two huge loaded trucks ground to a stop outside the gateway to the school compound. The trucks were bright green with large pink flowers painted on their sides and a collection of coloured flags dancing wherever they could be attached.

'They are food trucks,' I said in excitement to Jaya Narayan. 'Let's pull up and I'll take some photos.'

'We'll go inside and see if they have fed the children yet,' he replied enthusiastically.

I was a little diffident to just turn up casually but Jaya Narayan, with his usual confidence, disappeared into the building. While he was gone I took photos of the trucks and the bullock carts in the courtyard. The carts were fully loaded with food and would slowly trundle out to the schools over roads impassable to the trucks.

Jaya Narayan emerged with the head teacher and I was greeted courteously. He explained that the food came from a grain godown (warehouse) at the Block. The food distributed was a porridge of crushed grain and milk powder. The midday meal was being prepared by a thin old village man who supervised the heating of two kerosene tins in which the porridge and milk bubbled. The cans were balanced on a low, open mud stove, which he fed with pieces of wood and cow-dung cakes.

To one side of the fire stood a line of large earthenware pots, which might have served as an illustration to the story of Ali Baba. An earthenware saucer balanced on top of each pot kept out the dust and flies. 'Do you have any problem getting the fuel?' I asked the head teacher, and he replied that he asked the adults to bring a stick or cow-dung cake; some contributed, some did not. The old man was paid twenty rupees a month by the Bihar Government.

This programme was feeding thousands of children and expectant and nursing mothers. Their daily free meal was the work of CARE (Committee for American Relief Everywhere). That evening I met Mr Sinha, one of CARE's ten field officers in Bihar. He had come in to meet me at nine o'clock in the evening after a full day's work and before he had eaten his evening meal. Normally he began at four o'clock in the morning. I might have expected him to be irritable with tiredness but he was courteous and indefatigable, eager to talk about his work and full of cheerful enthusiasm.

'Ma'am, my people are hungry,' he told me in his staccato manner of speech. 'It is my duty to serve them. They need help. If I love my people I will see their troubles and be able to assist them.'

He leaned earnestly towards me. 'I'm a hard-boiled realist, ma'am. All the little problems have to be met. There are not enough trucks. A number of godowns at the Blocks are going to become inaccessible when the monsoon breaks. Practical troubles. Today, for instance, I went to a village. All the children and their mothers had come to the feeding centre ... And do you know ma'am,' he said, 'so many of them had nothing to eat from. Too poor to have anything. Or went and sold their things. Only little plates they had, you know the kind, woven hastily from leaves. Or they just held out their cupped hands for the food. I ask you, ma'am. I'm a hard-boiled realist. I had to arrange for each school to be provided with bowls so that the children had something to eat from.

'And then in another place the headmaster took me aside. "Look, brother," he said, "there are many pregnant ladies in the village. They will not come to the feeding kitchen because their condition makes them shy. How will they manage without this food we can give them?"

'So when I had taken his reports and checked his supplies I went to the village, ma'am. The headmaster had told me where to find a respected elderly lady who might assist me. I called at her doorway, ma'am. Out she came. So thin she was herself. But she had good sons, she told me, who were working on a road nearby. One of the Government hard manual labour schemes, to provide access to the interior villages during the monsoon.'

"'Mother," I said to her. "The headmaster tells me there are many pregnant ladies not attending the feeding kitchens. How can they manage to exist in these times without food? Could you persuade them to come to the kitchen, Mother?"

"'It is not nice for women in their condition to go abroad,' she reproached me.

"'No, Mother, I quite understand their feelings," I said to her, "but these are very hard times for all of us. Every day food is at the school for these ladies. They must have it to keep themselves and their babies healthy. It is our duty, Mother, to help them come." By this time a crowd had gathered. Her sons came forward.

"'Yes, Mother," they said. "You should do as he says. We all need help these days."

'It is a mother's duty to take note of her sons – after her husband, ma'am – so she promised to help.'

He reached down into his brown leather satchel, full of his reports and accounts, and brought out a beautifully hand-drawn and hand-printed map of Palamau District. In clear symbols the map showed the Blocks, railways, roads, even possible river transport systems, sources of supply, locations of warehouses. Little packets marked CARE were coloured blue, pink or white to indicate the three stages through which the feeding programme had expanded, from 200,000 to more than six million beneficiaries. He told me this was a simplified system so that food could be quickly allotted when most needed.

'Today I went to seven different schools. I cover 1450 schools in the district. I visit them all if time permits. I like to see that the food is properly cooked and whether to all children there is equitable distribution.

'Now I am going, ma'am, to prepare a report to send to Patna, because I have to keep the information moving from the village level to the central office or how else can they plan the movement of supplies? Now as you know the drinking water supplies in the district are shrinking daily. Water will have to come in tankers. In some cases the headmaster of a school has to pay a bullock driver to bring water for the children. He should not have to pay out of his own money so I have arranged for a headmaster to be paid out of a special fund for this emergency.

'I am very sorry for my people, ma'am. I have no family. My mother is my weak point. When I am free I think about her.

'We will win through, ma'am,' he beamed at me, his eyes crinkling. 'I take life as it is, not as it ought to be. I am a hardboiled realist, ma'am. By the grace of God and a pinch of salt we shall overcome all obstacles.'

And I recalled the woman at the Fair Price shop, who after taking her ration of rice and picking up every grain that had dropped, took a handful of her precious food and placed it in a bin for the indigent. Umeshwar Charan, chairman of the Bihar Relief Committee in the area, said to me, 'One can be very proud of our people.'

Mr Sinha wished me goodnight, leaving me charmed by his manner of talking and full of respect for his compassion and devotion to his work. I was humbled by the number of people who had generously talked with me, giving me their precious time.

We returned to Patna and I was able to attend a coordination meeting of the voluntary relief agencies. It was held in a large two-storeyed, three-sided building with lawn and garden beds between the two wings. A verandah, supported by concrete pillars, ran the length of the building. The inside walls, like most Indian buildings, were white washed.

At the end of the downstairs corridor I came to an enormous heap of plain cotton saris in greens, blues and deep pinks. They jostled bales containing second-hand clothing that had been sent from all over the world. I too had brought a trunk of children's and babies' clothes. In a gap between the bales a door gave entry into another storeroom and as two servants carried my steel trunk of vitamin pills (kept in Patna until my return) into this second room a grey-haired man wearing shorts and sandals moved out from behind one of the benches to shyly greet me. He introduced himself as the doctor in charge of all vitamin and medical supplies donated to the Relief Committee. I handed my consignment over with the instructions for proper use of the tablets.

All the shelves in the room were bulging with cartons and the overflow of boxes covered most of the floor. He allowed me to peep into a number of the cardboard boxes and I noted that vitamin supplies had come from Germany and Sweden and powdered milk and baby food from Holland. I asked the doctor how quickly the supplies would go out and he explained that it was only now that the Committee was getting adequate reports, which would enable them to provide medical teams along with the feeding kitchens. And I appreciated how invaluable Mr Sinha's careful reports would be.

Suddenly Jaya Narayan dashed in and bustled me upstairs. We hurried past the control room where a retired Commissioner of Police kept precise records and day-to-day graphs of the aid being received by and distributed by the Bihar Relief Committee. Jaya Narayan briskly urged me into the room next to this one and installed me in a chair by the door. The conference room was full of aid workers and he had to search for a chair for himself.

JP, the secretary taking the minutes and Father Donahue sat facing the hundred delegates representing over a thousand field workers. I could see many of the people who had talked with me. David Henry passed the attendance list for me to sign and I scanned with interest the names of the delegates and the organisations they represented and guessed at their various nationalities.

He also handed me a sheaf of cyclostyled papers; each group represented had submitted a progress report and from these the Bihar Committee had prepared an overall report.

The speakers were mainly concerned to explain the particular difficulties that were hampering their work. Mother Theresa of the Sisters of Mercy explained that her nuns could not do their work because there was no transport to take them or their medical supplies to the villages.

'Everyone needs transport, Mother,' JP, his voice hoarse with exhaustion, replied dejectedly. 'Where can we get it from? You know I approached the army and for all we want to do they only gave us fifteen lorries. One unworkable ... The Public Works Department and the police need seventy more lorries themselves. Everyone has this trouble. Where to find trucks and vehicles.'

David Henry lightened the gloom by reporting, as he had told me earlier, the arrival of twenty-one jeeps and the Suzuki motorcycles.

There were persistent demands for increasing the number of free kitchens. It was pointed out that when half-a-million aged and infirm, expectant and nursing mothers, and children up to the age of ten were being fed by the

Committee it would still be less than ten per cent of the severely affected population in this category.

And one problem was worrying everyone, one fear, that in the coming July the next monsoon would fail again.

My thoughts drifted away to the white jeep with the blue UNICEF logo of the world encircling a mother and child, the jeep that I had seen at a feeding kitchen on the plateau. Perhaps the excitement I had felt had been at seeing a United Nation's Agency in action; perhaps even more than that it was a triumphant sense of the capacity people have for helping one another.

As a friend was to say to me on my return to Australia: 'It must have been wonderful to see such relief effort in a world bedevilled by war and race conflicts and prejudice and hatred.'

And it *was* wonderful. The relief workers inspired me. They were tired. They were fearful. They felt what they were doing was a day-by-day grind beset with constant anxiety and fear. But to me their work was a great fabric of sustained, intelligent and humane effort, the more remarkable that it was not only national but international.

The following morning JP repeated to me his concern about the effects of long-term malnutrition. 'The ration is so low, Wendy, and the food provided so limited in variety and the length of time this has to be endured is only half over now. The central Government must raise the ration. On what we are able to provide people are not dying. That is all I can say.'

Bert Stringer summed up his feelings about the aid effort. 'It's like walking on thin ice. One crack and at any moment the whole structure of information, collection and transportation of supplies might collapse. And all of us be submerged.'

And I again recalled Umeshwar Charan's fear that on the plateau the supply of drinking water was shrinking. People were walking up to two miles (3.2 kilometres) for drinking water and digging in dry waterbeds. He had commented, 'If they start to move in search of water, then the whole fabric of food relief will collapse and they will be doomed.'

Jaya Narayan invited me to have dinner with his wife and family. He had been a wonderful guide and friend and I could not have managed without his assistance. He gave endless instructions to people about my food, boiling my water, washing utensils, seeing that I was secure at night, organising accommodation and interviews. But he had also been an emotional strength, someone with whom I could discuss not only the day's events but also my many mixed feelings. He had been enthusiastic and always keen to see for himself how the relief effort was working.

His children greeted me with, 'We are having ice cream,' and I could see that my visit was a special event. I took a gift of a large, beautifully illustrated book of fairy stories. Immediately his twelve-year-old daughter buried herself in reading it but his five-year-old stared at me with big reproachful eyes and demanded, 'Did you only bring one book?' All I could do was apologise and agree that I should have known better. Jaya Narayan's wife was shyly hospitable but as she was not comfortable speaking

English and my Hindi after four years was very rusty we communicated mostly in smiles.

Jaya Narayan expressed his hope that I would be able to write a very fine book and I thanked him and his wife for their help. The evening before I left Patna the four American Peace Corps volunteers came to visit me. We sat in a downstairs room and they cheerfully installed me at a table with my notes open in front of me and then sat in a half circle facing me.

I had asked them to tell me about their work and about any of the village people who had helped them and what their reactions had been. But they kept drifting away into thoughts and reflections and worries of their own, and it soon became clear that they needed a sympathetic listener while they explored their reactions to India and the famine. Tom Cochrane tried to explain how he had attempted to reconcile himself to a tragic event for which he felt himself responsible. While he had been installing a pump in a village some farmers had asked him if they might borrow his equipment to deepen a well. He had loaned them the tools and while they were digging, the wall of the well collapsed on them and three men died.

'You know,' he said, 'they were trying to help themselves. It shouldn't happen when people are trying to help themselves, not when their lives have been so difficult.'

He shook his head with its thatch of red hair and bronze beard and looked at me with painful earnestness. 'Why should it happen? Is it fate or...' he stopped awkwardly.

There was no answer to this sort of injustice and his feelings ran too deep for me to offer some trite cliché of comfort. I shared with them the feeling that the affluent societies they and I had come from had shielded us from the stark cruelty of life lived in a Bihar village and he was wrestling with a bigger question of injustice. Why did some people in the world live in wealth and comfort while others died of starvation?

At the end of the evening they looked at the blank pages of my notebook in consternation.

'The lady hasn't written anything,' Hank commented, shaking his head. 'We've been of no use to her.'

I laughed. 'On the contrary,' I said. 'I have learned a lot about you.' They rose to go and I followed them to their jeep.

'Good luck with your book,' they called cheerfully.

'Thank you,' I replied, 'but it is not me who needs the luck. I wish you all the very best.'

They jostled each other into the jeep and Hank got into the driver's seat. With great gusto and cheer he broke into an American pop song and sang, *'I'm just irresponsible...'* No, I thought. You are certainly not that.

Prabhavati gave me parting gifts for our children and JP assured me that he would probably visit us in Australia in December. As I took the train towards a stopover in Varanasi I continued to be uplifted by the vast fabric of humanitarian aid I had witnessed. To leave the heat and dust, worry and sights of cruel suffering was a relief. But I also felt ashamed that I could simply depart while so many others must continue the struggle to keep people alive.

*

The Bihar famine was a bitter experience but ironically it brought about unprecedented development in Bihar. Dr Kumar Suresh Singh, District Commissioner of the Palamau district, summed up the changes that occurred. 'The famine helped indirectly to bring about an agricultural revolution. It brought backward areas of Palamau to a breakthrough not accomplished before. Farmers were shaken and bolted out of their old ruts.'

Because of the Food for Work programmes more dams were built, more wells sunk or deepened, more irrigation schemes started. Farmers were instructed and responsive to better agricultural methods.

Dr Donald Rugh, Director of CORAGS (Committee on Relief and Gift Supplies of the National Christian Council of India), paid tribute to those who suffered most. 'What augers very auspiciously for the future is that we have discovered some tremendous leadership potential among the village people themselves. We have had local people come forward with ideas which proved very effective and we have been impressed with the integrity of local people when they have conceived and carried out a plan of their own.'

The monsoon arrived between June and August. Farmers were jubilant; children shrieked ecstatically as they played in the falling rain and mud; mothers gave sighs of relief and fervent prayers of thanksgiving were offered. The rice seedlings were planted. The land was green again.

Wheat seed was obtained from the Punjab and Mexico. In November, Bihar's Food and Supply Minister withdrew his order, which had declared 'famine areas'. The Bihar Relief Committee announced that it was ending its relief work but joined with other groups in forming a permanent water development society for Bihar. The Halco drill continued to work on the plateau and Bill Casey brought a second drill, donated by Community Aid Abroad, by road from the port of Calcutta. Part of the cost of this drill was met from donations by Victorian schoolchildren.

Sadly, despite increased prosperity in India the gap between rich and poor has widened and according to Andrew Hewett, Oxfam's Australia Executive Director, who wrote to me in 2011, around '500 million people are still mired in deep poverty'. Bihar is now a state of over 100 million people. There have been steps towards the reduction of poverty and some areas, notably Patna, are relatively well off. However over one half of the population still live by agriculture, which is uncertain, and Bihar has a disproportionate share of India's poor. Thirty-six million people live below the poverty line and the poorest exist on Rs.600 per capita a month, the equivalent of twelve dollars Australian. There is still a long way to go for Bihar to provide a decent living for all its citizens.

I believe that the formation of so many international relief and aid organisations after the Second World War was one of the great humanitarian successes of the twentieth century. Their work in Bihar helped prevent a catastrophe of extraordinary magnitude, for later the Bihar Famine came to be called The Famine That Wasn't.

Our book, *Tiger on a Rein: Report on the Bihar Famine,* was published in London in 1969.

POSTSCRIPT

Allan and I continued to correspond with JP. In 1969 he and Prabhavati were invited by the Gandhi Centenary Celebrations committee to visit Australia for the Gandhi-birth celebration. He agreed to come as a guest of the Australian Government, providing time was set aside for a home visit to us in Warrnambool. It was in our kitchen that we asked him if he would permit and help us to write his biography. He demurred, 'What do you want to do that for?' But Prabhavati insisted, 'Let them do it. They will finish it.' No doubt thinking of past people who had made fine but empty promises.

In our summer Christmas vacation of 1970 we took our children to Queensland and left them in the care of my parents. For the first time in our travels to India we flew to Delhi to finish our research and spent the following weeks working in libraries and interviewing JP's friends of his Independence days.

JP: His Biography was published by Orient Longman in 1975 and re-published in 1998 as part of the celebration of fifty years of Indian Independence.

In 1973 we had received a letter from JP telling us that Prabhavati had died. JP died in 1979.

Wendy Scarfe, 2019

ACKNOWLEDGEMENTS

The authors are very grateful to the late Jayaprakash Narayan for permission to quote from personal letters and conversations.

The lines by W.B. Yeats quoted in section entitled "THE HOUSE WITH THE POMEGRANATE TREE" are from 'A Prayer for my Daughter' and 'Meditations in Time of Civil War', and are reproduced by kind permission of M.B. Yeats, Esq., and Macmillan and Co Ltd. The authors' thanks are also due to *Now, Overland* and *New Horizons in Education* for permission to reprint material which first appeared in article form in these magazines.

My thanks to Michael Bollen for the privilege of being published again by Wakefield Press My gratitude to my friend and editor Julia Beaven whose sensitive editing makes the creative process of producing a book rewarding and a shared pleasure. To Clinton Ellicott who has typeset *A Mouthful of Petals* thank you for coping with some unusual and unexpected challenges. I appreciate your skills and dedication. Liz Nicholson's cover designs are always beautiful eye-catching and engaging. Thank you, Liz.

This edition of *A Mouthful of Petals* is my tribute to my late husband, Allan. With his inexhaustible patience and perseverance, his irrepressible sense of humour and his kindness and compassion he comes alive in these pages.

Wakefield Press is an independent publishing and distribution company based in Adelaide, South Australia. We love good stories and publish beautiful books. To see our full range of books, please visit our website at www.wakefieldpress.com.au where all titles are available for purchase. To keep up with our latest releases, news and events, subscribe to our monthly newsletter.

Find us!

Facebook: www.facebook.com/wakefield.press
Twitter: www.twitter.com/wakefieldpress
Instagram: www.instagram.com/wakefieldpress

BACK COVER MATERIAL

At the invitation of India's venerated political leader and activist Jayaprakash Narayan, Wendy and Allan Scarfe, two dedicated but far from solemn young Australian teachers, travelled to the remote village of Sokhodeora in Bihar in 1960. They had been asked to take charge of the educational activities of his ashram, but over the three years they lived there, their activities extended far beyond that.

This humane and important book recounts their efforts in helping local people counter the misery, poverty and ignorance that afflicted so much of the region. By the time they left, the Scarfes had succeeded in teaching both children and adults much that would help them to lead better and fuller lives. And they left behind, for the young at least, something to hope and work for.

This new edition of *A Mouthful Of Petals* includes an account of Wendy Scarfe's return trip to Sokhodeora during a famine in the late 1960s, and how those who live in Bihar state fare in the early twenty-first century.

*

'A wonderful story – both inspiring but also distressing. It's deeply imbued with a sense of humanity, of ordinary people's quest to improve their lives and the significance of what seem from the outside very small steps. But also distressing because the level and nature of poverty and inequality is so preventable.'
–Andrew Hewett, Oxfam Australia Executive Director, 2011

'Magnificent – among the most important documents of our time on the nature and problems of our great neighbour. It is to Australia's international credit that the Scarfes are now widely known abroad, especially in Asia, for their sensitive and important works on Indian themes ... their achievement has been remarkable.'
–*Overland*, 1977

'A startlingly vivid picture of this one small remote spot on our earth.'
–*New Statesman,* 1967

'Not only beautiful but also important ... a work of deep understanding and major importance. Perhaps it is its profound humanity that is the most lasting impression of this book.'
–J. Jordens, *Overland,* 1968